S0-EDQ-710

Becoming a Psychologist

SCANDINAVIAN UNIVERSITY BOOKS

Universitetsforlaget, Oslo/Bergen/Tromsö

Munksgaard, Copenhagen

Läromedelsförlagen, Stockholm/Gothenburg/Lund

BF
204
S53
1972

1-20-74

Jan Smedslund

Becoming a Psychologist

*Theoretical foundations for
a humanistic psychology*

A Halsted Press Book

UNIVERSITETSFORLAGET

Oslo/Bergen/Tromsö

© UNIVERSITETSFORLAGET 1972

Cover: Bjørn Roggenbihl

Published in Europe and the United Kingdom by
Universitetsforlaget, Oslo, Norway

Published by Halsted Press,
a Division of John Wiley & Sons, Inc.,
New York

Library of Congress Cataloging in Publication Data

Smedslund, Jan.
Becoming a psychologist.
"A Halsted Press book."
Includes bibliographical references.
1. Humanistic psychology. 2. Psychology—Methodology.
I. Title. [DNLM: 1. Psychology.
BF 121 S637b 1972a]
ISBN 0-470-79915-3

Printed in Norway by Edgar Høgfeldt A/S, Kristiansand S.

TO

Åsebrit

Contents

Preface

A view of psychology will be presented which differs from the traditional academic ones, both in the conception of the data, the methods, and the theories of psychology. Psychologists are seen as depending on the social meanings of peoples' activities, as checking on the adequacy of communication with people, and as using tautological theoretical formulations, derived from common sense, to guide them in constructing procedures intended to work in the historically given socio-cultural conditions. The critical reader may, perhaps, discover latent contradictions in this position. Even so, it involves radical and probably irreversible changes in theoretical perspective. A return to the isolated academic psychology of a decade ago seems impossible.

The book is written for students of psychology at all levels, and for psychologists and others who are interested in deeper reflection about the theory and practice of psychology. It should be very suitable reading in introductory and advanced courses in general psychology, since it deals with important problems of general interest that are seldom touched upon in standard textbooks. It is particularly recommended to instructors who are interested in meeting the challenge of the student revolution by presenting a critical view of psychology, while at the same time maintaining rigorous academic standards. At the end of each chapter is a set of fairly difficult questions intended to stimulate critical discussion of the contents of the book.

I have dedicated this book to my wife Åsebrit Smedslund for a reason opposite to what is typically the case. By pursuing her own academic career and taking only fifty per cent of the responsibility for our children and our household, she has made me feel relatively free from the guilt of oppression. The joy of cooperating on an equal footing has been to me a source of considerable strength.

I want to express my gratitude to Leif Braaten, Carl Erik Grenness, Kenneth Junge, Johan Lindstrøm, Thorleif Lund, Per Schioldborg, and Olav Skårdal for their constructive and critical comments. Many other colleagues and students have also helped me directly or indirectly on various occasions.

Finally, I want to mention the members of the Far Left at the Institute of Psychology in Oslo. Their activity led me to realize, for the first time, the full extent and relevance of the brutality, fanaticism, and suffering in the world in which universities, and psychologists, are supposed to function. Without this painful lesson in political activism, the book would surely not have been written in its present form.

Oslo, December 1971

Jan Smedslund

I. Introduction

What does it means to become a psychologist? In what ways do psychologists come to differ from other people in their thinking? What are the essential features of understanding in psychology? The aim here is to provide a partial answer to these general questions by describing certain important aspects of being a psychologist, which have remained implicit or have been more or less ignored in the traditional type of textbook. The reason for this relative neglect can be found in the restricted frame of reference within which psychology has developed as a science and a profession. In what follows, this frame of reference will be extended by taking into account certain perspectives provided by philosophy, social science and, above all, by ordinary common sense. As a first part of this undertaking, certain basic premises will be made explicit.

Psychology is reflected in the professional activity of psychologists

Psychology is not here regarded exclusively as an intellectual discipline, defined by the sum total of existing written documents in the field. Hence, students are not seen only 'studying psychology' in the sense of acquiring in reproducible form a sample of the information contained in these documents. Rather, we will frequently take the perspective that psychology is defined by the total of professional activities of psychologists, and that students are in the process of 'becoming psychologists'. Becoming a psychologist means, among other things, reading textbooks and articles, listening to lectures, discussing psychology in seminars and elsewhere, conducting empirical studies, doing practical work, etc., and reflecting upon all these experiences. The experiences are gradually integrated by each individual student into a more or less unitary and more or less generalized whole, which is *his* way of functioning as a psychologist. From the point of view of cognition, this whole can be described as a *conceptual framework,* from the point of view of action it can be seen as a *system of strategies,* and from the point of view of valuation and affectivity it appears as a *system of values* (professional and scientific ethics and methodology). Our concern here is with the essential features of the integrated whole involved in becoming a psychologist, and particularly with some features which are relatively neglected in the usual textbooks.

It may be very hard indeed to discover one single and definite set of features behind the activities of all psychologists. Not only are their thinking and performance highly uneven in quality, but they are also extremely variable in content, due to differences in thematic and theoretical background. The commonality that perhaps exists may therefore be deeply hidden. However, the purpose here is not really to find out how psychologists today actually think and function professionally, but rather to point out certain ways in which they *should* think and function professionally. The task will be to describe certain perspectives and ways of thinking with which, it is believed, every psychologist should be familiar, regardless of his particular interests and specific theoretical inclinations. It should be noted that the perspective of defining psychology on the basis of the psychologist's professional activities is not regarded as the only possible or the only desirable one. Rather, it is seen as a useful corrective to the tendency to regard psychology exclusively in terms of the content of its textbooks and journals.

The interplay of theory and practice in the psychologist's activity

There are two different modes of understanding which occur in psychology, as well as elsewhere, namely, the *practical* and the *theoretical.* In the former mode one understands and deals directly with people in given concrete contexts, and awareness of the concepts and considerations involved is marginal or entirely absent. One typically perceives and acts spontaneously, i.e. with very little preceding analysis and reflection. When there is reflection, it is directed towards concrete goals and is formulated in concrete everyday words. In the theoretical mode of understanding, the focus is on describing and explaining the events or processes involved in general and precise terms. The theoretical mode involves detachment from immediate practical purposes and a concern with the abstract and universal, with concepts and principles. Also, it involves a critical attitude towards the very concepts and assumptions with which one works, whereas practical understanding at any given time takes its own presuppositions for granted and involves doubt only in concrete matters. For an interesting further discussion of these matters see Levi-Strauss (1966, chapter One).

Although the two modes of understanding are different, they can both occur in every normal adult person in any situation, and even in alternation in one person in the same situation. Furthermore, it is generally recognized that processes in one of the modes can influence processes in the other and vice versa. One can change one's theoretical views as a result of practical experiences and one can apply one's theoretical understanding to practical problems.

Some practical understanding of psychological matters is a necessary condition for living with others in society. Hence every normal adult person must have a considerable degree of such understanding. In this sense we are all relatively experienced psychological practitioners. On the other hand, the infrequent attempts at theoretical formulation by laymen are typically, and for obvious reasons, vague, fragmentary and weakly founded. Therefore, theoretical sophistication is what most clearly sets the professional psychologist apart from other people.

The characterization of the psychologist as being above all a theoretican may evoke the picture of an esoteric and practically useless profession. However, this is not what we want to assert. It is true that theoretical understanding is frequently not a necessary condition for doing successful practical work. You may do some good practical work in psychology merely because you are gifted, sensitive, and adequately experienced, even though you lack theoretical background. Occasionally, someone may even do wonders in the way of counseling and therapy for reasons that are quite remote from psychological understanding, such as being in the powerful role of a Catholic priest, a shaman or a psychologist, by being warm and spontaneous, by being pleasantly authoritarian, etc. Theoretical understanding is also not sufficient, since it may be of little help in practical work, if you lack appropriate experience, relevant technical training, or if you happen to have some kind of hampering personal qualities. Even so, one must believe that, in general, adequate theoretical understanding tends to improve the quality of practical work, and that the universal custom of training psychologists at universities rather than in practical institutions is therefore justified. One must also believe that advances in theoretical understanding represent the only way in which the overall quality of practical work can, in the long run, be substantially improved. Without the critical theoretical tradition, psychology would be in much the same position as e.g. psychiatric practices in many primitive cultures. Apparently, these may continue in generally unchanged form over centuries. However, lest the discussion of theory and practice appear too one-sidedly in favor of the former, it should be added that it is frequently doubtful whether theorizing which has not grown out of practice is of much value. The power of our Western intellectual tradition has been achieved at the expense of the frequent emergence of isolated scholastic 'worlds' with little bearing on what goes on outside the study chambers. In this book the vital importance of a steady interplay between theory and practice will, therefore, be strongly emphasized.

Psychology is reflexive

Psychology is regarded here as a *reflexive* undertaking. The two first dictionary meanings (Webster) of the term reflexive are: '1. Capable of bending back. 2. Directed or turned back upon itself.' In the present context, the most adequate definition of reflexive would be 'capable of being turned back on itself'. Applied to psychology this simply means that the psychologist's professional activities such as observing, interviewing, testing, experimenting, thinking, writing, lecturing, counseling, etc., themselves belong to the subject matter of psychology. Take for example the case of a psychologist who formulates a theory of persuasion based on observations of how subjects influence each other in discussions arranged in the laboratory. Reflexivity here implies simply that the psychologist should recognize that his own efforts, through writing, lecturing, and discussing, to convince his colleagues that his theory is plausible, are themselves examples of persuasion and hence should be explainable by the theory. All too frequently one observes glaring examples of ignorance of this principle. Thus, one may visit congresses devoted to the discussion of perception where all the participants walk around with name badges so small that one must grab hold of a person and bend down close to him in order to read his name. Similarly, there are conferences on educational psychology where you may observe one lecturer after the other reading his manuscript with a dull flat voice and expressionless face to a bored and sleepy auditorium.

Reflexivity is a quality that psychology shares with the other social sciences, but which sets these sciences sharply apart from the natural sciences. Botany or geology is not in this same sense relevant to the description and understanding of the professional activities of the botanist or geologist. The reason is simply: the botanist is not a plant, and the geologist is not a piece of mineral, but the psychologist is a person and his professional activities involve mental processes, describable by psychology.

Before discussing the consequences of reflexivity for psychology, it is important to point out certain limitations in its applicability.

First, many parts of psychology such as the study of animals, infants, sensory and motor processes, etc. may be only remotely and peripherally relevant to the understanding of the professional activities of the psychologist. Hence, reflexivity is not always important to the same extent.

Second, although it should not be ignored, it may for many purposes be bracketed, i.e. deliberately excluded from consideration. The important thing to remember about reflexivity is this: All the topics studied by the psychologist may not be equally relevant for the understanding of his own activities, but all of his own activities belong to the subject matter of psychology. Hence, self-reflection is a professionally relevant activity.

Third, many essential perspectives on psychology as a science and a profession fall outside the scope of psychology proper and belong to the domains of other disciplines such as sociology, social anthropology, economics, political science, and history. Psychology can be seen as a cultural sub-universe situated in a larger society. In order to understand certain aspects of the psychologist's activities, one must see them in relation to the surrounding social realities. These continuously changing realities lie outside the scope of psychology proper, but although they may be temporarily bracketed for the purpose of specific projects, they cannot be ignored, if one wants to understand the activity of psychologists. In summary, this means that the psychologist must consider his own activities, not only in the light of psychology itself (reflexivity), but also in the light of various other disciplines.

Let us now try to make explicit some consequences of the reflexivity of psychology.

The psychologist encounters fellow human beings

Since psychology also applies to professional psychological activity the psychologist himself can be a subject or a client, and not only have subjects and clients. Being a person himself, the psychologist encounters another person, a fellow human being. This means that the psychologist may have an attitude towards those he is studying and treating, which differs fundamentally from the attitude that is evoked by a non-human entity. Your fellow human beings experience things basically as you do, they are existentially in the same position, they feel and dream and think much like you do. They require respect and affection as you do and they evoke feelings of sympathy and antipathy. The preceding may be regarded as commitment to a *humanistic* position in psychology. The reader who thinks that such a position is rather self-evident and trivial is in a way right. Yet, one should remember that much of academic psychology is still inclined to view the matter in the way expressed by Bergmann and Spence in a classic paper (1944):

... the empiricist scientist should realize that his behavior, symbolic or otherwise, does not lie on the same methodological level as the responses of his subjects ... In studying his subjects, including their symbolic responses (object language), the behavior scientist himself uses a different language (pragmatic metalanguage).

This position would seem to exclude reflexivity as well as a study of such processes as communication between psychologist and subject or client about psychology.

The psychologist can be subjected to psychological investigation

The basic similarity between the psychologist and his subject or client means that the same conditions and factors that influence the subject or client may also influence the psychologist. Empirical research can be and has been applied to ascertain this. The preceding means, for one thing, that theorizing about and dealing with subjects and clients becomes considerably facilitated. The principle of this is best expressed in the famous statement by Edward Tolman, 'what would I do if I were the rat?' This is a special case of the utilization of common sense knowledge that will be described at length in chapters V and VI. Conversely, the psychologist should be able to profit in his understanding of his own research and practical work from what he has learned about subjects and clients. Many potential sources of error and misinterpretation can be avoided if the psychologist himself is regarded as in many ways similar to his subjects and clients. Some aspects of the psychology of the researcher and the therapist will be further elaborated in chapters II and III.

Subjects and clients have 'psychologies' of their own

The psychologist encounters fellow human beings who, like him, have a practical understanding of psychology, as well as at least some theoretical conceptions. This means that psychological descriptions frequently must include the subject's/client's practical and theoretical understanding of psychology as an integral part. This is a particular example of what is meant by Alfred Schütz's observation that

... the constructs of the social sciences are, so to speak, constructs of the second degree, that is constructs of the constructs made by the actors on the social scene, whose behavior the social scientist has to observe and to explain in accordance with the procedural rules of his science (Schütz 1967, p. 59).

Even our unreflected practical understanding in every day life involves routine second order constructions such as what A thinks about B's opinions about C, what A thinks B thinks A thinks of him, etc. It is a sign of the relative immaturity of our science that a complete conceptual framework attempting to incorporate the practical common sense psychological conceptions of subjects and clients has not yet been constructed.

In passing, it should be noted that there is an openness in the theoretical task at this point. Thus, it may be argued that the second degree constructs employed by the psychologist in order to understand his own and his fellow beings' practical psychological understanding, must themselves be analyzed by means of third order constructs etc. For examples of such higher order analyses see e.g. Mills (1967).

Psychological theories may generate realities, which serve to verify the theories

A final consequence of the preceding considerations is that developments in psychology are communicated, not only to other psychologists, but eventually also to the general public, i.e. to the potential subjects and clients. As already mentioned, such communication about psychology between psychologists and subjects/clients cannot be accommodated by the methodological scheme of Bergmann and Spence (see above). On the other hand, it has wide-reaching implications for the scientific status of psychology. Generally speaking, a psychological theory is a special case of what may be called 'theories of identity'. Such theories attempt to describe what we are, who we are, how we function, i.e. the 'nature' of Man. A new theory becomes accepted by the general public, perhaps because it appears to confirm certain aspects of their already existing self-picture, while at the same time appearing to resolve or explain certain important uncertainties. This means that there may occur, in the general public, a change, not only in self-image and in the conception of other adults, but also in the conception of children and of what they are to become. Hence, new generations may grow up, whose identity will progressively tend to accord better with the prevailing theory.

Although we will return to these problems it may be important to quote Berger and Luckmann (1967, p. 178) here, in order to make the point somewhat clearer:

> Another way of saying that psychological theories are adequate is to say that they reflect the psychological reality they purport to explain. But if this were the whole story, the relationship between theory and reality here would not be a dialectical one. A genuine dialectic is involved because of the *realizing* potency of psychological theories. Insofar as psychological theories are elements of the social definition of reality, their reality-generating capacity is a characteristic they share with other legitimating theories: however, their realizing potency is particularly great because it is actualized by emotionally charged processes of identity-formation. If a psychology becomes socially established (that is, becomes generally recognized as an adequate interpretation of objective reality), it tends to realize itself forcefully in the phenomena it purports to interpret... Psychologies produce a reality, which in turn serves as the basis for their verification.

Thus, the theoretical psychologist encounters a dilemma in attempting to verify his theory: Psychologist to potential subject/client 'This is human nature, this is how you are.' Potential subject/client: 'Yes, I believe you are right, this is how I am, just look at me.' An alternative version of the dialogue is just as troublesome: 'This is human nature, this is how you are.' Potential subject/client: 'No, you are quite wrong. I'll show you, just look at me.'

Two anecdotes from the history of psychoanalysis may serve to concretize the point that psychological theories generate new realities. In one of the early psychoanalytic congresses, some time after Freud had published his treatise on the nature of humor, it was observed that when a lecturer told a joke, the audience looked at Freud to see whether he was laughing, before they laughed themselves. Apparently there was a general wariness about displaying behavior that could be unfavorably interpreted, and perhaps this was followed, among the initiated, by a gradual deeper change in the conception of what is funny.

The other anecdote serves to illustrate how psychological theories may very well have serious consequences in changing behaviors. It is said that Freud and his disciples were walking on a mountain outside Zürich, and that they arrived at an observation point with a not very solid rail at the edge of a steep cliff. To savor the anecdote it must be remembered that Freud had written that fear of heights was a definite sign of sexual anxiety. Soon the whole party was leaning against the old rail, talking higher and higher and ever more gaily. Gradually every one leaned more and more heavily and trustingly against the rail, until there was a breaking sound, upon which every one threw himself backward at the last moment so as to escape certain death.

What has been said above about the premises accepted in this treatise can be summarized in the following practical conclusion: The psychologist should never forget that he himself is not exempted from psychological scrutiny even in his most professional and scientific moments. Psychology is not an elevated platform from which one may serenely look down on what human beings do and experience. Rather, we all participate in the dramatic scenes we observe, and our scientific and professional activity is inextricably bound up with the surrounding sociocultural matrix. We may deliberately and temporarily bracket this matrix, but we must not pretend it is not there.

Questions after Chapter I

1. Discuss the relative merits of regarding psychology as an intellectual discipline embodied in existing written documents, and as an entity embodied in the conceptions, strategies, and values of psychologists.

2. Discuss the question of whether one ought to regard theoretical or practical sophistication as the most important characteristic of qualified psychologists.

3. Are you really convinced that reflexivity is an important feature of psychology and that this makes a difference.

4. What are the relative merits of treating subjects/clients as respectively fellow human beings and as organisms?

5. Are you really convinced that psychological theories may generate new realities?

II. The psychologist as researcher

In order to be able to describe what it means to become a psychologist, the integrated whole involved (see chapter I, pp. 15-16), must be broken down, analytically, into manageable parts. One obvious such breakdown is into the roles of researcher and practitioner. These two roles are felt to be relatively distinct. They can also be seen as, in some ways, primary, relative to the third main role of the psychologist, namely that of *teacher,* which involves communication with students.

Every role involves *prescriptions* as to how it should be played. As far as professional roles are concerned, a major distinction can be made between *ethical* and *methodological* prescriptions. A main difference between them can be formulated as follows: If you break an ethical rule *you* are bad, if you break a methodological rule your *work* is bad. Ethical rules regulate the psychologist's ways of dealing with subjects, clients, colleagues, institutions, and the general public. Many of these rules are the same that apply to every role in the given society. However, some of them are relatively specific and involve, e.g. the definition of certain communications as confidential, and elaborations of under what conditions the injunction to 'tell the truth, the whole truth, and nothing but the truth' can be dispensed with. The latter example is especially important, since, as will be shown later, neither psychological research nor psychological practice is conceivable without certain forms of deceit.

Methodology contains relatively general prescriptions for how to avoid critique of one's work. Methodology means precorrection of error, in so far as this error stems from the way a given research on practical work is carried out. The most definite and uncontroversial advances in psychology have not, so far, been made in the form of acquisition of scientific knowledge, but rather in the form of increasing methodological sophistication.

In this chapter, a few of the prescriptions for the role of psychological researcher will be described, as well as some problems involved in actually playing the role.

What does it mean to be scientific?

In order to be a psychological researcher you must be committed to search for a particular kind of knowledge, namely scientific knowledge. This may be simply defined as the knowledge which can only be established by maintaining a constant critical attitude. In a critical attitude one is all the time attuned to the question of what evidence exists for and against any particular statement or set of statements. The researcher is always looking for logical and statistical fallacies, empty statements, tautologies, ambiguities, alternative interpretations, hidden presuppositions, sources of error, overgeneralizations, etc. In playing this critical game he is trying to establish maximally dependable, exact, and generalized knowledge. He is continuously balancing between the strong wish for sweeping generality and revolutionary novelty, to which the layman often succumbs, and over-pedantic concern with petty trivialities. When the scientist frequently seems to err in the latter direction, he often does so for two good reasons. First, he knows that maximum dependability is a necessary criterion for scientific knowledge and that he must make sure that what little he can establish in the way of new knowledge has this quality. Second, he knows that difficult general problems that have resisted all the obvious and easy attempts at solution, can sometimes be solved only as a result of persistent and exhaustive inquiry into what, to the outsider, may seem to be unimportant details.

Scientific knowledge changes continuously as a result of ongoing research processes. It consists not only of what one at a certain time believes to be true, but also of what one believes to be false. Contemporary psychology has accumulated considerable knowledge of what hypotheses are wrong, what points of view are untenable, and what methods and ways of thinking are indefensible.

In summary, being scientific can be very simply defined as a commitment to the critical attitude. In recent years, a number of criticisms have been raised against the traditional conception of science. The most important of these criticisms will be discussed in the following sections.

The scientist attempts to be neutral

It is often said that science is not neutral (*wertfrei*). Four different interpretations of this statement are obviously true and are listed below:

1. The direction of research is influenced by political pressures on the channeling of funds and on the establishment of different types of institutions and positions.

2. The individual researcher's choice of theories, concepts, and problems is influenced by his general and special background.

3. The researcher may have vested interests in certain types of outcomes and interpretations and these may unwittingly influence what he actually comes up with. See Rosenthal (1966) and Friedman (1967).

4. The researcher himself and others may use findings in the service of very different kinds of interests. When the possibility of 'misuse' of results is imminent, the researcher may get into a legitimate ethical conflict. Examples of this are studies of nuclear, chemical, and bacteriological weapons, 'brainwashing', torture, etc.

In the preceding four senses science is indeed intimately related to values. Furthermore, the commitment to the critical attitude is itself a normative matter. Even so, the validity of our initial definition of what characterizes the scientific attitude is not affected by this and it can be reformulated as follows:

5. The researcher is under obligation to try to maintain his critical attitude. This means that, in his research, he must try to be equally critical of those alternatives that he favors as of those he tends to reject. Hence, he is under obligation to bracket his evaluations and to proceed in an impartial and detached manner. If he does not do this he will, per definition, not produce scientific knowledge. This does not exclude that a highly biased and emotionally involved researcher *can* hit upon results which *later* become established as scientific knowledge. The point is that *he* did not so establish them.

Thus, there is a built-in dilemma in the role of the researcher. On the one hand, he is obliged to be neutral and impartial. On the other hand, he must be strongly engaged and highly interested in order to endure the intellectually strenuous and patience-trying work. The result is a continuing conflict between the obligation to retain an open mind, and a wish to accept certain interpretations as being the definite truth.

In summary, the recent emphasis on the importance of value and interests in science in no way changes the researcher's obligation to be neutral and disengaged in his work. However, we may have become somewhat more skeptical about his ability to approximate this ideal.

Relevance cannot always be known in advance

The psychological researcher is often accused of concentrating on trivial or practically irrelevant questions. This criticism can neither be fully dismissed nor fully accepted.

On the one hand, it is a legitimate pressure put on scientists by other members of society to help solve our growing and, in the long run, desperate problems. On the other hand, it is in the nature of research that one must play the critical game in order to achieve dependable knowledge. The consequence is that scientific work proceeds much too slowly and through too many detours to please politicians, who are supposed to do something about the problems now. As a solution to this dilemma, psychologists have sometimes participated in so-called *action research,* i.e. studies of the carrying out and consequences of practical undertakings. Action research will be directly valuable to the extent that it produces scientific knowledge, i.e. to the extent it allows one to assemble relatively solid evidence for and against different interpretations of the outcome. Unfortunately, the complexity of the actions that have potential practical importance is usually so high that one is left at the end of the project with about as much uncertainty as when one started. This means that action research is usually no direct short cut to scientific knowledge, but is likely to leave one disappointed. However, it may also have another function, namely to provide new data and new ideas, which may, in turn, stimulate and direct further research, perhaps in more realistic and fruitful directions.

Besides action research proper, it is also possible to re-direct conventional research to practically relevant areas. Frequently, such areas have obvious *face relevance:* changes in psychiatric treatment are obviously relevant when one attempts to improve the outcome of such treatment, etc. However, practical relevance is not always a highly visible relationship. The history of science contains numerous examples of how research turns out to be relevant in quite unexpected contexts, and conversely, that research on seemingly directly relevant problems resulted in no advance. Frequently, we do not know what is relevant for what and in what ways. Relevance has no independent distinguishing characteristics — it is a post-facto characteristic. We may *try* to do something of practical relevance, but there is no recipe that can guarantee that we succeed.

In conclusion, the cry for practical relevance should be heard and taken into account as far as possible. In view of the doubtful efficiency of such short cuts as action research and of the difficulty of determining in advance what will be relevant, one must, however, allow the main stream of science to proceed at its own speed and in those more or less strange directions that at any given time seem intellectually plausible.

Reflection and dialogue alone do not establish scientific knowledge

Since we all have extensive experiences and considerable practical under-standing, it is natural that we *think* about these experiences and this understanding. Such reflection is a powerful instrument for arriving at new ideas and conceptual insights. The same can to some extent be said about dialogues (and discussions between several people at a time). In a dialogue there is a mutual stimulation and criticism which may enhance the quality of each participant's consequent thinking. Reflection and dialogue are clearly important parts of the scientific work. How-ever, the would-be-researcher in psychology should realize quite clearly that reflection and dialogue alone cannot establish scientific knowledge, and that, when carried too far, they can lead one into a trap that is hard to escape from.

The dangers of prolonged reflection about empirical phenomena with-out reliance on other methods, can e.g. be illustrated by the work of Sartre on the ancient and psychologically important problem of nega-tion ('not-being', 'nothingness'). For a brief description see Stern (1967, pp. 54-64). The history of this topic in philosophy would fill several volumes and will not even be touched upon here, except to note that, already in antiquity, the philosopher Parmenides seems to have recog-nized a major difficulty in describing nothingness when he says: 'Never let this thought prevail that non-being is; but keep your mind from this way of investigation.' (Stern 1967, p. 59). He may have had in mind the contradiction inherent in all definitions of the type 'nothingness is . . .' Many philosophers have failed to heed this warning, in our time notably Heidegger and Sartre, who have struggled with the attempt to characterize and define nothingness.

In defense of Sartre, it must be said that he has realized how deeply real nothingness and negation are in our lives, and that somehow we cannot accept defeat and remain silent about this aspect of life. Yet, the outcome of his reflections in *L'Être et le néant* includes long passages which few people seem to understand, and linguistic monsters such as 'Le néant n'est pas, il est été' or 'il est néantisé. In English this must be translated as approximately 'nothingness is not, it is been', or 'it is naught' (where the neologism 'naughting' is a translation of Sartre's 'néantiser' (and Heidegger's 'nichten'). Prolonged reflective undertak-ings of this type may easily fail and the reason is very simply formulated by Levi-Strauss in his comment on Sartre's *Critique de la raison dialec-tique.*

He who begins by steeping himself in the allegedly self-evident truths of introspection never emerges from them. Knowledge of men sometimes seems easier to those who allow themselves to be caught up in the snare of personal identity. But they thus shut the door on knowledge of man . . . Sartre in fact becomes the prisoner of his own Cogito (1966, p. 249).

Successive reflection about the true nature of a phenomenon (in our example nothingness) is 1) entirely dependent on the starting point, i.e. on a person's initial conceptions, and 2) is subject to a very strong interaction between reflection and what is reflected on. The net effect of these two preconditions may be that the reflecting person is successively more tightly enmeshed in his own web. Furthermore, the relentless requirement of inner consistency in these advanced thought processes forces the person to develop his own language in communicating with himself. The more determinedly the lonely thinker pursues his introspection, the farther he gets from his fellow beings. The typical symptoms of such states of advanced cognitive 'encapsulation' (Brunswik) are 1) impenetrable soliloquies, 2) linguistic monsters, 3) neologisms. They are all well illustrated in the case of Sartre.

Dialogues with other persons widen the scope of the reflective process, but again there is dependence on the initial conceptions of the two participants and very strong interactions between their respective points of view. This means that there is a diminishing return involved. What participant A says to participant B is progressively more influenced by what B has previously said to A and vice versa. The homogenization of thinking within in-groups is a very pronounced phenomenon. One of the reasons why introspection was abandoned relatively early in the history of scientific psychology was, indeed, the fact that introspective data from one laboratory could not be reproduced in other laboratories with different theoretical views. In other words, what we observe in introspection is highly influenced by what we think we should observe, and this can spread to entire groups.

The weakness of isolated reflection and of isolated dialogues and group discussions is that you do not encounter anything which is truly *independent* of your thinking. This means that you do not allow the world around you to break through into your encapsulated existence. There is no denial that your preconceived notions always influence what you choose to observe, how you are selective, and how you interpret. However, you *can* decide to expose yourself, under prearranged conditions, to outcomes of which you are openly uncertain and over which you have no control. In this way you can make yourself, at least pointwise, open to the world. This is the essence of the *empirical* position, to which, I think, every psychologist must be committed.

In conclusion, reflection and dialogue are necessary and valuable, but alone they cannot establish new scientific knowledge. In the long run they may lead to evil circles of intellectual stagnation and to communication problems. Therefore, the psychologist must also expose himself to phenomena which are *independent* of his thinking about them. This is what empirical research is about.

Psychological research involves the study of other persons who do not know the full purpose of the research

We have said above that empirical research should confront the researcher with outcomes which are independent of his thinking. One direct consequence of this is that he should study other persons than himself. The mental processes in the researcher are more or less influenced by his conceptions of them, and thus can only be the starting point for his work.

Sartre's endless struggles with the meaning of words as they appear to him, and the contradictions involved in attempting to describe e.g. nothingness, can be ended only if the focus is shifted from the thinker himself to other persons. Instead of asking of oneself 'what is nothingness', one may ask 'what is nothingness under circumstances C1, C2, C3 . . . Cn to persons P1, P2, P3 . . . Pn?', and other similar questions. Experimental psychology may, for instance, provide some interesting material on how people deal with negative information (see Wason and Johnson-Laird, 1968). Nothingness, negation, emptiness, absence, which, when considered as independently existing, are impossible to describe in positive terms, change into positively existing phenomena when they are considered as processes, operations, or states in living persons. This is a transition from existence 'en soi' to existence 'pour lui/pour elle.'

However, as we have seen, it is not sufficient to say simply that the researcher must switch to a study of the other person, because this would include acceptance of the dialogue as a useful procedure. Why this is not the case should be clear from the following schematic example: Researcher: 'This is what I think about nothingness . . . and this is what I expect you to think . . .' Subject: 'I think . . .' Here the subject may be strongly influenced by the experimenter's thoughts and no truly independent information will be forthcoming. The prototype of a proper procedure should rather be something like this: Researcher: 'Tell me what you think about nothingness?' Subject: 'Why do you ask me?' Researcher: 'I won't tell you that until later.' Subject: 'What do *you* think about nothingness?' Researcher: 'I won't tell you that until later.' Subject: 'I think . . .' In this case the subject's answer may be reasonably independent of what the researcher expects him to answer, would like him to answer, and of what the researcher himself thinks about the topic involved.

In general, it is a basic methodological requirement in psychological research that the subject shall not be influenced by the researcher's thinking and expectancies. This means that all psychological research must involve *deceit,* in the general sense that the researcher, for a period of time, does not tell 'the truth, the whole truth, and nothing but the truth'. The information given to subjects never contains the whole truth, and very frequently there is misleading or confusing information, or even direct lies. This withholding and manipulation of information are necessary in order to place the subject in exactly the kind of situation one wants to study. Ethically, it is justified by reference to the 'cause of science', to the fact that it is only temporary, that it leads to no unnecessary or lasting harm, and that the subject has voluntarily agreed to participate in the study.

Finally, the reader with some historical knowledge will note that we are siding with the behaviorists against the old introspectionists in defining scientific psychology as the study of the other person. However, it will become apparent later in this book that we subscribe neither to the physicalism of behaviorists, nor to their postulate of 'epistemological loneliness' (Bakan, 1968). At this point, however, we are restricting the discussion to basic aspects of doing psychological research, i.e. to prescriptions that must be followed by all researchers.

Making observations and having experiences are not research

In these days of revolutionary talk, it is sometimes asserted that if you make observations and subject yourself to experiences in connection with some given project, then you can write down your impressions and present them as a piece of research. In order to evaluate this, one should keep in mind that every observation or experience in itself is ambiguous, i.e. can be interpreted in many different ways. Research is the process of accumulating evidence for and against these various possible interpretations. The problem, then, is whether observations and experiences, e.g. in the course of practicing psychology or in one's every day life, enable one to decide between specific alternative interpretations. In the sections to follow, it will be shown that our experiences are very likely to lead us astray in the matter of interpretation, unless we resort to highly disciplined research projects.

Since antiquity, philosophers have recognized two basic principles according to which people seem to connect events, namely the association laws of *similarity*, (a thing evokes thoughts about similar things), and *contiguity* (a thing evokes thoughts about things which occur in spatiotemporal contiguity with the original thing). These principles were taken over and further developed in the new scientific psychology. Similarly, a classical line of thought in social anthropology began with Frazer (1922) who pointed out that magic beliefs seemingly belong to two groups, homeopathic magic depending on a law of similarity and contagious magic depending on a law of contiguity. The very existence of magical beliefs in all human societies in itself indicates that our daily experiences indeed tend to lead us astray when it comes to interpretation. In technologically advanced societies the law of similarity has come to be regarded as a psychological principle only, whereas the law of contiguity has been further refined into scientific views of causality. However, it is easy to show that in psychological practice and everyday life our dependence on contiguity is just as likely to lead us astray as it is in so-called primitive societies (see below). Hence, we must firmly reject the view that the mere practicing of psychology in every day life, or in professional contexts, is likely to lead to any genuine scientific advance. At most, such practice may furnish clues and ideas that *may* turn out to be fruitful. In what follows, this skepticism will be documented in some detail.

Dependence on positive correspondences only

Let us assume, as an hypothetical example, that we are interested in knowing how bedwetting in children relates to a particular type of toilet training. More specifically we may have the hypothesis that this type of toilet training (from here on called T) is an important factor contributing to the emergence of bedwetting. Let us furthermore assume that our observations are made in the course of work in an out-patient psychiatric clinic for children.

The most elementary, but very human, attitude is to be overly impressed with and keep track of the cases of bedwetters who have been subject to T. These correspondences are remembered and emphasized, much in the same way as the child tends to remember and emphasize the time he became ill exactly on his birthday, on Christmas Day, etc. It is quite hard for the untrained person to accept that the instances of positive correspondence between bedwetting and T or between illness and important holidays, *may* be entirely coincidental, i.e. *may* represent the outcome of two quite independent chains of events. It is even more difficult to believe in coincidence when there are *several* positive correspondences. Examples: In each of the last seven years there has been sunshine on my birthday. Now I have observed altogether 21 bedwetters with a background of T.

In Table 1 is shown a frequency table in which two categories of events are quite unrelated, even though there is a very high number of positive correspondences. In fact the number of positive correspondences is three times as high as the number of any other category of combinations. For further comment, see below.

Levi-Strauss has pointed out that so-called primitive thought is even more deterministic than scientific thought (1966, pp. 10-11). To primitive thought everything must have a definite place in the system of things and *all* contiguous occurrences of salient events are felt to be meaningful and in need of specific explanation. Even in our society it takes a long time for children to overcome, even partly, the tendency to reject the notion of coincidence (cf. Piaget and Inhelder, 1951). For experimental evidence that even highly educated adults tend to fall into this and the other types of error to be described below (see Smedslund 1963).

Dependence on presence vs. absence of one type of event, only when the dominant type of event is present

Very frequently, one of the two types of event involved is the more conspicuous, accessible, or important one. In the example given, this is clearly the case with bedwetting, whereas T is a set of historical happenings of considerable complexity, which were embedded in the lives of the parents and their child and which probably were not recognized as such by any of the persons involved. In this case the practitioner would probably think of his hypothesis only when he encounters a bedwetter and would try to keep tally of how frequently T seems to have been involved. If the bedwetters with T are clearly more numerous than the bedwetters without, he would be inclined to think there is a connection. On the other hand, when a child is *not* a bedwetter, the practitioner is inclined to be concerned with *other* hypotheses, such as ones concerning the background of thumbsuckers, nailbiters, children with nightmares, overaggression, overdependency, asthma, etc. It requires a very considerable amount of abstraction and distancing to see e.g. an asthmatic child who is not a bedwetter as relevant to the hypothesis of the origins of bedwetting, and to check whether or not he has been subjected to T. Yet this is precisely what one must do in order to test the given hypothesis. In Table 1, 45 out of 60 bedwetters have had T, but this is no evidence that bedwetting is related to T. In order to decide this, one must also look at the relative number of non-bedwetters who have and do not have the assumed background.

In our daily experience we can frequently recognize absence in the *concrete* sense that something that we expected to find is not there. Hence, we do notice the absence of T in some bedwetters. However, it is very hard for us to recognize as relevant the absence of the initial type of event, in this case bedwetting, because nothing leads us to expect it. On the other hand, each child who arrives at the clinic is referred on the basis of some kind of complaint, and this complaint typically defines the context in which we proceed. We see the child as bedwetter, asthmatic, aggressive, anxious, etc. rather than as 'non-bedwetter' 'not-asthmatic', 'not-aggressive', 'not-anxious', etc. However, at this point we must be careful, lest language lead us astray. The 'not' in the preceding sentence is what is called a contradictory rather than a contrary negation. This means that not-aggressive and not-afraid simply mean not aggressive and not afraid, rather than asserting the opposites timid and brave. The contradictory negation refers to the absence of a trait or characteristic without any implication about what is present. The contrary negation, which is not involved here, means that the opposite is the case.

In conclusion, we tend to think of our hypothesis about bedwetting only when bedwetters are encountered, just as we think about our hypothesis about asthmatics only when asthmatics are encountered, etc. As illustrated in Table 1, this tendency can contribute to make our inferences unreliable, since it leads us to consider only half of the four-fold table.

The logical structure of the concept of statistical relationship with dichotomous variables

We must now make explicit the general logic of inferences about the statistical relation between two variables. The illustration will be in terms of dichotomous variables, i.e. variables with only two values, but the logic is equally valid for multivalued and for continuous variables.

If we have two types of events A and B, each of which may be either present (+A, +B) or absent (—A, —B), four kinds of combinations are logically possible, namely +A+B, +A—B, —A+B, and —A—B. In order to form an opinion on whether or not the occurrence vs. non-occurrence of A is related to the occurrence vs. non-occurrence of B, we must keep a record of how many times each of the four combinations has occurred. The frequencies shown in Table 1 illustrate the fallacies involved in depending only on the positive correspondences (+A+B), or only on the presence vs. absence of one type of event when the other one is present (+A+B/+A—B, or +B+A/+B—A).

Table 1. 2×2 frequency table for illustrating the concept of statistical relationship with dichotomous variables

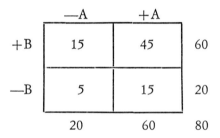

There are 45 positive correspondences (+A+B's) in the material. This is by far the most frequent category. However, there are 60 cases (or 75%) both of +A's and of +B's. If A and B were completely unrelated we would, by pure chance, expect $75\% \times 75\% = 56.25\%$ cases of +A+B, which is exactly what is found, namely 45 cases. Hence, the frequency of positive correspondences alone can lead us completely astray. Furthermore, although the probability that a + A will also be a +B and vice versa is .75 (45 out of 60 cases), this again is no more than could be expected by chance. Applied to our example, the numbers would mean that three out of four bedwetters turn out to have the given background T and, vice versa that three out of four with the given background turn out to be bedwetters. However, the lack of relationship in the data also means that three out of four non-bedwetters have T, and that three out of four without the background T are also bedwetters. This means that the chances that someone is a bedwetter are the same, irrespective of whether or not he has the given background, and the chances that he has the given background T are the same whether or not he is a bedwetter.

In the example of Table 1, we could also have pointed out that the probability of getting a +A (e.g. bedwetting) without knowing anything about whether or not B (e.g. background T) is positive or negative, is also three out of four or 75% (lower marginal numbers). This is also the probability of getting a +B without knowing whether A is positive or negative (right-hand marginal numbers). The marginal frequencies tell us about the total frequencies of the types of events in the given material, and are frequently called the *base rates*. In the given example, dependence on one of the types of event to predict the other does not improve the chances of being correct, beyond what can be achieved by depending merely on the base rates. Judgments of relationship between types of events are essentially estimates of the extent to which prediction can be improved above the base rates. Since, as we have shown, we tend to ignore the base rates, we are also susceptible to extreme misinterpretations of our experiences.

Samples, universes, and representativeness

The data in our hypothetical example of bedwetting and toilet training background (T) are assumed to have been gathered in an out-patient psychiatric clinic for children. A consequence of this would be that the children observed include proportionally many more bedwetters than groups of children taken at random from the homes or nursery schools in the surrounding area. The subjects and the behaviors we observe all consist of *samples,* in the sense that we seldom include *all* the individuals or *all* the behaviors of the *population* or *universe* in which we are interested. Furthermore, it is obvious that samples can be biased or selected in various ways. An example is the sample of children consult- ing the clinic. Another example more easy to visualize would be the strawberries we can *see* in a basket in the supermarket. Very commonly this sample consists of very fine and not overripe specimens, whereas many of those farther down in the basket may be reduced to a sad state of sogginess. In such a case, we say that the visible sample is not *representative* (i.e. typical or characteristic) of the population taken as a whole. There are two ways in which a 2×2 sample, such as that given in Table 1, may lack representativeness relative to a given universe. We have already mentioned the elementary case of differences in marginal distribution, exemplified by the inflated frequency of bedwetters in the clinic sample. The other, theoretically more interesting, way in which representativeness may be lacking, is when there is a difference in the relative cell frequencies, i.e. when the relationship between the two variables is not the same in the sample as in the universe. The following is a hypothetical example: Suppose that toilet training of type T is much more frequent in socio-economic group X than socio-economic group Y, whereas bedwetting is equally frequent. Suppose furthermore that people in group X much more frequently than in Y, regard bedwetting as a matter to be taken to the Doctor. In group Y, one may be inclined to 'keep the matter in the family'. The result of this could be that, although bedwetting and T are completely unrelated in the population as a whole, they would be highly related in the clinic sample. Most of the children referred for bedwetting would come from group X, and most of these would have a background of type T. On the other hand, a high percentage of the non-bedwetters may come from group Y and these would tend not to have background T. The important point here is that, even if we were able to judge the degree of relationship between variables in our experience (which we cannot do), our experiences may lead to completely erroneous conclusions because they do not include access to the base rates in the universe in which we are interested. Needless to say, we would tend to ignore these base rates even if we knew them.

In conclusion, one of the basic prescriptions for the role of researcher in psychology is to realize clearly why practical and every day experiences do not tend to furnish reliable knowledge. In order to arrive at such knowledge, e.g. about the relationship between two dichotomous variables, we must record observations of all four categories of events, including the double negative category (not-bedwetters, not-T). In addition to keeping track of the sample cell frequencies and base rates, we must be aware of the matter of representativeness and obtain estimates of the population cell frequencies and base rates. The weakness of man's inductive powers is such that, even after societies have existed for ten thousands of years, the daily lives of people all over the world are still filled with practices and beliefs that have no valid empirical foundation.

Misinterpretations of statistical measures

In the preceding sections some weaknesses involved in inductive inference from practical experience were described. The conclusion was that these weaknesses can only be corrected by research. Turning now to the research practices in psychology, we note that there is a heavy dependence on statistics for the description and evaluation of results. All psychologists are trained in statistics, and sound statistical thinking is undoubtedly an asset for a researcher. The uninitiated reader is referred to any one of the numerous existing text-books for an introduction to this aspect of a psychologist's intellectual background.

However, despite the relatively advanced formal training of psychologists, statistical measures often tend to be implicitly misinterpreted in directions that protect the researcher from uncertainty. Generally speaking, statistics often seems to be implicitly regarded as a sort of magical short cut to empirical truth. The would-be researcher should be keenly aware of the traps to be described, in order not to succumb to empty formalism.

Error. From the very beginning of scientific psychology it was observed that different individuals get different results in apparently identical situations and that the same individual tends to get different results with repeated measurements. This inter- and intraindividual variability is typically quite strong, even in rigorously controlled studies. In analogy with the tradition in the natural sciences, the variability not accounted for by the observed factors has been labeled *'error'*, and this term is still widely used (see e.g. Scott and Wertheimer, 1962). However, strictly speaking, the term error should be used *only* about that portion of the variation which can be explained by the imperfection of the measuring instruments involved. In the natural sciences the error variation is the variation that stems from the sum of the known or estimated imperfections in the instruments and procedures involved. Errors are deviations from 'true' values, and, to the extent that their origins are known, they can safely be ignored for many purposes.

However, in psychology, the term error is often used in another sense, referring to all the variation not explainable by the investigated variables. It would perhaps help if the word *error* in the widely used analysis of variance tables were replaced by the word *unknown* (i.e. unknown source of variance).

Mean. In order to introduce some order in the data, psychologists frequently calculate the average or mean value for many subjects and/or many responses. This mean usually cannot be legitimately regarded as an estimate of a 'true' value, since one cannot explain the deviations from it as error, i.e. in terms of known imperfections of the measuring instruments (see above). The most correct interpretation of the mean is usually to regard it as an indicator of a *tendency* or *trend* in the material. One should be aware of the danger of treating it as if it were a direct description of concrete individuals or concrete responses. One may, for example, find a significant (see below) difference in one direction between two means, even though, let us say, one-third of the individuals involved display a difference in the opposite direction. Example: on the average subjects learn faster in condition A than in condition B, but one-third of them learn faster in B than in A. For this third, then, a conclusion based on the mean would be false. Hence, one should avoid interpreting means as being representative of tendencies in individual subjects.

Correlation. There are many types of correlations, but they all involve a measure of the extent to which two variables tend to co-vary, i.e. of the extent to which they are statistically related. A perfect correlation means that to each value of one of the variables there corresponds a definite value of the other variable and vice versa. A zero correlation means that the variation in one of the variables cannot be predicted from the variation in the other and vice versa. One mistake, which, although warned against in all text-books, continues to occur, is to treat the correlation as if it refers to an established psychological linkage. This is definitely not the case. In terms of our earlier example, we could very well have found a high correlation between bedwetting and toilet training of type T, even though there was no psychological relationship between these variables. As was pointed out, the observed correlation could be entirely a byproduct of the biased selection of the clinic sample.

In general, there is a tendency to forget that the correlation, like the mean, is only an indicator of a tendency or trend. Just as deviations from the mean may be incorrectly treated as error, one may incorrectly consider the imperfection of a correlation as being due to error and hence as being of little consequence. This may be temporarily comforting but not very realistic.

Significance. Given two samples of observations, we can, by means of the elementary calculus of probability, and relying on the sample variability as an estimate of population variability, determine the likelihood that any given difference between means or any given correlation could have occurred by pure chance. If this likelihood is lower than a conventional level, usually 1 out of 20 or 1 out of 100, the difference or the correlation is said to be *significant* at the given level. A significant difference or correlation is one which is very unlikely to be the outcome of pure chance.

The concept of statistical significance can very easily come to function, in the mind of the researcher, as a kind of magical short cut to truth, and this must be very clearly recognized.

A difference or correlation, significant at the .01 level, means that it would occur by chance less than once in a hundred times. However, this does not imply that the theoretical interpretation of this difference or correlation has a similar likelihood of being true. A significant correlation between bedwetting and toilet training of type T in the clinic sample does not mean that the hypothesis that these factors are psychologically linked is strengthened to any particular degree. Nor does it mean that observation of T in a family is a practically useful prognostic sign of future bedwetting in the child. The correlation may be highly significant, yet of such a low order that it is of no practical importance. It is vital to recognize that the degree of statistical significance of an observed trend in the data has no logical connection whatsoever with the degree of certainty we can assign to the corresponding theoretical interpretation, or with which we can rely on given practical measures. In addition to the possibility of biased sampling, it should be noted that level of significance is a direct function of the size of the observed samples. Every difference or correlation becomes significant if the sample is big enough and loses significance if it is small enough. Increasing or decreasing the number of observed persons or responses obviously has no bearing on the magnitude of the relationships involved. In other words, *statistical significance does not mean, and has no definite relation to, theoretical or practical significance.*

These were a few of the ways of thinking about data that should be avoided by the researcher in psychology. After this discussion of formal methodology, we will now turn to some other aspects of the 'praxis' of psychological research.

The researcher as a high-status person

The meeting between a psychologist and his subject is a social interaction process and involves a number of aspects and problems which are unique to the social sciences. The psychologist must induce subjects to participate and to perform properly; he must also communicate with them, both in order to inform and to deceive. A precondition for all this is that he must attempt to see things also from the subject's point of view, a task which is non-existent for the natural scientist.

In order to understand what goes on in psychological research, it is, among other things, important to recognize that the researcher is a high-status person. The principal investigator has a good personal income, servants (assistants, technicians, secretaries), ample material possessions (valuable instruments, work space, money for salaries, and expenses), etc. The investigator is also a person with a higher form of wisdom. What he does and how he thinks is often more or less incomprehensible to ordinary people and to the lower categories of servants. Likewise, his ulterior motives for doing things this way rather than that may be beyond the understanding of others, sometimes also beyond his own understanding. Even so, his instructions are to be accepted and obeyed. The preceding is also true in the case of a team of investigators, or when the principal investigator and his assistants work on relatively equal terms. The freedom of research is sacred, and not to be interfered with by the uninitiated. The position of the researcher, once his grant is approved, is highly privileged and protected.

Until he becomes so senior and so important that he no longer personally participates in his projects, this high-status person, who is the researcher, goes to his laboratory and meets with fellow human beings who are typically in quite different life circumstances. They may be undergraduate students, school- or nursery-schoolchildren, job applicants, enlisted men, clients of various kinds of treatment centers, inmates of institutions for the handicapped, retarded, mentally ill, criminals, etc. Common to these categories is that they are moderately to extremely low-status persons with small means and little power.

The difference in social position must be recognized as a frequent precondition for psychological research, because only the high-status person has the necessary material means to launch a study and the necessary coercive power to get subjects. Conversely, low-status persons are most accessible as subjects, because their resistance to coercion is low. Financially independent adults (providers for families), especially those of relatively high status, are typically felt to be too 'busy' or too 'important' to be bothered, tend to be reluctant or inaccessible if one nevertheless attempts to bother them, and anyhow tend to be 'bad' subjects. They may have difficulties in adjusting meekly and flexibly to instructions and tend to cancel their appointments because of 'more important' business. Although there are many kinds of exceptions, psychological research is typically a game that is played between high-status researchers and low-status subjects. This has consequences both for the technical execution of research and for the results.

Why subjects participate and behave properly

Subjects participate in psychological research because they have to, because they are paid, because of social pressures, and, occasionally, because of curiosity. The various types of inducement will not be commented upon in detail. However, it is obvious that low-status subjects are more frequently than others in positions where they can be directly ordered to participate, or where they are willing to work for a modest financial compensation. The presence of social pressure is not always so easy to observe. Yet it occurs very clearly in classrooms, institutions and other groups of subjects, when the question of participation arises. Its hidden strength is well illustrated in the case of a pale little girl of five years who meekly followed the present author into the laboratory, after all of her friends had been subjects. In the doorway she turned and asked her teacher in a small resigned voice: 'Will I come out again?'

The nature of the game, from the point of view of the child subject, also came out vividly although somewhat ambiguously in the remark by another small girl to her mother, upon seeing the author on the street. 'There goes the man who takes me to the basement and gives me candy!'

Usually, an empirical study proceeds smoothly enough, once a subject has agreed to participate. However, one should not forget that this is possible only because one can rely on the immense capacity of the normal adult for behaving socially correctly. This is part of the *Randbedingungen* of psychological experiments, and must be included in whatever theoretical framework you choose to accept. Conversely, if politeness and cooperativeness on the part of molecules or enzymes were preconditions for microbiological research, this would have corresponding consequences for microbiological theory. Briefly, psychological research presupposes parts of the sociocultural matrix in which it occurs.

Small children are not yet completely socialized, and consequently, they are the ones most likely to disturb the experimental proceedings. They are likely to forget instructions, let their attention stray to other aspects of the situation and volunteer crude remarks such as: 'You have a blue tooth', 'Why do you look so strange?' 'Why do you ask those dull questions?' 'Don't you have any real work to do?', etc. However, children do not really count (except as subjects), so the experienced experimenter can relatively easily detach himself from these disturbances, except perhaps for a nagging irritation — 'Is that tooth really so visible?'

On the other hand, if a slightly drunk princess of the street happens to have volunteered as a subject, matters can get quite complicated. This type of subject may display a bottle of beer and offer it along with other things to the experimenter. She may regard the entire set-up with utter lack of comprehension, and, above all, may get personal, i.e. look deep into the eyes of the researcher, call him by his first name, touch him, etc. How different will the laboratory look when you see it with a swaying, yet friendly lass sitting on the table, and your papers soaked in beer! The science game, being an important and highly respectable, but entirely impersonal activity, is broken to pieces. You feel confused and warm and try to concentrate on how to remove your visitor and her traces in a firm yet humane way before the next subject arrives.

In many specific research projects one may perhaps safely bracket one's knowledge of the social preconditions. However, when it comes to the question of general conceptual framework, these preconditions cannot be ignored.

The researcher must deceive and the subject must be honest

Empirical research in psychology must, as already mentioned, occur in conditions where the subject does not know what the researcher expects to find. Hence, *all* psychological studies depart at some point from the injunction to tell 'the truth, the whole truth, and nothing but the truth'. Minimal witholding of information occurs, e.g. in a study of perceptual judgments where the subject is not told exact properties of the presented stimulus-objects and what the experimenter's hypotheses are. Maximal deception is exemplified, e.g. in the studies of obedience by Milgram (1965), where the real subject is falsely led to believe that he is merely working as an assistant, required to administer successively more severe electric shocks to a subject, who is seen and heard screaming in agony (all make believe).

It is generally recognized that varying degrees of deceit are necessary, since the whole purpose of psychological studies would otherwise be defeated. Ethically, there is usually no problem, as subjects can always be told the truth afterwards. The border line cases are those studies, such as Milgram's, where there may occur genuine suffering in the subjects.

The converse requirement that the subject must be honest may seem rather trivial. It appears obvious that if the subject seriously attempts to deceive the researcher, then the results become useless and the purpose of the study is defeated. Actually, we are here touching upon a fundamental problem in psychology, namely the nature of the relationship between the outer and the inner man, between the objective and the subjective. Irrespective of one's theoretical position, one must acknowledge that deceit on the part of the subject is a real, even though frequently improbable, possibility. Every researcher always tries to establish a situation and a relationship with the subject which will ensure that deceit will not be attempted. Three consequences of this will be briefly mentioned here:

First, the opposition honesty-deceit leads us to realize how the research situation is merely one variant of the possible interactions between two persons. When two people are telling each other the whole truth about what they think, we have an open symmetrical dialogue. We have already pointed out that this type of interaction has limited value for scientific purposes (p. 30). When one person is completely open, whereas another is intentionally holding things back or distorting them for a purpose, the latter may be said to try to 'manipulate' the former. The situation in psychological research is a normally ethically defensible and institutionalized subclass of manipulatory interactions.

Finally, there is the case when both partners in an interaction to some extent withhold information and/or lie. This is a normal type of everyday interaction. A possible subclass would be the case of two researchers confronting each other. The following is a concrete example:

In the thirties, a young philosopher, interested in what was then called 'science of science', underwent treatment by a well known psychoanalyst. The analyst was a prolific writer and presumably kept notes about what happened in the treatment. Also, in accordance with the rules of his trade, he must have kept many of his thoughts about the patient to himself. The philosopher, on the other hand, was not quite an ordinary patient. He was, in addition to his personal motivations, interested in gathering material on how psychoanalysts think, and he got some data on this, by, inadvertently, having the identical dream hundreds of times during the therapy. In this way he could observe how the therapist changed his interpretations and general ways of reacting to an identical input.

This was an illustration of the potential symmetry between researcher and subject. Another is the well-known cartoon showing two rats in a

Skinner box, one saying to the other: 'Now I've got him conditioned. Each time I pull the lever, he delivers a pellet'.

One of the lessons of the preceding runs as follows: Your subject is really a double being. The outer man you can observe, but the inner man is inaccessible to you, unless he chooses to reveal himself. Your subject is probably not pulling your leg, but some of your scientific curiosity should be directed to the question: 'How do you *know* he is not (pulling your leg)?'

The preceding question leads directly to our second comment on the problem of deceit vs. honesty. In most situations, including practically all psychological research, we are pretty convinced that no deceit is involved on the part of the subject. In others, we think deceit is possible, but very frequently we are able to decide in a subjectively convincing way whether or not this is actually the case. The question of how we can do this leads us to common-sense psychology, i.e. to what we all know about *when* people tend to deceive others and *when* they tend to be honest. The structure of this knowledge and its validity are taken for granted in most psychological research. The investigation of the common-sense psychology of deceit vs. honesty is a task which is of considerable importance in order to understand the 'praxis' of psychology, scientific as well as practical.

Finally, the acceptance of deceit as a real possibility has profound implications for psychological theory. Above all it means acceptance of *meaning* as a datum in psychology, because only actions which have meaning can be true or false. Furthermore, it means recognition that the subject, to a considerable extent, controls the relationship between his inner knowledge and feeling and his outer behavior. This again means that one cannot postulate any absolutely fixed 'behavioral indices' of mental processes. In other words, mental processes cannot be operationally anchored in any simple way, and any attempts at such anchoring must be provisional and relative to situation or culture. The preceding also applies to psychophysiological relationships (see pp. 223—225). The general reluctance to admit data from so-called *lie-detectors* as legal evidence, reflects common-sense understanding of this fact. Hence, we may conclude that the conceptual framework of psychology is in many ways different from that in natural science. The natural scientist makes inferences from his data, based on theory. The psychologist *communicates* with his subject.

Questions after Chapter II

1. In addition to maintaining a critical attitude, the researcher is usually expected to be creative, original, patient, courageous, etc. Try to clarify how the latter group of requirements are related to and compare with the requirement of maintaining a critical attitude.

2. Are you really convinced that the scientist must attempt to be neutral?

3. To what extent is it true that empirical study, but not reflection and dialogue, establishes contact with an independent reality?

4. Try to clarify further the relationship between degree of statistical significance of a difference or correlation and the theoretical and practical conclusions one may draw.

III. The psychologist as practitioner

The researcher and the practitioner both rely on ethics as well as on methodology as regulators of their work. In science, methodology is very much in the foreground, since it attempts to specify how one can best satisfy the requirements of the critical attitude in particular areas and with respect to particular types of problems. Ethics is usually not quite so salient, probably because scientific work relatively seldom involves any direct intervention in the personal lives of individual persons. On the other hand, the practitioner is strongly concerned with ethics, precisely because he is all the time intervening deeply in people's personal lives. Methodology is also important for the practitioner, but usually more from a pragmatic than from an abstract critical viewpoint.

In the chapter on the researcher we mostly discussed methodology. In this chapter it seems more appropriate to begin with a description of professional ethics as it regulates the practitioner's conduct.

Professional ethics

The following is a translation into English of the main points in the 'Professional-ethical directives for members of the Norwegian Psychological Association'. These generally accepted directives give a fairly detailed description of the ethical rules that for a period of time have been accepted as reasonably adequate by the population of Norwegian psychologists. In content they differ very little from similar directives adopted in other Western countries.

In the introduction to the directives 'O' is defined as any individual person with whom the psychologist has dealings, in a professional capacity. O is explicitly said to include subject, client, patient, student, etc. A 'professional relationship' is defined as 'any formalized situation in which the psychologist engages in professional activity relating to O'.

It is pointed out that the professional-ethical directives presuppose that the psychologist otherwise acts according to the norms of general ethics, common sense of justice, and regulations anchored in public law. The fundamental directives are formulated as follows:

It is a fundamental prinicple that the personal integrity of every human being should be respected, and should be protected against interference. The psychologist shall, in his professional activity, always attempt to act according to this principle. He must, therefore, at any time be on guard against factors in the work situation, as well as in his own personality, that may lead him, in his professional activity, to violate the principle of personal integrity.

The psychologist should regard it as a duty to attempt to become conscious of aspects or traits in his personality that may be an obstacle to responsible treatment of the client, so that he can have a clear picture of his limitations and a well-founded idea of what task he can — and cannot — take on. It must furthermore be considered important that the psychologist tries to keep up to date on the technical development in his field, and that he constantly works to increase his theoretical, methodological, and practical competence.

When a psychologist works for others he shall ensure that the regulations in his contract, and possible other rules applying to his work, do not conflict with the professional-ethical directives valid for members of the Norwegian Psychological Association.

Many of the tasks of the psychologist entail the definite possibility that there will be radical effects on other persons, and this means exacting requirements as to the personal maturity of the psychologist. The professional relationships that the individual psychologist may enter into, may be of kinds that cannot be regulated by anticipatory rules. *In the last resort, the ethical consciousness, sense of responsibility, and professional competence of the individual psychologist must be decisive.*

Finally, the following relatively detailed rules are formulated:

A. The psychologist shall in his work establish and maintain a professional relation. relation.

1. The psychologist shall see to it that psychological methods and instruments are not used unless a professional relationship has been established.

2. The psychologist shall not abuse his own superiority in psychological knowledge in private company.

3. The psychologist shall not seek information about O through private channels.

4. The psychologist shall not seek information about O from other persons or institutions without letting O or the person who represents O's interests know about it in advance.

5. The psychologist shall refrain from giving information about his own personal life to O, unless he has a conscious purpose, beneficial to O.

6. The psychologist shall not abuse O's confidence and possible dependence in order to further his own interests or to promote causes in which he is himself engaged.

7. The psychologist shall refer O to another competent professional if it appears that his relationship with O cannot maintain its professional character.

50

B. The psychologist shall inform O about the professional relationship.

1. The psychologist shall, when the professional relationship is established, make certain that O understands the purpose, nature, means, supposed duration and economic terms of the relationship, except when such information destroys the work situation.

2. The psychologist shall inform O about the extent to which the psychologist is bound to, and has a right to, professional secrecy.

3. The psychologist shall not hold out to O the prospect of any other help than the one he expects to be able to offer.

C. The psychologist shall show respect for O's personal identity and right to autonomy.

1. The psychologist shall attempt to arrange the situation in such a way that O can realistically feel that the relationship is in his own interest. It shall be a basic principle that O's participation in the relationship should be voluntary.

2. The psychologist shall be impartial in his professional work, i.e. he shall not let himself be influenced by racial, linguistic, religious, or political considerations in his relationship to O.

3. The psychologist shall attempt not to influence O with his norms or his ideology.

D. The psychologist shall take into consideration limitations in methods and in his own personality.

1. The psychologist shall attempt to clarify for himself the limitations that exist in methods and in his own personality relative to the tasks with which he is confronted at any given time, and he shall make due allowance for these limitations in his dispositions.

2. The psychologist shall, in general, refrain from using methods that are still in the pilot stage or that do not satisfy general methodological requirements. If such methods are used, it is of special importance to be aware of their tentative nature and not draw conclusions that go beyond what the method warrants.

3. The psychologist shall not use methods that are unfit for the problem involved. The psychologist is obliged constantly to consider the problems he is confronted with in relation to the methods that are available to him, and to pick out the methods or techniques that he, from a professional point of view, considers most adequate.

4. The psychologist shall, in general, refrain from establishing a professional relationship or from using a method, when the necessary conditions for examination, or certain factors in O's situation which are necessary for a positive result, are absent.

5. The psychologist shall not on his own use methods or techniques that he does not master with the sufficient degree of theoretical and practical competence.

6. The psychologist shall not establish a professional relationship or use methods and techniques when emotional factors in the psychologist himself may be an obstacle for a professionally and ethically defensible treatment of O.

Thus the psychologist shall not establish a professional relationship if:

a) he is closely related to O by way of family ties or friendship,

b) he feels antipathy or a too strong positive attachment to O,

c) it is conceivable that unresolved emotional conflicts in the psychologist may influence the relationship to O.

E. The psychologist shall see to it that the professional relationship does not harm O or cause him unnecessary suffering.

1. The psychologist shall not use his knowledge or his acquaintance with O in such a way that it may harm O or cause O unnecessary suffering. He shall refrain from seeking information about O that is unnecessary for solving the task involved.

2. The psychologist shall not place O in a situation that disturbs his mental balance, unless preparations have been made for restoring this balance.

3. The psychologist shall avoid a situation where O objectively or subjectively becomes dependent on further psychological assistance, unless the professional relationship has a therapeutic purpose.

4. The psychologist shall not exploit special circumstances in order to gain an unjust or disproportionate financial profit.

F. The psychologist is bound to professional secrecy.

1. The psychologist shall, with those limitations that are legally stipulated, be bound to professional secrecy concerning what is confided to him in the course of his professional work, or concerning what he gets to know about people's private lives and illnesses.

2. With the consent of O or of the person who represents O's interests, the psychologist can give such information as is covered by his professional secrecy to persons or institutions agreed upon.

Psychologists who work as members of a team must, in general, give that information that they consider necessary for the treatment of O to those persons who are involved in the treatment, provided that these persons are bound by the same professional secrecy as the psychologist. However, if he finds it expedient to do so, the psychologist may suppress information or reserve it for some members of the treatment team.

3. The psychologist shall see to it that results of examinations, etc., are securely filed, so that they cannot be appropriated by outside persons. Examination materials concerning O belong to the psychologist who has conducted the examination, or the institution he works for, provided that this institution has qualified persons to take care of the materials.

4. The psychologist shall avoid the possibility of disclosure of clinical examples or other personal material. If the psychologist, for teaching purposes, in case reports, articles, or lectures must give examples informing about O's personality or life, he, shall camouflage his information in such a way that it becomes impossible to recognize the person involved. If the psychologist is not certain that the camouflage is sufficient, he shall drop the example, or present the manuscript to O for approval.

G. The psychologist shall show responsibility and forethought when delivering statements.

1. The psychologist shall, when delivering statements to others, try to survey the consequences that his statements may have for O, and, out of regard to this, show responsibility and forethought.

2. The psychologist shall always include in his statement the methodological and situational reservations that are necessary, in order that the receiver of the statement can get a clear picture of what importance can be attached to the information involved.

3. The psychologist shall not incorporate his data in a conceptual framework that is inadequate relative to the methods used.

4. The psychologist shall refrain from using a special terminology if this can lead to misinterpretation or incomplete comprehension.

5. The psychologist shall only leave to persons he considers sufficiently qualified the task of evaluating and drawing conclusions from the psychological examination material he has presented.

6. The psychologist shall attempt not to let himself be influenced by personal considerations such as prestige, special expectations, etc. in the direction of either not examining O extensively enough to justify a conclusion, or of refraining from presenting certain findings.

7. The psychologist shall not give examination reports in written form to O himself, to relatives of O, or to persons who are not professionally or officially involved in the work on O's problem and/or situation.

8. The psychologist shall not give individual advice without having personally conducted an examination. If it becomes necessary, in the course of official educational work, or in reply to written inquiries, to give statements in the form of advice, the psychologist shall express the necessary reservations.

H. The psychologist shall be concerned about facts when he discusses professional questions in public.

1. The psychologist shall, when he informs the public about psychology, psychological methods, and psychological professional activity, attempt to give the information in such a way that it does not lead to misinterpretations among the public and to damage of the profession.

2. The psychologist shall, in public debate, see to it that normative statements do not come to appear as derived from the results of psychological research.

I. The psychologist shall see to it that psychological auxiliary materials and techniques are presented, distributed, and stored in a way that guarantees their usefulness to professional psychologists.

1. The psychologist shall, in presenting a method that he has devised, attempt to give an accurate and objective description of the method.

2. The psychologist shall see to it that psychological auxiliary materials are distributed only to competent professionals, and that professional considerations determine the way and extent of distribution.

3. The psychologist shall see to it that psychological auxiliary materials and techniques remain professional secrets. Thus, he shall refrain from presenting tests or parts of tests for teaching purposes, in popular articles, etc. When he publicly mentions methods, he shall avoid giving information that weakens the usefulness of the methods.

It is a shared duty of psychologists to ensure that psychological auxiliary materials are stored in such a way that they are not available to outside persons.

K. The psychologist shall show respect for and solidarity with his colleagues.

1. The psychologist shall contact those other psychologists who have had a professional relationship with O earlier, before he himself establishes a professional relationship with O. Members of the Norwegian Psychological Association shall mutually inform each other in such cases.

2. The psychologist shall, when there are no special reasons for an exception, charge his fees according to the normal rates set by the Norwegian Psychological Association. When no normal rates have been stipulated, the fee should be set according to a reasonable estimate, in relation to corresponding fees in professions with a similar length of training.

3. The psychologist shall, when he advertises or in other ways offers his services, avoid giving the offer a form that emphasizes his own competence at the expense of his colleagues.

4. The psychologist shall not publicly criticize his colleagues and their work in a way not concerned with facts. Pertinent criticism shall by preference be published in professional journals.

5. When ready to be used, psychological techniques and auxiliary materials shall be accessible to every psychologist qualified to use them, unless professional or ethical considerations lead to a contrary conclusion.

The preceding lengthy quotation contains a very detailed description of the ethical rules that one has felt the need to formulate explicitly. Some of them are, by necessity, rather vague and a few may be controversial. To revolutionaries, they may appear to have a conserving function (acceptance of law and order, maintenance of political neutrality, etc.). Yet, together, they give a vivid picture of the network of rules within which the practitioner in Western society must work. The researcher is also bound by these rules, but he meets them primarily in the relatively uncomplicated professional relationship with subjects, in connection with the treatment of methods and auxiliary materials, and in his relations with colleagues. To the practitioner, a constantly functioning ethical sensitivity is a *sine qua non*.

The student should seriously consider and discuss each one of these rules. Although ethics is not learned by reading alone, the discussion of the rules should bring to light the underlying reasons and attitudes, and facilitate the development of the specific kind of ethical awareness required.

Meanwhile, we will turn to a more direct consideration of the problems involved in functioning in the role of a psychological practitioner. Ethics may be part of the background of such functioning, but there are also more salient aspects which come to the foreground each time one interacts with a client.

The psychologist is a person who 'sees' and 'can' help

Becoming a qualified psychologist entails entering into a role. As far as people have any conception of psychologists at all, they ascribe to them certain very definite characteristics. How many times have you heard a variant of the classical remark, 'Oh, you are a psychologist, then you can see right through me, can't you?' Even when there is no overt comment, you can often see that people go through at least a brief inward shudder when your profession is mentioned.

We all take it for granted that people have a surface that is accessible to others, and a private inner world that is partly kept secret because it would lead to unforeseeable, awkward, or painful consequences to express it openly. The psychologist has the role of the one who can penetrate the surface and see what is private. In other words, he is seen as one who is particularly good at understanding people. This image of the psychologist derives partly from psychoanalysis. Established psychoanalysts are therefore frequently experienced as vaguely threatening, even among their non-clinical colleagues. A particularly clear expression of how the 'expert' psychologist may affect his surroundings is given in the following example. A newly appointed professor of psychology was interviewed for a student newspaper by a rather nervous and awed freshman. In the printed interview, which was brief and superficial, the professor was described as having 'eyes that see'.

Another aspect of the ascribed role of the psychologist is that he is expected to be able to do something with what he sees, i.e. he is supposed to be able to give wise and successful advice on how to solve personal problems, and to treat people for mental illness. He is also expected to be able to take care of himself in matters of mental hygiene.

Finally, the picture of how people often view psychologists is not completed if one forgets to mention that there are many jokes about psychologists and much hostility directed towards them. This is to be expected in the case of such a powerful and threatening role. The jokes and the gossip always, in one way or another, involve denial of those very abilities that define the role of psychologist. In the jokes and in the gossip psychologists tend to be exceptionally blind and clumsy socially, have children who become juvenile delinquents or mental cases, fail miserably in their married life, etc.

At first, the newcomer in the profession may be tempted to reject the belief in the magic eye and the magic touch as nonsense, and to contradict it openly by saying 'I am just an ordinary guy, I don't "see" things,

I don't know how to help people better than the next man. True, I studied psychology, but that does not make me a magician.' Yet this open denial must somehow be toned down, for one obvious reason. Without the magic eye and the magic touch, the definition of the psychologist and his justification is erased, as far as the public is concerned. Why should we, then, have psychologists, why should we spend taxpayer's money on educating them, and on establishing positions for them? The denial takes away an essential part of the psychologist's subjective identity too. After all, the study of psychology must have left something more in us than esoteric theoretical knowledge!

Most psychologists probably feel that, in some ways, they *do* see and understand more and *can* help better than the layman, even though there is nothing magical about it. This makes their denial of unusual powers halfhearted and unconvincing, and their image as experts may be left largely undamaged. The problem of reducing the exaggerated expectancies of the public to a realistic level is a recurrent theme in the practitioner's life.

Officially, the image of the psychologist is powerfully upheld by the insistence that the profession should have expert status as far as mental phenomena are concerned, that this should be stipulated by law, that the quality of training of psychologists should be strengthened, that there is a need for more positions as qualified psychologists, that one should avoid letting 'quacks' examine and treat people, etc.

As a further protection of the profession, general introductory textbooks are careful to point out that the reader should not expect to become better adjusted or to be able to deal with people better merely by reading, since the books are only about scientific psychology.(!) To become a 'real' psychologist, a much more elaborate and prolonged professional training is deemed necessary.

In conclusion, we have pointed out that the ascribed role of the psychologist as having the magic eye and the magic touch must be upheld in order to safeguard the social identity of the individual professional and in order to legitimate the profession as such. Yet, within the circle of professionals there is considerable doubt about exactly in what ways we see and touch better than others. A frequent position is that, although we have quite ordinary eyes and touch, we are more experienced than most people, and we have learned to master certain theories, technical tools, and skills that give us an advantage over ordinary common sense. The extent and nature of this supposed advantage will be discussed later on (chapters VII, VIII, IX, and X). Meanwhile, we will turn to the question of what inner and outer adjustments are necessary in order to live in the ascribed role of a psychologist. These adjustments can be roughly classified as having to do with controlling respectively the magic eye and the magic touch.

Handling expression of attention

While I was working on this book, a student called me and complained about acute attacks of anxiety. He also mentioned that he had chosen to contact me because I was not a psychoanalyst, and because, as he expressed it, he hoped to 'avoid the diagnostic stare.' This reflects a very common problem in the mutual adjustment of the psychologist and another person. When a layman meets a psychologist, especially when the latter functions professionally, or is interpreted as doing so, the layman will tend to become conscious of being observed, i.e. he will tend to become *self-conscious*. This, naturally, will vary according to who the person is and what the situation is. Many clients may simply feel safe by being under competent observation, or they may be so absorbed in their worries that they forget to be self-conscious. However, when dealing with unmotivated, ambivalent, or shy clients, with relatives of clients, institution personnel, etc., the psychologist frequently meets the problem of balancing between showing too clearly or too little that he is seeing and hearing. An open, uncontrolled and quite absorbed attention, where the observer literally stares at the person, can be embarrassing, distracting and quite inhibiting. It calls forth too much self-consciousness, i.e. consciousness about how one appears to the other. In fact, all normal adults have learned to apply a considerable degree of restraint when it comes to giving expression to one's attention to others. We have all learned that it is not nice to point at someone or to stare with gaping mouth, and that it is a delicate matter to describe someone present.

It is usually more acceptable to flatter and praise than to criticize, yet even praise is frequently felt to be embarrassing. We all know how a person who is unashamedly praised will blush, look pained, look down or away, etc. He is likely either to contradict or to moderate the praise, or rapidly start talking about something else.

In the same way as too strong attention, too pronounced friendliness, enthusiasm, openness, etc., can be felt as unpleasant and restraining, because the receiver feels pressured to return the feelings and the confidence, in a situation where he is not inclined to do so. Related to this is the unfortunate tendency to talk *as if* one has already agreed to a 'you-and-me' conspiracy or alliance, *as if* one shares viewpoints, *as if* one has already established a deep understanding. All the preceding too strong expressions can easily be felt as illegitimate and premature instrusions on the client's privacy.

Another variant of overplaying the role of an attentive observer can occur when the psychologist, either in a professional or a private context, says 'mm' when the other person has posed a question or expressed an opinion, clearly intended to be answered or commented on. The 'mm' with a certain pronunciation clearly communicates something like 'yes, please continue to talk and expose yourself while I listen.' Irrespective of whether the other person is a client or not, this may lead to serious irritation or to an embarrassing feeling of being ignored. The psychologist does not seem to take what one says seriously and at face value, he only concentrates on the fact *that* it is said, *how* it is said, and *what it reveals* about the person. Although it is true that certain psychological techniques, notably the variants of psychoanalysis, have institutionalized such behavior on the part of the psychologist in the treatment situation, it is generally very risky to deviate in this way from established 'good manners'. In general, the psychologist must, even more than other people, be very careful about how he expresses his observing attitude to the person in question, and he must avoid communicating the slightest disrespect for the person's intentions.

Incidentally, the particular form of sharp gaze cultivated by some clinical psychologists (and psychiatrists) may quite probably have little value for grasping more of the subject's behavior. On the other hand, it functions importantly to signalize to the observed person that he is indeed being observed and by a very competent expert at that. 'See, I am looking at you and nothing is likely to escape me!' This reinforces the belief in the magic eye, which again may have some direct or indirect therapeutic or pseudotherapeutic consequences. A notable passivity or restraint in self-expression (expressionless face) on the part of the psychologist may also communicate the same thing. 'I am not expressing myself, see — I am all occupied with watching you!'

The hazards of overcommunicating attention are matched in a symmetrical way by the hazards of undercommunicating attention. If you give the slightest sign of being uninterested or inattentive, the other one may become hurt or resentful because of the implied lack of respect. He may also experience his own behavior as meaningless and empty. His self-expression will rapidly come to an end, if he feels he is talking to a wall or where the audience appears to be 'deaf', 'blind', or generally 'insensitive'. By saying 'mm' and by numerous other minor signs we communicate that we are attentive. For the psychologist, the maintenance of adequate signs of attention is especially important, because he is already so threatening that lack of attention will be a direct invitation to escape through silence or deceit, and is also a cause for resentment and increased distrust.

In general, persons probably express themselves most adequately when they are neither overwhelmed by attention nor deprived of any sign of attention. The optimal supply of attention is an extremely delicate matter which varies from moment to moment, context to context, and person to person. The problem of adjusting to this is shared by everyone, but it is especially important to the psychologist, who, by definition, is regarded as one who 'sees'. If he is not personally very skillful at this point, he will risk becoming the prey of all kinds of systematic illusions, in the sense that, e.g., certain types of people will tend to be relatively self-conscious and/or uncommunicative in his presence.

Eliciting information

So far we have described the problem of delivering signs of attention with optimal strength. However, the psychologist must be other things than a passive listener, in order to function adequately. In situations where this is institutionalized (orthodox psychoanalysis), and also in other contexts where he has achieved the client's confidence, it may be sufficient for the psychologist to be only a listener for long periods. However, before he has achieved such confidence, and in situations where he cannot expect the client to be inclined to expose himself, it is clearly necessary for the psychologist to take the pipe out of his mouth (metaphorically speaking) and say something too. The greater part of the professional time of many practitioners is taken up with encounters where the client does not really come of his own free will and/or where he is in no way motivated or able to be particularly trusting and open. Examples would be encounters with, e.g., the parents of a delinquent youth or with the problem child itself, with inmates of various kinds of institutions (asylums, prisons, institutions for retarded, etc.), job applicants, draftees, prospective foster parents, etc. Finally, all the shy, withdrawn clients, and those with small powers of expression or with little training in talking about emotional and interpersonal matters.

In many of the preceding cases, one may not get ahead by merely remaining silent and by nodding and saying 'mm' to whatever communications may be forthcoming. Sometimes, there is even an element of cruelty in 'out-waiting' the client, who finally feels he *must* talk. The task must be to find more natural methods of getting the person to talk about informative matters and to express himself in some way. The most direct way is to question him, but this may too clearly define the situation as an interrogation, and may allow the other to play whatever game he is up to, whether this is to talk about irrelevant matters and cover up, to make a good impression, or to appear innocent and misunderstood. If the game is not to give any important information, the client may grow increasingly silent, finally answering only in monosyllables or by incomprehensible mumbling. Among various solutions to the problem of getting a person to expose himself in a spontaneous and honest way, a very important one is to try to engage him in a *natural conversation* about any, preferably relevant, topic that can be brought up. (In work with small children, the parallel is to provide materials for play and to observe and talk with the child while he is playing.) This may take away some of the feeling of being observed and some of the awareness that the psychologist is trying to find out things. Instead, the topic of the conversation consumes the client's attention. This technique is popular with dentists and doctors, e.g. while preparing a tooth-extraction or taking the blood pressure. Needless to say, the technique may not work at all with very anxious clients, simply because they are too scared to be willing to listen and talk. Perhaps the psychologist is in a better position here, simply because he uses no objects that directly represent the threat, and because the threat is usually not so sharply defined and localized in space and time.

The task of engaging someone in a natural conversation or to steer such conversation in a desired direction is in itself extremely delicate. First, it must not be immediately obvious that this is done. Caricature: 'Now, let's sit down and talk about something!', or 'Now, what shall we talk about?' Second, the conversation itself must continue to have all the appearance of being indeed natural. We all know the very embarrassing and perhaps deeply hurting feeling that the other one is merely conversing with one, without being really interested in the topic, and in what one has to say about it. Examples: 'He is just talking absentmindedly with me, while waiting for X', 'She is just talking with me because there is no other place to sit', etc. In the case of the psychologist, the client might feel 'He is just talking to make me talk. He doesn't care anything about what we are talking about, nor is he interested in what I have to say, except where it tells him something about me that I don't know.'

As in all such matters, it is clearly impossible to formulate explicitly all the fine nuances and devices that are involved. Yet it is clear that at least two principles are important in engaging someone in a natural conversation. The first is to select topics and points of view that are interesting in themselves to the person. This may lead one to take up matters in connection with his profession or work, his hobbies, interests, etc. In cases where there is little advance information, this involves a certain sensitivity to what makes the other one think. The other important principle is to expose oneself to a certain extent. This is a natural ingredient in any normal conversation; it serves to create interest and take away the other one's feeling of being observed.

The degree to which the psychologist exposes himself must be finely adjusted. It must be enough to stimulate the other one and give the conversation some balance. On the other hand, it should not be carried too far. The inexperienced psychologist may occasionally and momentarily find himself maneuvered into a state where *he* is doing all the talking and the client is saying 'mm'!

The psychologist should be wary about expressing opinions in matters that may be controversial, since this may lead the client to become silent and/or antagonized. Frequently, psychologists choose to be careful, tentative, and perhaps a little ambiguous in their self-expression, and to let their comments focus on what the client has said, in such a way that he is stimulated to continue. However, through all that the psychologist says and does, there must run a strong emphasis on optimal attention, and on the expression of respect for the client's individuality and integrity.

'Manipulating' the client

Despite all qualifications, the preceding may have left an impression of a rather manipulatory and dishonest attitude on the part of the psychologist. This theme must be further discussed.

We have already seen that it is strictly impossible to do psychological research without deceiving the subjects. In a similar way, it appears difficult to practice psychology without deceiving the clients. However, most of the deception is in the mild form of withholding information, which, after all, is typical of many human relationships.

The client is not informed of some of the examination results, he is not informed of the psychologist's varying tendencies to feel aversion or attraction to him, he is not informed of the psychologist's momentary or persistent doubt about whether or not he can help him, etc. The psychologist engages the client in 'natural' conversations which are not always natural on the part of the psychologist, etc. In general, the professional relationship is such that the psychologist must be careful about what he does and does not communicate to the client. Even apparently spontaneous reactions occur against a constant background of careful intuitive judgment and a feeling of strong responsibility. Many therapists have emphasized maximal openness and honesty, but this may be more of an ideal than an actual reality.

The balance between simply being an open and understanding fellow human being to the client, and technical considerations about how to achieve the *purpose* of the relationship is of crucial importance. To varying extents all psychologists recognize that achievement of the purpose of helping is not always compatible with complete openness. In any situation, and at any time, there are limits to what the client can understand and limits to what he can take emotionally. Furthermore, everything the psychologist communicates may influence the development of the professional relationship, and therefore must be carefully selected and programmed.

Some experienced practitioners may object that the preceding pages tend to overemphasize some trivial details of the work, and that the focus of attention is usually on the problems of the client as such, and on relatively global features and strategies. This is probably a true account of how it *feels* to do many types of practical work. However, this does not preclude an attempt to analyze more closely some of the processes and considerations that are usually taken for granted. After all, since the psychologist's 'natural way of being' is one crucial determinant of what he may achieve in his practical work, it must be important to analyze what ways of being are important, and see to it that the students of psychology who are too deviant in their personal form can get some kind of correction before they graduate. The preceding must not be understood to mean that the psychologist's attitude and personal way of functioning is the only determinant of what he can achieve. Obviously, technical training and theoretical framework must also be taken into account. In connection with the latter and as an appropriate end to this chapter, it should be mentioned that the most fundamental weakness of practical work is its concrete and uncritical nature (see p. 16). Since the practitioner must rely on an explicit or implicit theoretical framework to guide him, he cannot easily detach himself from, and be critical of this framework. Hence, practice alone may easily lead to stable traditions, that, other things being equal, may remain basically unchanged for generations.

Questions after Chapter III

1. Discuss the ethical problems that may arise when the psychologist's client is not a person, but, say, an institution or a corporation.

2. Discuss the requirement not to let oneself be influenced by racial, linguistic, religious, or political considerations, and not to influence the client with one's norms and ideology (C2 and C3, p. 51).

3. Discuss the requirement to take into consideration limitations in one's own personality. (D, p. 51.)

4. Discuss the requirement that psychological techniques and auxiliary materials remain professional secrets. (I 3, p. 53.)

5. Is the psychologist really a person who 'sees' and 'can' (help)?

6. Discuss the extent to which deceiving (manipulating) the client is necessary.

IV. The psychological sub-culture

The picture of the psychologist as researcher and practitioner is not complete before we have considered the particular environment or subculture in which he lives. Like all subcultures, it has rules for the adoption of new members, special languages, hierarchies of positions, 'religions' (methodology and ethics), and 'mythologies' (behaviorism, psychoanalysis, information processing, etc.). The very existence of this subculture creates certain problems for the psychologist that should be clearly understood by every novice who wants to enter the sacred halls, and by people outside who have contact with psychologists.

The danger of becoming 'encapsulated' in the subculture

The transition from the world one lived in before one started to study psychology seriously, and the world one will live in as a psychologist is more radical than may always be apparent.

The only way to become a psychologist goes through being a student at a university. There one encounters a new world of concepts, procedures, and values. One learns terms, theories, methods, and ways of thinking that were more or less unknown in one's pre-psychology life. There soon occurs the problem of how to integrate this new 'reality' with one's everyday realities. One starts to look at one's own problems and at those of others in term of new concepts, one sees other aspects of people than earlier and one's manners and conversation become more or less infused with the new psychological background.

However, the effect of studying psychology includes other aspects of life too. One gets to know one's fellow students, and perhaps some of the teachers. Gradually, one's circle of friends will become dominated by other students of psychology and more of the daily conversations will tend to focus on matters psychological and on matters related to the

65

study and the profession. This process no doubt proceeds at different speeds and with more or less extreme end results depending on the person and the circumstances. However, the typical outcome is that the number of other psychologists in a psychologist's circle of friends and acquaintance is fairly high.

Selectivity with respect to acquaintances and friends is not a special characteristic of psychologists, but is a characteristic of occupations in general. In particular, it is valid for academic professions and also includes a tendency for one's friends, if they are not psychologists, to belong to other academic groups or at least to groups within the same socio-economic strata. The frequency of blue collar workers, office and shop personnel, etc. is quite low among the friends of people with advanced college education. For the botanist, geologist, or surgeon, this may have few evil consequences in their work. However, for the psychologist it may be a serious drawback to interact exclusively with people with academic backgrounds, and especially to interact mostly with other psychologists. If he is not a psychologist in private practice he is likely to meet among his clients a high proportion of people from the lower socio-economic strata. This means that he is supposed to understand and be able to help people with little education, difficult material circumstances, and otherwise quite unfamiliar cultural backgrounds. The paradoxical outcome is that the psychologist, who occupies a role supposedly involving unusual perceptual and therapeutic powers, may be severely handicapped, precisely with respect to his ability to understand and help. Although he may seek consolation in the belief that, after all, we are all quite similar, the middle class and academic background of most psychologists may make it quite difficult for them to perceive and understand the background and the life situation of the low-status client. A possible remedy for this would be to require that all psychology students should have the experience of working in unskilled jobs and living in the corresponding neighborhoods for some specified period, preferably early in their studies, before they get too established in the psychological subculture. However, it is admittedly hard to know the extent to which such a requirement would really improve the psychological services rendered later.

In meeting his clients, the psychologist is not only handicapped by his particular experiential background, but also directly by those external characteristics that reveal his position in society. His physical (racial) characteristics, his language, his hair-cut and clothes may all serve to identify his social position, and hence to evoke possible hostility, anxiety, or withdrawal. Dramatic attempts to scale the barriers created by external appearance have been described by Griffin in *Black Like Me* (1960) and by Morris West in *Children in the Sun* (1966). However, normally, there is no way around these barriers. In the United States, the estimated need for qualified psychological assistance is very high among Negroes, Puerto Ricans, Mexicans, and American Indians, yet the vast majority of the available professionals are white. Here social distance becomes very salient indeed. Another matter is whether an abundant supply of psychologists is really a sufficient or even a necessary condition for helping the underprivileged, or whether the social system and material conditions as such will frustrate all efforts to provide more than extremely limited and pointwise assistance.

Seen in a wider perspective, no applied psychologist can avoid this question. He must see that sometimes he is part of a treatment system with a paralyzing inefficiency. E.g., he may be occupied with diagnosing and attempting to help delinquent youths in treatment homes and youth prisons, all the time knowing that perhaps 80 or 90 percent of the clients will return to criminal activity within a couple of years after their release. Similarly, he must consider that this profession is a luxury that can be afforded only by technologically developed societies and that the majority of the world's peoples are grappling with more basic problems such as preventing their children from dying from undernourishment and illnesses, or trying to keep illiterally from increasing. These questions must penetrate into the psychological subculture itself, simply because they concern the very meaning of the practitioner's life work.

The semitechnical language

The student of psychology has to learn a vocabulary of technical terms with more or less precise meanings. Gradually, as he becomes acquainted with the terminology, his conversation and his writings get infiltrated with these terms. This process continues and the qualified psychologist can, in his most inspired moments, become completely unintelligible to everyone, except perhaps a few fellow specialists. The linguistic change is paralleled by a deeper cognitive change. The psychologist begins to experience, describe, and interpret the actions and interrelations of people in relation to his technical conceptual system, and this again determines the wording, not only of his scientific publications, but also of his examination reports and professional statements. Members of teams in treatment institutions talk with each other about the clients in a jargon, which is unintelligible to outsiders. This jargon can be described as semitechnical, since only some nouns and perhaps adjectives and adverbs are technical, whereas the syntax and most of the words are those of the native natural language.

One consequence of this is that the psychologist is faced with a formidable communication problem vis à vis his client. He talks with his colleagues and writes in semitechnical language, but he must talk with the client in ordinary everyday language. Consequently, the psychologist must continuously translate the message he gets from the client into his own theoretical frame of reference, and then translate his own messages to the client, in the opposite direction. A similar problem arises when the psychologist communicates with other people involved in a case, such as parents, spouses, administrators, teachers, etc. In all these cases, he must use ordinary language, and yet communicate the essential aspects of what he himself may have formulated in semitechnical terms. Psychologists handle this more or less successfully, varying from noticeable clumsiness to some fair degree of fluency, yet they all acknowledge the problem involved.

In order to get ahead in this matter, it becomes essential to understand better the relationship between the semitechnical and the ordinary language. The ordinary language is rich and flexible and excellently suited for describing and dealing with everyday problems.

Everything important in human life can to some extent be described in this language. On the other hand, the semitechnical languages in psychology describe certain selected and highly abstract properties of events. Their vocabulary and their flexibility and richness are very much smaller than that of ordinary language. Their main advantage is that they permit a clear and brief formulation of presumably important, highly complex facts and relationships, which would require unmanageable lengths of everyday language sentences. A well-known example is that a two-line proposition in symbolic logic may require half a page in ordinary English.

Only a brief preliminary comment on the problem will be given here. One may try to lessen the strain on the psychologist by providing the students with systematic training in translation from technical to nontechnical language and vice versa. However, this cannot be done efficiently without analysis of the relationship between the two languages. Here we touch upon a general theoretical problem, namely that of the relationship between scientific and common-sense psychology.

The psychologist must function within a given socio-cultural matrix and must communicate with his subjects and clients in the language imbedded in this matrix. On the other hand, he must develop what Schütz (1967, p. 59) has called 'second order constructs' in order to understand how people function on the basis of their first order constructs. In the realm of psychological phenomena these second order constructs make up what is called the *science* of psychology. The relationship between the first order and the second order construct must be clarified, not only in order to make possible a further development of the science, but also in order to facilitate solutions of the practitioner's communication difficulties. Chapters V through XI are all relevant to this problem in various ways.

The hierarchical structure
of the psychological subculture

Up to now, the psychological subculture has been described as if it was made up of equal colleagues. Yet, we all know how misleading this is. The system is an hierarchical one, with *competence* as the differentiating criterion. The exact steps on the hierarchical ladder differ from country to country, but the lowest is always the beginning student and the highest is the professor with tenure, at the university, and 'director', 'chief psychologist', 'diplomate in clinical psychology', etc., in applied work. Each successive step on the ladder involves increasing prestige, power, and income. Every advance is decided on by persons higher on the ladder than the climber involved. This is characteristic of all hierarchical systems and, as always, it is legitimated by the assumption that those higher in the hierarchy are more competent than those lower. One major positive aspect of such a system is that it is stable and thereby ensures the maintenance of the value system involved. Furthermore, it has a strong incentive function, thereby furthering work promoting the basic values involved. Thus, the hierarchical nature of the profession of psychology may be thought to be a contributing reason for the widespread efforts to achieve scientific and professional excellence.

Among the negative aspects of the system are stress, competitiveness, and unhappiness among those who are losers. There is also overwork among those high in the hierarchy, who are constantly called upon to function as judges in matters of examinations for degrees, applications for positions, awards and grants, publication of articles, books, etc. Furthermore, the ideal freedom of research is somewhat curtailed by the system. Persons who disregard or offend the idiosyncrasies and preferences of their superiors can sometimes take a relatively dim view of their future as climbers on the ladder. Genuinely unorthodox suggestions and ideas may also be dismissed, if they are too threatening to cherished beliefs of superiors. The climber who plays safe is strongly inclined to choose work in traditional areas, in order to avoid criticism.

In considering the arguments for and against maintaining this kind of a system, one should keep in mind the words of the Norwegian poet Stein Mehren, who wrote, 'every unveiling is a veiling of something else.' Those who point out the hidden negative aspects of the system tend to forget the hidden positive ones, and vice versa.

In deciding whether one should work to maintain the present hierarchical structure, or whether one should prefer, e.g., some kind of egalitarian structure, where everyone is simply a psychologist, one must consider two fundamental questions, one normative and one empirical. The normative question is: To what extent are you willing to uphold a given interpretation of the values of science and the profession, notably when they conflict with other humanitarian or political values? Every psychologist also has other identities, such as being, e.g., a Socialist, a Catholic, a citizen of his country, and many other things. Sometimes his other values may come into conflict with his professional values, and in these cases his strongest commitments in the given context are revealed. In our examples below we will show how psychologists differ in their interpretation of professional values and in their strength of commitment to these values.

The simplified empirical question is: Which kind of structure, hierarchical or egalitarian, is more likely to further any given set of values?

In what follows, two empirical examples will be described. They are interpreted as supporting the tentative hypothesis that, at least under typical conditions, in Western societies, only an hierarchical organization will uphold the traditional scientific and professional values, and that an egalitarian organization may, in the long run, be incompatible with the maintenance of the traditional standards of scientific and professional excellence. The reader should be warned that the complexity and ambiguity of these matters are so strong that any definite interpretation can easily be challenged. Yet, we have chosen to present the data and some interpretations, because they do provide a starting point for further discussion of these vitally important questions.

The fight over open admission

Over the years 1968 to 1971, when this was written, a bitter conflict has divided the Institute of Psychology at the University of Oslo into two camps. One faction has taken the position that the overcrowded Institute should, in principle, remain open to every interested student with certain minimum qualifications, whereas the other faction has maintained that the number of students admitted should be limited to fit the given estimated capacity of the Institute. For most of the period the former faction had the upper hand, and the Institute maintained a policy of open admission, in spite of constantly deteriorating conditions for studies, teaching, and research. In order for the reader to understand this, a few of the circumstances must be explained.

A relatively egalitarian system of government of the Institute had been established on January 1 1969, in response to the first impact of the 'student revolution'. The policy of the Institute in this period was determined by a council consisting of every person working full time at the Institute (except for the office personnel, who had one representative only), as well as of 8 student representatives. At the time of the last voting, shown in Table 2 (February 9 1971), the persons with voting rights were distributed over the four main hierarchical positions as follows: Professor/Associate Professor: 7, Assistant Professor (with tenure): 26, persons with temporary appointments (mainly Assistants and Scholarship holders + 3 Assistant Profesors): 26, Student representatives: 8. This meant that power within the Institute was not related to hierarchical position at all. Actually, the upper half of the hierarchy, i.e. the teachers with tenure, made up a minority in the council.

The influence of the student group was higher than indicated by the nominal numbers, since, alone of the four groups, they always met in full strength (due to a system of substitutes) and always voted *en bloc*, on a Far Left platform. Conversely, the influence of the highest hierarchical group (Professors/Associate Professors) was lower than indicated by its nominal strength, since this group always had the highest relative number of absences due to sabbaticals. This trend happens to be only incompletely shown in the sample of three votings shown in Table 2.

The arguments presented in the council and elsewhere for reducing admissions were, explicitly, that this was necessary in order to maintain time for research and time to keep professionally up to date, and thereby to maintain a high level of excellence in the teaching itself. The main arguments for maintaining open admission were reference to the needs of the Norwegian people for more psychologists, the interests of the would-be students, and the importance of open admission as a means of forcing the government to provide more money for the university, etc. The secondary arguments on both sides disputed the validity of the opponents' primary arguments, and, as usual in such disputes, both sides

71

maintained that, in the long run, there was really no conflict between *their* preferred alternative and the values stressed by the opposite part. The arguments on both sides were much more complex and subtle than can be reproduced here. However, those who worked for continued open admission did this partly on the basis of values other than those of the science and the profession, whereas those fighting to limit admissions depended primarily on traditional scientific and professional values. in hierarchy and tendency to vote for one of the alternatives.

Turning nov to the figures in Table 2, we note that a very strong majority of those in the upper half of the hierarchy (the permanently appointed teachers) voted for limited admissions, whereas a very strong majority of those low in the hierarchy (assistants, scholarship holders, and student representatives) voted for open admissions.

Table 2. Frequency of voting for and against limited admissions among four groups of voters in three meetings of the Council of the Institute of Psychology, University of Oslo, Norway

	5—5—70		9—15—70		2—9—71	
	Ag.	For	Ag.	For	Ag.	For
Prof./Assoc. Prof.	0	5	1	5	0	3
Assist. Prof.	7	10	7	19	7	15
Temporarily appointed	8	5	13	5	10	5
Stud. repr.	8	0	8	0	8	0
	23	20	29	29	25	23

On every occasion there is a clear relationship between position in hierarchy and tendency to vote for one of the alternatives.

One possible explanation of this goes as follows: As long as one does not feel directly threatened in one's work situation by the increasing number of students, one tends to vote according to humanitarian and/or political opinions. On the other hand, when one begins to feel in a concrete way the heavy and steadily increasing pressure of administrative and teaching duties, the interest in restricting admissions becomes dominant. This hypothesis is supported by the existence of a positive relationship between tendency to vote for limited admissions and number of years since appointment to permanent position. Thus, in the voting on September 15 1970, when the number of voting permanent teachers was unusually high, only 2 of the 8 who voted against limited admissions had more than 3 years of seniority. On the other hand, 15 of the 24 who voted for limited admissions had such seniority.

Extrapolating from the data presented in Table 2, one may surmise that, with an even more egalitarian system, i.e. with a higher number of student representatives, admissions might have been kept open indefinitely, or, at least, until the conditions became considerably more chaotic. Conversely, it seems clear that a council where those higher in the hierarchy had more power, would have clamped down on admissions much earlier. In general, the data seem to fit the general hypothesis, mentioned above, that, in concrete choice situations, those who are relatively high in the hierarchy will tend to uphold the traditional values of the system more strongly than those who are relatively low in the hierarchy.

The fight over the requirement of a scientific work to become a diplomate in clinical psychology

Until September 1969, the Norwegian Psychological Association (NPA) had four requirements for becoming a diplomate in clinical psychology (no details will be given here):

1. University degree in psychology
2. Special practice (at least five years of clinical practice under specified conditions)
3. Diplomate course (arranged by the Association)
4. Scientific work. (The work did not have to be published, but it was expected to be of a certain standard, as judged by a permanent committee, consisting only of diplomates, and appointed by the Association. A thesis from the university in clinical psychology was also acceptable.)

Point 4 created great difficulties for many psychologists who had graduated from the university in a period when a thesis was not yet required as part of the final examinations. These psychologists did not feel properly prepared for the task, nor did their work give them sufficient time to carry it out. As a consequence there was a sizable group of members of the NPA who had fulfilled or expected to fulfill the requirements nos. 2 and 3 (no. 1 being a condition for membership in NPA) and who were interested in abolishing no. 4, in order to be able to advance in the hierarchy. Like all such advances, becoming a diplomate entails noticeable increases in prestige, power, and income.

At the request of members of the mentioned group, a special meeting of the General Assembly of the NPA was held in Oslo on September 5 1969. The main argument for abolishing the requirement of a scientific work was that it is a ritual with no genuine value for professional functioning. On the other hand, many of those who were already diplomates and some of the teachers from the university argued that the whole profession depended on whatever scientific support could be mustered and that diplomates ought to have documented experience with and ability to carry out a scientific investigation.

After a highly emotional debate, it was decided, by 75 votes against 35, to abolish point 4 in the requirements for a diplomate in clinical psychology. No record of the individual voting behavior has been preserved, but it was clear from the debate and the advance votes that nearly all of the participating established diplomates voted with the minority and that most of the prospective diplomates voted with the majority. At the time when point 4 was abolished there were 29 diplomates in clinical psychology, all *with* scientific works, out of a total NPA membership of around 300. In the period from September 5 1969, when point 4 was abolished, to March 19 1971 a total of 49 *new* diplomates, nearly all *without* a scientific work, had been registered with the NPA.

This event, in which a group of psychologists voted to award themselves a diplomate title, has the consequence that this title will in future be awarded to most psychologists with five years of clinical experience, provided they take care to arrange this experience according to the rules. The main conclusion is that, when an hierarchical system allocates decisive power to those low in the hierarchy, it will tend to disintegrate in an egalitarian direction, as soon as those in power have something to gain and become sufficiently eager. In such cases, the traditional values of the system need not be upheld.

In conclusion, becoming a psychologist not only means becoming a researcher and/or a practitioner and/or a teacher. It also means becoming a member of an organized subculture in which continuous political activity occurs, and where positions must constantly be taken. No student of psychology should avoid facing the complicated and important questions of how the power should be distributed in order to further the interests *both* of the profession *and* of the people in the surrounding society.

Questions after Chapter IV

1. To what extent is it true that you yourself are becoming 'swallowed up' and isolated by the student or the professional subculture? Discuss the problem involved.

2. To what extent does your own daily conversation and writing contain technical terms? Do you have any trouble communicating with people who have not studied any psychology? Discuss the problems involved.

3. What are the merits and drawbacks of respectively an hierarchical and an egalitarian system at the university and in applied work?

V. The basic nature of common-sense psychology

In the first part of this book some aspects of the psychologist's interaction with subjects, clients and colleagues have been described. We have seen that the qualified psychologist is robed in the sacred garment of Science, equipped with a magic eye and a magic touch, and is securely placed somewhere on the competence ladder.

The next question, which arises quite naturally, is what substantial backing can be given to this imposing external role? What does the psychologist really know and what can he really do? To be true, a partial legitimation of his work lies in his firm commitment to the rules of the critical game and to the rules of professional ethics. However, this only establishes honorable intent, whereas we must also ask for actual ability.

As an introduction to the problem of the psychologist's ability, suppose that a layman for some reason decides to pretend that he is a qualified psychologist. How would he fare, how soon would he be unmasked as an impostor? No general and valid answer to this question is available. However, it is a good guess that, unless there are other psychologists around, who can discover his lack of knowledge of the folklore and jargon of their profession, he may not be unmasked at all. The reason for this is, as we have already pointed out, that the impostor, as well as all other normally developed adults, already has a 'psychology'. Everyone has a certain practical understanding of himself and of his fellow beings, and this understanding can, at least to some extent, be formulated and communicated in the language of every day life. We constantly understand, explain, and predict our own and other peoples' experiences and acts, with considerable success. Without this ability we could not live in a reasonably normal and independent way in society.

The existence of a widespread and rather advanced common-sense psychology and of ordinary languages well suited for the purpose of communicating psychological thoughts, means that the psychologist is in a somewhat special situation. A fake mechanic, baker, or radiation expert would fairly soon commit blunders that would make them unambiguously unpopular in the vicinity. However, the fake psychologist could, if he is reasonably sensitive and gifted, and provided that he avoids colleagues, live happily ever after, listening to and advising people. This does not mean that his services would be as good as those of a genuine professional — it only means that the public need not necessarily notice the difference.

The preceding means that the task of analyzing lay or common-sense psychology becomes important. Not only must the achievements of scientific and professional psychology be evaluated in comparison with those of common-sense psychology, but it is also clear that the former can only be understood as a further development of the latter. In order to grasp the deeper nature of the scientific and professional achievements, we must attempt to make explicit what we already know implicitly in our daily lives.

The structure of common sense

The following three definitions in 'Webster (1967) together indicate approximately what we have in mind when talking about common sense. 'Good sound ordinary sense.' 'Good judgment or prudence in estimating or managing affairs esp. as free from emotional bias or intellectual subtlety or as not dependent on special or technical knowledge.' 'The unreflective opinions of ordinary men.'

Common sense has three well known important features: it is normally unreflected or unconscious, it is shared by all 'ordinary' persons, and, when made explicit, it is self-evident in a compelling way. All three features will be discussed here.

Philosophers concerned with the problem of common sense have commented on its unreflectiveness and on the fact that, usually, it is explicitly formulated only when contradicted.

If there is some artificiality in saying that common sense has beliefs, there is none in speaking of its rejection of an opinion; the reason — it might be suggested — is that common sense does not declare itself in advance of attack upon it. The man of plain, ordinary common sense cannot readily be said, for instance, to believe that the things around him continue to exist in his absence — the idea of their not doing so does not cross his mind. But when he encounters the contrary opinion, his common sense asserts itself. (Grave, 1967.)

An analogous example from the field of psychology proper would be the problem of other minds, which will be discussed later in this chapter. In our ordinary daily lives we cannot be said to 'believe' that others have minds, we simply take it for granted, and only when some-one asserts the contrary does our common sense get aroused.

It should be added that common sense need not necessarily be directly contradicted in order to become explicitly formulated. Obviously, it can become so in any problem situation when alternative solutions are contemplated, when reasons must be formulated, or when reflection is indicated. However, it remains generally true that common sense is largely unreflective and that what is made explicit in daily life are only minor and unrelated fragments.

The assumption that common sense is shared has two severe restrictions that should be mentioned already at this point. First, common sense is a characteristic that is clearly present to a variable extent, both within the same person, and from one person to another. In some moods and situations a person is more apt to do 'foolish' things than in others, and some persons generally handle their affairs of living more success-fully than others. Furthermore, a substantial part of the population lacks even the minimum of common sense necessary for independent life, and therefore must be taken care of by others. We refer here to children of all ages, to seniles, the mentally retarded, the mentally ill, etc. To the extent that these persons have understanding, it only involves certain fragments and partial aspects of what adults in the given culture regard as common sense.

The other limitation in the sharedness of common sense has to do with its cultural and historical boundaries. Since understanding of foreign cultures and other historical periods appears to be limited and hard to establish, it is also hard to know to what extent and in what respects common sense remains invariant from one culture and period to another.

The third central feature of common sense is its quality of compelling self-evidence. This has led philosophers to the intriguing question of how common sense can be proven correct or falsified if it is self-evident (cf. Grave, 1967).

In order to analyze in detail the structure of common sense, we will turn to the research of the child psychologist Jean Piaget and his col-laborators and followers. In the course of their studies of the cognitive development of children, they have made explicit hundreds of presup-positions about objects, space, time, movement, velocity, quantity, num-ber, probability, etc., which all normal adults in our culture unreflectedly take for granted and which, if challenged, are asserted as self-evident truths. Piaget's famous studies of conservation of length may serve as our paradigm of the structure of common sense.

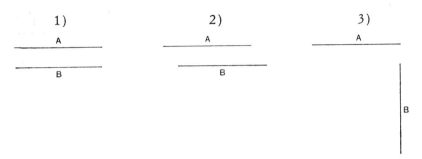

Figure 1. Schematic illustration of observation of conservation of length.

Suppose we place two sticks A and B parallel to each other in such a way that both ends coincide, 1) in Figure 1. The observer will conclude from this that A and B are equally long. Stick B is then displaced somewhat to the right (position 2) in Figure 1. Upon a question such as 'is A longer than B, are the sticks equally long, or is B longer than A?' all adults (but not all preschool children) state that the sticks are still equally long and that this is self-evident. When pressed for an explanation, they may volunteer answers such as 'they are still the same sticks', 'we didn't change the sticks in any way', 'if you push B back you'll see that they are still the same,' etc. Adults clearly find the question quite strange and, until asked, they have unreflectedly taken for granted that the length remains the same.

A frequent explanation of the self-evidence of common-sense beliefs is that they are *empirically* based. In the situation depicted in Figure 1, position 2), one may simply argue that one can literally *see* that the two sticks are still equally long and that this makes the statement self-evident.

However, the insufficiency of this explanation is clearly revealed if stick B is, instead, placed in the position indicated in 3). Now B looks longer than A (the vertical-horizontal illusion). In other words, if the observer had not first seen A and B in 1), he would have tended to judge B as longer than A, in 3). The contents of his direct experience then, tend to *contradict* the assumption of conservation, rather than *support* it. In general, and especially in more complex situations, the self-evidence of common sense clearly cannot be said to be a reflection of direct empirical evidence.

An alternative empiricist hypothesis, namely that common-sense beliefs are directly taught to children by others, is equally implausible. It is unlikely that anyone is prepared to argue that children acquire conservation of length by being told by their parents or others that sticks maintain their length when moved around (provided they are not broken or otherwise tampered with). On the contrary, the typical case seems to be that the thought that it should *not* be as indicated by unreflected common sense has never crossed the mind of the person involved, nor of those who could have taught him. This seems to be true of most common-sense beliefs, irrespective of content. For instance, it is most certainly true of the belief that others have minds and are not merely complicated robots. In general the acquisition of common sense seems to proceed in a *submerged* way, without any conscious recognition on the part of the individual person involved.

A third explanation of self-evidence in the particular case of conservation is that it is based on the observation that sticks which are returned to their initial positions retain their initial length. However, this argument fails to account for the belief that the sticks also maintain their length while being in positions where, perceptually, they appear longer or shorter.. As a matter of fact, a rubber string could be stretched simultaneously with the change in position, and could be restored to its original length while being returned to the initial position. This situation could be made perceptually equivalent to the one described in Figure 1, 3), and the only difference between them would be that in one case the perceptual impression of difference is interpreted as reflection of a real change (the rubber string) and in the other case it is seen as merely apparent. This is not merely an hypothetical example. It is well known that, in the ordinary conservation experiment, a considerable number of preschool children predict that the sticks will be equally long again when returned to 1) (Figure 1), *while at the same time* maintaining that in 3), stick B is longer than stick A. In other words, it is quite possible simultaneously to deny conservation and affirm reversibility (possibility of return to the initial state).

The final acquisition of conservation of length presupposes a distinction between 'apparent' and 'real' length, the crucial problem being to account for the self-evident quality of the belief in the conservation of the 'real' length. One may speculate, e.g., that this self-evidence is based on such implicit premises as, 'A and B are rigid solid objects', where 'rigid' means retaining its spatial properties (including length) up to the point of breaking or being crushed. It follows that since B is not broken or crushed, it has retained its spatial properties, including length. In the parallel case of conservation of quantity (two equal balls of plasticine, A and B, B being deformed into another shape) one may envisage the following variant of premises: A and B contain equal amounts of plasticine, nothing is added to or taken away from B during the deformation, which means that B is not changed in quantity, hence it remains unchanged and continues to be equal to A.

In these two examples, typical of hundreds of others, the common-sense statements take the form of tautologies, i.e. they are necessarily true, because they follow from given premises and definitions. This means that common-sense beliefs are established as a consequence of the acquisition of the *meanings* of terms and situations. As the full social meaning of terms and situations becomes understood, the common-sense beliefs come to be established as latent possibilities that are activated at the moment they are needed or challenged. A common-sense belief, then, has the status of a latent or potential implication from a given set of premises. It differs from other latent beliefs, in that it is derived from established social meanings, and hence is shared by every normal adult in a given culture.

Understanding and logic

At this point, it becomes necessary to comment explicitly on the relationship between, on the one hand, meaning, as defined by how something is understood by the person, and the beliefs, defined as the implication that follow from the meanings. The special case that interests us here is the relation between the social meanings of events in a given culture, and the common sense in this culture.

Our position here was expressed as follows in a recent article:

Consider the way in which it is decided how a person has understood a given statement. There seem to be only four major procedures for determining such understanding: Observing agreement or disagreement as to (1) what statements are *equivalent* with the given one, (2) what is *implied* by the given stateemnt, (3) what is *contradicted* by the given statement, and (4) what is *irrelevant* to the given statement ...

These procedures are useful only if we assume that the person is logical — in a general sense of the term. If he is not assumed to be logical, the observations of agreement or disagreement can carry no information with respect to how he has understood the original statement. In other words, if the person is liable to make faulty judgments of the relations of equivalence, implication, contradiction, and irrelevance, as such, the four methods cannot help us to find out how he understands the given statement.

How, then, can it be determined whether or not a person is in fact logical in a given situation? The answer appears to be that we can decide whether or not a given judgment or inference is logically correct, only if we can assume that the person has understood correctly the premises involved. If we cannot assume correct understanding — or more generally, if we do not know what the person's premises are — we cannot evaluate his judgments and inferences as far as logicality is concerned.

In conclusion, decisions about understanding must take logic for granted, and decisions about logicality must take understanding for granted. This circle can be transcended only if one of the factors is defined *a priori* as a constant.

Here — as in other matters psychological — we should take a clue from every-day life. It seems quite clear that common-sense thinking (cf. Heider, 1958; Schutz, 1967) always and automatically takes logic in a wide sense for granted and regards understanding as the variable which must be determined. In conversations we always assume that the other person is logical, i.e. that he will accept statements which are equivalent to or follow from his earlier statements, and that he will refuse to accept statements which contradict his earlier statements or which, to him, are entirely irrelevant. When our expectations are not fulfilled, we normally attribute it to a lack of understanding on our part, or sometimes to a change in the other person, but not to genuine illogicality on his part. Apparent illogicality which resists reduction to any specific lack of understanding, is experienced as 'making no sense.' Exactly similar considerations apply in the case of non-verbal interactions. Understanding must be a variable since it is a function of the relation between the meaning experienced by different individuals with different background. On the other hand, logic must be presupposed, since it is a characteristic of the activity of any integrated system and is a part of the very notion of person. (Smedslund, 1970, pp. 217-218.)

It follows from the preceding that common-sense beliefs, being logical implications from social meanings, cannot in themselves be empirically testable. Either they are consistent with subsequent observations, or they are seen as being based on erroneous premises.

This is especially clearly illustrated in the case of transitive inferences, since, here, the premises are explicit and less ambiguous than in the case of conservation. If $A>B$ and $B>C$, then the adult or older child infers that $A>C$. If this coincides with actual observations, it is taken to indicate that the two premises were as assumed. If, on the contrary, one observes $C>A$, this is interpreted to mean that at least one of the premises is not valid. Under no circumstances is the validity of the principle of transitivity itself questioned. In other words, the structure of common sense is unassailable, and its fallibility is explained by faults in the information with which it works. Empirical studies cannot have the purpose of validating common-sense beliefs, but they can function to reveal lack of mutual understanding (communication) between researcher and subject. Thus studies of children and of the mentally retarded and mentally ill can serve to map out in what ways these categories of people lack understanding of and ability to deal with what is the social reality of adults.

Since communication between individuals is, by definition, dependent on social meaning, the psychologist must presuppose his knowledge of such meanings when dealing with subjects and clients. When communication breaks down, i.e. when researcher and subject disagree on the interpretation of given situations, the former must attempt to diagnose the source of misunderstanding, i.e. the difference in implicit premises that explains the lack of mutual understanding. As long as we do not succeed in explaining the actions of our subjects or clients in terms of some common-sense formulation, these actions per definition cannot, indeed, make any 'sense' to us. A common-sense explanation then is one which can be communicated to others in the given society and which has a tautological form, i.e. follows necessarily from the shared premises involved.

In this section, a first attempt has been made to describe the structure of common sense. This structure is seen as the network of implications of such premises as are shared by normal adult members of the given society, in the given situation. Before we proceed to analyze how the psychologist gets his knowledge about particular subjects or clients, psychological common sense must be set apart from other varieties of common sense, notably the sociological one.

The distinction between psychological and sociological common sense

The general area of common sense can be subdivided into several broad regions. One is the region of what may be labeled *physical* common sense. This region has, as mentioned above, been thoroughly explored by the investigations of Jean Piaget and his collaborators and followers in their studies of the cognitive development of children. We all take, e.g., conservation for granted. Ordinarily, the thought that it could be otherwise never crosses our mind. Only after having observed that young children apparently do *not* reason this way, have we become aware of this aspect of our common sense. One may, no doubt, define other important categories of common sense, such as the *technical* one. For example, it is evident to us that an appliance, such as an electric shaver without batteries, can only work when connected with the network. However, our main interest here lies in these aspects of common sense which have to do with people. In this area, it is particularly important to notice and consider the distinction between psychological and sociological common sense.

Sociological common sense is the unreflective understanding of the *objective* order that exists in given social situations. Objective means here an order existing *in advance* of any given individual, *independently* of him, and relative to which individuals are *interchangeable*. As a concrete image we may envisage a marathon performance in square dancing, where both dancers and leaders are constantly being changed without interrupting the dance. The rules of the dance are objective in the sense that they exist in advance of the entrance of any individual participant, they are approximately independent of him, and any individual is interchangeable with any one of the others. Yet, they are dependent on people in the sense that they exist only as people agree upon them and master them. Sociology is in no way a discipline concerned only with *static* phenomena — the rules of square dancing may change — but at any moment in their change they maintain their objective character in the above-mentioned sense.

On the other hand, psychological common sense is the unreflective understanding of the *subjective* order that exists in given social situations. Subjective means here an order existing *for* any given individual, and *dependent* on him. In the example of the marathon dance, the psychological interest is focused on one individual at a time, how and why he learned the rules and how to perform according to them, how and why he enters and leaves the dance, what variations he introduces and why, what he experiences and what he expresses during the dance, what he thinks and feels about the dance in advance and afterwards, etc.

The distinction between sociological and psychological points of view should be understood as a pragmatic indication of a rough boundary between two disciplines and two professions with somewhat overlapping and closely related interests. It should be noted that many sociologists, notably Goffman, explicitly introduce a certain amount of psychology in their descriptions in order to get a reasonably complete picture of social interactions.

> I assume that the proper study of interaction is not the individual and his psychology, but rather the syntactical relations among the acts of different persons mutually present to one another. None the less, since it is individual actors who contribute the ultimate materials, it will always be reasonable to ask what general properties they must have if this sort of contribution is to be expected of them. What minimal model of the actor is needed if we are to wind him up, stick him in amongst his fellows, and have an orderly traffic of behavior emerge? What minimal model is required if the student is to anticipate the lines along which an individual, *qua* interactant, can be effective or break down? ... A psychology is necessarily involved, but one stripped and cramped to suit the sociological study of conversation, track meets, banquets, jury trials, and street loitering.
>
> Not, then, men and their moments. Rather moments and their men. (Goffman, 1967, pp. 2-3.)

Rules can only be maintained, deviated from, and changed, given participants with definite psychological characteristics. Therefore, *socio-*

logical common sense presupposes psychological common sense. Conversely, psychological methods presuppose knowledge of the network of rules that define 'meaning-in-context' in the given culture, and psychological common sense, as well as research and professional practice are impossible without such knowledge. In other words, *psychological common sense presupposes sociological common sense.*

In order to give a picture of a sociological point of view, which will not explicitly concern us in the following, but which will be constantly presupposed, the following excerpt from sociological common sense is offered:

What should one do when one is invited to a party? At the moment of the invitation one expresses that one is delighted to be invited, the exact nuance of excitement is delicately balanced according to the circumstances. If one does not want to go to the party, one must devise an excuse that cannot be revealed as such, i.e., one must make it clear that one wants *very* much to go, and that one is *very* disappointed, but that one simply *cannot,* for some, apparently clear, yet not easily verifiable reason. Example: 'I am so sorry, we would have liked to come, but we are already engaged on Friday.' Occasionally, there are vulgar and curious persons who attempt to circumvent the rule of not indicating disbelief, by saying, sweetly and innocently, 'that is too bad, who are you going to see?' This leaves you with little choice, but to say something like, 'oh, you don't know them, they are from out of town', or 'business, as usual' in a vague casual voice, and then you hurry to change the subject (without appearing to hurry).

When one has accepted an invitation one is obliged to go, and if, for some reason, one cannot or changes one's mind, one is obliged to inform the prospective hosts as early as possible, and in a proper way, emphasizing that the impediment was impossible to foresee, that it was impossible to give the information earlier, etc.

One arrives at the party certainly not too early, but also not too late. If one transcends the boundaries for a reasonable time of arrival, one must offer suitable apologies, again emphasizing circumstances beyond one's control. One shakes the hand of the host and hostess, one looks happy, sometimes it may be particularly appropriate to bring flowers, a box of candy, or some small gift for the house, etc.

One is introduced, or introduces oneself, to guests one does not know, and one greets people one knows more or less formally, yet taking care to include everyone present.

In choice of topic of conversation, many delicate considerations are unreflectively made. One must attempt to say something which is of interest to the other one(s), but it need not be interesting to oneself. One should moderate one's outflow of speech in such a way that others also have a chance to say something. Conversely, one should show interest in and attention to what is said and answer direct or indirect questions. Ordinary topics of conversation that are eligible in many situations (but some of them not in all) are 'children', 'youth', 'travel recollections and travel plans', 'whatever happened to ... (persons, gossip)' 'car', 'houseowner', 'gardening', 'food', 'clothes and fashions', 'who won (sports)', 'prices, taxes, salaries', 'do-it-yourself-themes', 'politics (local, national, international)', 'books, articles', 'movies, TV, theatre, concerts, exhibitions'. (See Berne, 1966, especially pp. 41-47.) Topics, ordinarily quite inappropriate, are the mutual sexual adjustment of couples present or their extramarital affairs, the merits of the present party as compared to other parties with other hosts, etc.

When the conversation has started, the main rule is to stick to the topic selected. The matter of changing the topic, without being rude and inconsiderate, is very delicate indeed. If the current topic is not clearly exhausted, as witnessed by noticeable pauses, etc., one's best chance may be to treat an ambiguous remark as a starting point for an apparently unreflective and innocent 'à propos what you said there — I just heard ...' One such sentence, if not countered by someone who stubbornly wants to pursue the original topic, can elegantly lead to a new topic, namely the one favored by the person who engineered the change.

Let us leave the party at this point, with the passing note that some rules, but not all, can be broken in certain ways after one has signalled that one is 'drunk', particularly when several people have mutually agreed that they are roaringly and happily plastered.

The point made here is that a tremendous amount of finely structured knowledge (sociological common sense) is required in order to participate in any event in adult life. This becomes particularly clear when one considers, for the sake of comparison, a birthday party for a four-year-old. Whatever structure there is, is introduced and maintained by the adults. The children are dressed up and bring a gift. Some of them mechanically, or after being prodded, say 'congratulations', but their facial expressions are not adequate and the receiver doesn't care anyhow, nor does he(she) necessarily remember to say 'thank you' (not that the giver cares). The wrapping is torn away brutally, and the gift is honestly commented upon by those present. Crude remarks such as 'I already have one like that' are not heeded, because the giver has already disappeared somewhere else. At the table one can observe disorder, lack of self-discipline, immodesty, and a general absence of orderly conversation. Only the somehow pitiable and oversocialized child feels obliged to eat everything on his plate, abstain from making a mess on the table and of himself, and to ask permission to leave the table. The adults organize plays and entertainment. The farewell is chaotic and arbitrary and seldom involves polite statements about how pleasant it all has been. If courtesies are offered, they are rendered in a mercilessly mechanical way. Yet this means little, because no one, except adults, listen, and these exclaim 'how cute'.

The well known novel *Lord of the Flies* (Golding, 1969) is an interesting speculation about what may happen when immature individuals are left to govern themselves. Here it can be seen that when the participating individuals lack certain psychological characteristics, the ordinary objective social order cannot be maintained. (Cf. Goffman's considerations about a minimum psychology, quoted above.) Conversely, it is known that if a person is kept in prolonged isolation, combined with various sorts of mental torture, his social surroundings may become insufficient to support his normal psychological functioning, which may deteriorate in drastic ways. In summary, sociology and psychology are concerned with respectively an objective and a subjective aspect of human lives. They mutually presuppose each other, not only at the level of conceptual analysis, but also at the level of factual interdependence.

In chapter II, p. 31, the subject matter of psychology was defined as the realm of events that exist in the mode 'pour lui/pour elle', i.e. *for* the other person. In order to pursue this theme, we will now turn to the problems involved in getting to know other minds.

Other minds

In our daily lives we take it for granted that other persons have minds. When I write this I take it for granted. We may play with the thought that all other people are merely complicated automatic robots or images in one's own dream, but this solipsistic attitude cannot be maintained. Even when writing such thoughts down or talking about them, we forget ourselves, again taking for granted that we are communicating with someone. The vital importance of the axiom of other minds and of community with others has been painfully experienced by philosophers who have attempted to analyze its foundations. Towards the end of Book I of *A Treatise of Human Nature,* the great empiricist philosopher David Hume vividly describes his conflict as follows:

I dine, I play a game of back-gammon, I converse, and am merry with my friends; and when after three or four hours' amusement, I would return to these speculations, they appear so cold, and strain'd, and ridiculous, that I cannot find in my heart to enter them any farther. (Referred to in Bakan, 1968, p. 82.)

Yet, even if it is accepted that the existence of other minds is an essential and absolutely necessary assumption in human life, one cannot deny that there is a philosophical and a psychological problem involved. How do we know that other minds exist, and how do we gain access to them, when the only things available to us are words and acts? The philosophical part of the problem is to determine what logical necessities, possibilities, and impossibilities are involved, given various interpretations of terms such as 'know' and 'mind'. The psychologist's task is to determine which possibilities are actually realized, i.e. what actual processes are involved. This is one fragmentary and superficial way of distinguishing between philosophy and psychology in the present context.

The philosophical problem of other minds has not been, and perhaps never will be, entirely clarified. However, it may be regarded as partly a matter of ambiguity of the term 'know' as revealed in the following quotation from the philosopher Wisdom (1952, p. 208):

When someone says, 'we never know the mind of another' we need to ask him whether (1) he wishes to say that the sort of thing we would ordinarily call 'knowing the mind of another' doesn't happen — if so he makes in quite ordinary language a statement of fact which is false, or whether (2) he wishes to say that the particular sort of intimate, telepathic knowledge of another's mind which would give us knowledge of his mind comparable to our knowledge in memory of the past seldom or never occurs — if so he makes in a readily acceptable caricature of ordinary language a statement of fact which is true or whether (3) he wishes to say that we cannot know the mind of another in exactly the way he does himself — if so, in a readily acceptable extreme caricature of ordinary language, he makes a statement which is necessarily true, couldn't possible be false.

Nearly always the truth of the matter will be that the sceptical speaker is neither definitely doing one of these things nor definitely doing another.

In the preceding quotation, Wisdom, in a sense, leaves the reader where he started, namely with alternative (1), the common-sense solution. The task of the psychologist is then to determine what processes are involved in the knowing of other peoples' mind in the ordinary sense of the term.

This general question may be subdivided into two somewhat more specific empirical questions, namely, how do people in general conceive of other minds and get to know about them (common sense) and how does the psychologist as a professional go about this same task (scientific psychology)? The psychologist can ask both these questions as a consequence of the reflexivity of psychology (see chapter I, pp. 18-19) and he can also relate his results in the two cases. In other words, the insights of common-sense psychology and the insights of scientific psychology can mutually influence each other, to the extent that they are not identical. As we shall see, they usually are indeed identical.

This may all sound very confusing and very abstract, so let us take a concrete example. Suppose a woman says 'I am so happy' and looks very happy. The answer of common sense to the question 'how do you know how she feels?' obviously is that one knows because she says so and so and has such and such an expression. 'We infer it from her behavior' echoes the research psychologist. Yet the structure of our inferences about the woman's mind has nothing simple to it. For one thing, we may be misled — people can simulate happiness, both openly and covertly (cf. chapter II, pp. 44-46). Looking at a drama we know that the person who plays the role may not be particularly happy, yet the character portrayed may somehow be experienced as genuinely happy. We also know that the young bride of an aging millionaire may have quite mixed feelings, yet she may appear to radiate happiness in front of the photographers. We know of the possibility of simulation and we estimated its likelihood on the basis of preceding, simultaneous and succeeding evidence. Also, we all know, from within, the double experience of simulation, and the peculiar balance which must be maintained. Sometimes the underlying sadness may be so strong as to infiltrate the facade and spoil the impression, sometimes the gay happiness somehow invades one's 'deeper layers' and makes one actually feel an incongruous yet momentarily genuine happiness. What then is 'really' occurring in one's mind?

But there are more complications to be mentioned. How worried can a father be when his teenage daughter with a radiant smile utters the words 'I am so happy, Dad!' when all the surrounding circumstances indicate a deep depression. Common sense recognizes degrees of self-deception in such matters and is not blind to the possibility of sequences such as 'she desperately wanted to feel happy and she said she was happy again and again in order to convince herself and others. Sometimes she succeeded'. Such instances indicate that common sense does not automatically accord to a person a privileged status of having direct access to what he (she) 'really' feels. Sometimes the other may be in a better position to observe: 'Do you know you look so radiantly happy these days!' 'Do I really? Well, I suppose I must be. I haven't had time to think about it really.'

The peculiarity of happiness as of every other mental process is that it has not other external defining properties except those that may be labeled 'signs of happiness'. Happiness may be overwhelmingly real when behavior, context, and bodily impressions coincide completely. Yet it is full of paradoxes such as 'I ought to be happy, I should be happy, yet I am not' and 'I am so happy, yet there is absolutely no reason I know of, on the contrary I ought to be deeply depressed.'

There is a close interaction between the cognition of a mental process and its identity. Within wide limits the process 'is' what it is seen to be, and, in addition, it is changed by being seen in a new way.

Mental phenomena become, or are influenced by, what they are cognized as, especially if this is communicated.

Suppose you go about your business in a relatively serene and calm mood. Suddenly, a member of your household looks at you very irritatedly and says 'what are you so angry about today?' The question implies that your anger is not a matter of doubt, the puzzle is only why you are angry. You reply (feeling quite irritated) 'I am not angry', yet your serenity has disappeared and you may, quite possibly, start to feel a little angry. Perhaps the other one persists, and says, 'is it because of what happened yesterday?' The memory of that anger-provoking occasion becomes vivid in your mind and your anger is quite well established.

What was 'really' on your mind before this episode started? Could it be that you were unconsciously angry and that the other one sensed this? Or could it be that the other one, thinking of the events of yesterday felt that you ought to feel angry and saw your behavior as expressing this? Anyhow, the problem of what 'really' happened must be solved or disposed of somehow. Perhaps you concede, 'yes, when I come to think of it, I still am angry' or the other one says, 'well I suppose I was mistaken, I guess I was thinking about yesterday and I felt that you must be angry' or one just leaves the matter open, turning to other themes or activities, letting it fade quietly into relative oblivion.

What we have said above about the problem of getting to know other minds, fits in with what was said in Chapter II about the weakness of reflection and dialogue as methods of establishing psychological knowledge. One of psychology's methodological dilemmas lies here. On the one hand, one must avoid influencing what is observed. On the other hand, one must try to elicit sufficiently complex information to be able to reach a reasonably well founded conclusion. In the area of diagnosing intellectual development in children, this is exemplified by the extremes of Piaget's *méthode clinique* and the so-called non-verbal methods. The *méthode clinique* involves flexible and prolonged conversation with the child, whereas the non-verbal method involves completely standardized procedures, where the child does no talking, but is occupied with such things as pointing, finding candy under sticks of different lengths, etc. Both methods have dangers. Piaget gathers a maximum of relevant information at the risk of strongly influencing what he finds. The adherents of non-verbal methods, on the other hand, gather a minimum of information which is probably not very much influenced by the observer, but which on the other hand is maximally ambiguous (see Smedslund, 1969).

Throughout the preceding discussion, it has been assumed that we get to know other minds by means of communication, i.e. by means of a shared frame of reference or social meanings. We will now turn to a closer examination of this assumption.

We get to know other minds through communication

It is often said that we have immediate access to our own mental processes whereas we know of mental processes in others only through their behavior. This common-sense truth must be further examined. Our knowledge of our own mental processes may be quite incomplete and fallible. Yet it remains true that we have a direct access to them that is unique. Our access to the minds of other people is said to be indirect and to occur via inferences from their behavior. This is necessarily true if by behavior we mean every aspect of their activity including not only what they say and literally do, but also how they say and do it, and furthermore what they could have said or done and did not say or do, their mimic, gestures, posture, their writing and other products, etc. It should be added here that, although we may not think about it, a substantial part of our knowledge of ourselves stems from exactly the same sources as our knowledge of others. We hear ourselves talk, laugh, shout, we feel and see parts of our body move, feel that we blush or get pale, observe our examination results, etc. Beyond that we know about ourselves mostly through how others react to us.

Let us now consider more closely the concept of behavior. It is quite obvious that it is not physically defined behavior in itself which yields information about the other one's mind. The physical activity and the physical products of this activity are certainly the carriers of this information, and in this sense they are necessary conditions for the achievement of knowledge of other minds. However, they are not sufficient conditions. If we visit a totally foreign culture with a totally unknown language and totally unknown customs in general, we will understand nothing of what goes on, even though all the physical information is plainly available. We see and hear people move around, emit sounds, and do things, yet all this may tell us nothing about what goes on within them and between them. In other words, the sights and sounds may carry no *meaning* to us.

Everything, or almost everything, a person belonging to a given culture does or refrains from doing has some meaning to an observer belonging to or familiar with this culture. Human beings are so formed by the society in which they grow up that most of the things they do tend to have the same meaning to them as to an observer. This means that almost everything we do or refrain from doing can be characterized as *communication* in the sense that it involves *shared meanings*. Watzlawick, Beavin and Jackson (1967) have expressed this by the postulate that 'we cannot not communicate'. The fact that there exist intended and unintended, ambiguous, and even misleading communications has already been touched upon several times, and will be returned to below.

The psychologist, then, communicates with his subject/client and his knowledge of the subject/client's mental processes is entirely dependent on the adequacy of this communication.

Even when the psychologist looks at the subject through a one-way screen and the communication appears to be literally one-way, it is usually a phase in a more extended process, where the psychologist has contributed his share, especially by his initial instructions and explanations. Furthermore, the preceding means that psychology can only be practiced *within* the framework of the given society. Its irreducible and ultimate data are social or public meanings as they exist in this society. Crosscultural research depends on the similarity between the cultures and on the possibility of 'translating' from one to the other. One basic methodological difficulty is how to explicate the meanings involved in every communication. Consulting Webster (or equivalents in other languages) only leads to lists of possible interpretations of given words. Some more complicated meanings are given in works of law and in works on 'Good Manners', but most of the meanings are left implicit. Also, we all know that words, sentences, facial expressions, etc. are ambiguous, when considered in isolation, because their meaning depends on the context. On the other hand, it is a necessary condition for organized human interaction and for the continued existence of all institutions that *meaning-in-full-context* is relatively unambiguous. In fact, the preceding sentence probably can be regarded as analytic in that we tend to explain ambiguity and misunderstandings as stemming from incomplete knowledge of context. Hence the full relevant context of an act (verbal or otherwise) may be defined as the set of circumstances which make it wholly unambiguous or in other words fully intelligible. Although this is an ideal limit rather than an actually realized empirical fact, it may prove to be a useful assumption.

The psychologist in practice or in research utilizes the rich store of potentially unambiguous shared meanings that can be produced especially by means of language, in order to make sure that he is properly understood by the subject/client. Conversely, he applies all kinds of controls and precautions to make sure that he also understands the subject's expressions. In fact, the very term 'understand', when used in communicational contexts, means precisely the achievement of shared meaning. We have already analyzed the peculiarly circular relationship between understanding and logic, and described the basic procedures for checking understanding (pp. 82-83). Here, it should merely be noted that shared meaning is by no means a punctiform coincidence of interpretation. Since meanings form complex networks involving both absolute and probabilistic logical relations, understanding means that whole areas of commonality including possibility of mutual prediction and control are activated, sometimes only by a single word or gesture (cf. Vygotsky, 1962, pp. 140-141).

Another point is that there are interesting levels involved in most communications. Not only is it true that P and O may attribute the same meaning to an act (verbal or otherwise), but they may also explicitly recognize that the other one does likewise. P knows that O knows what he himself knows and vice versa for O. Furthermore P knows that O knows that P knows X, and vice versa for O. More complicated levels are seldom involved, and if they are, probably only as a kind of recursive reasoning, i.e. an assumption of 'limitless mutuality'.

A distinction should be made between the unreflected (centered) assumption that one's own world is *the* world and hence shared by all others, and a differentiated (decentered) recognition of variations in the degree of commonality of experience. Children (and also adults) frequently talk about experiences they have had, as if the recipient of the communication had shared these experiences. Hence, communication may become unintelligible, even though language is used correctly. This stems from a failure to recognize the necessity of informing the recipient about those parts of the context that he does not know. The dimension centration-decentration is of central importance in the study of communication. For recent discussions, see Flavell (1968) and Piaget and Inhelder (1969).

Finally, since communication involves more than one actual person (there is always at least a potential or fictitious receiver to every communication), it must normally contain some explicit or implicit reference to the relationship between the sender and receiver. Watzlawick, Beavin and Jackson have formulated a distinction between the content of the communication and the part of it which serves to characterize the communication. This may be diffusely built into the already existing general context, but, more specifically, it may be the inflection of the voice, the facial expression accompanying the utterance, the choice of words, or explicit communications about the communication such as 'this is an order', 'I was only joking', 'I didn't mean to say that', etc. This has been labeled 'metacommunication' (Watzlawick, Beavin and Jackson, 1967).

In summary, psychologists, like other people, get to know other minds through communication. This puts a heavy methodological and theoretical burden on the notion of social or shared meaning and on the problem of understanding how it is construed, apprehended, maintained, and changed. Especially, it should be noted that the not infrequent occurrence of misunderstandings must be given a theoretical rationale. Common sense clearly indicates that misunderstandings occur under conditions of reduced availability of context. As we have seen, this can be regarded as an analytic proposition.

Questions after Chapter V

1. How can one ever transcend common-sense psychology?

2. Should one ever regard an activity or attitude as irrational?

3. How can one compare common-sense psychology in one culture with common-sense psychology in another culture? Discuss the general kind of problems involved.

4. Try to take a consistent solipsistic attitude for a while. What kinds of conclusions and comments occur to you as a result of this experience?

5. Think of some examples of failure of communication that you know of. How do they fit in with what has been said above? How do you know communication failed and why do you think it failed?

VI. Some main concepts and principles of common-sense psychology

The general concepts and principles underlying common-sense psychology have, until recently, remained largely unexplored. They appear to have been hidden from our view by their very obviousness. Thanks largely to the efforts of the Austrian-American psychologist Fritz Heider (1958), it is now possible to formulate tentatively at least some of the general features of our shared intuitive conceptions. Much of what is said in this chapter is based on or influenced by Heider's work. Throughout the section, the reader will note the three main features of common sense: apparent commonality, earlier unreflectiveness, and self-evidence. At the end we will return once more to a comment on the peculiar structure of common sense, which, somehow, leaves us with little room between the analytic and the arbitrary.

With this overview of common-sense psychology as a background, it will then be possible, in the last part of this book, to discuss some of the refinements and developments of common sense that have been effected by scientific psychology.

Some fundamental concepts

The list to be presented is highly tentative. Other concepts could have been included, different distinctions could have been made, etc. However, the following concepts appear to be among those of basic importance.

1. *Consciousness of the world.* Expressions such as 'he thinks . . .', 'he believes . . .', 'he feels . . .' are used in describing how the world appears to a person. It is an *axiom* that other persons have minds and intuitive psychology clearly distinguishes between the world as it appears to a given person (the subjective world) and the real or objective world. One gains access to a person's mind through what he says and does. The problem of other minds and how we gain access to them has been discussed in the preceding chapter, and will not be further treated here.

2. *Perception and inference.* This category covers processes whereby the person gets information about the world. Terms such as 'see', 'hear', 'taste', 'read', 'infer', are used in this connection.

3. *Central processes.* Even when a person is motionless in a dark quiet place mental processes may be going on. Words such as 'thoughts', 'images', 'fantasies', 'recollections', 'dreams' describe varieties of these inner events, which are not related to any momentary perception.

4. *Can.* This auxiliary verb and related expressions indicate that it is possible for a person to perform an act or cause a change. The two main factors influencing can are *ability* of the person and *difficulty* of the task.

5. *Try.* This verb and synonymous expressions state that a person is actively attempting to do something or to reach a goal. Two main determinants of try are *want* and *ought* (may). Can and try and their determinants are the main elements in every analysis of action.

6. *Want.* This category involves personal motivation and must be clearly distinguished from try. The person may want or wish something without trying to get it, because he believes he cannot achieve the goal, because other, more important, activities take precedence, or because he feels he ought not to try to achieve it. Conversely, he may try to achieve something, not because he wants it but simply because he ought to do so.

7. *Ought and may.* The network of prescribed, forbidden, and permitted act-categories is of crucial importance in common-sense analysis of action. The cultural setting determines the boundaries of legitimate action in very definite ways.

8. *Causes and effects.* Sentences such as 'he made me change my opinions', 'she did it', 'x gave him permission' indicate the direct causes of mental changes and acts. The specification of who or what caused something is of central importance in common-sense psychology. The passive form in expressions such as 'he was hit', 'she was robbed', 'he was insulted' indicate how a person is affected by events.

9. *Like and dislike.* This category is basic in the analysis of interpersonal relationships. Knowledge about whom or what a person likes and dislikes is necessary for the prediction and control of his behavior.

10. *Knowledge.* What a person knows and doesn't know is obviously vital in understanding his feelings and actions. Knowledge, as also like and dislike, characterizes fairly stable domains of the mind, relatively remote from the momentary activities. They have the character of *dispositions*.

11. *Belonging.* Things may belong to a person as property, they may belong to him as products of his work, people and things may be seen as belonging together because they fall under the same category, etc.

Examples of belonging are: a person and his name, a person and his totem, an artist and his creation, man and wife, two whites in a crowd of Negroes, etc.

The other person as perceiver

Other persons are seen as perceivers and we all know much about the conditions of perception. We infer that a person is perceiving or not perceiving something from observing whether his eyes are open or closed, from the direction of his gaze, and from the relation between external changes and his reactions. As an example, we conclude that a person has perceived the traffic signals if he starts crossing the street when the green light comes on, and if he halts when he comes to a red light. We also know that visual perception is facilitated by good illumination, proximity, clear contours, etc. Conversely we attempt to prevent perception of an object by camouflage and by drawing the person's attention to other objects. We know that the 'span of apprehension' is limited and that 'one thing at a time' is a good rule.

We also manipulate others' perception by showing or pretending that we have certain feelings or opinions. We pretend that we like a gift, produce laughter to show that we understand a joke, look appropriately grave at the funeral of an acquaintance, hide irritation with a smile, play 'tough hero' while we are scared 'inside', etc. In these and other more complicated ways we try to control other people's perception of us.

Being perceived means being controlled. If someone else sees where I am or where I am going, hears what I say, sees how I feel, he has some power of influencing me and predicting my behavior. When another person looks at me, knowledge of this restrains me and everything I do becomes more or less influenced by how I think he will perceive it. To be perceived is also to be *evaluated,* and the other one's evaluation usually has some importance, because our self-image is partly dependent on what others think of us. Some problems of the psychological practitioner relating to this have been described in chapter II, pp. 57-59.

When the other one looks at me, I also get some power to control him. His attention is centered on what I do and say. I can influence him and call forth reactions in him. Holding someone's attention thus not only may yield self-consciousness, but also some power.

It follows that the mutual glance has a special place in the interaction between people. They completely hold each other's attention and one is mutually observed in one's process of observation. Eye-contact is maintained only in brief periods, if the relationship is not very close and/or colored by strong feeling.

Action

A simplified version of the implicit common-sense model for analyzing action is shown in Figure 2. According to the model an act or problem-solution will be carried out only if the person both can do it and tries to do it. The remaining combinations of can and try (can and does not try, cannot and tries, and cannot and does not try) do not result in the act. Exceptions from this rule are *unintended results* (I unintentionally pushed him over the brink while trying to save myself) and *luck* (when an unskilled dart-thrower hits the mark). A person tries to do something because he personally wants to and/or because he feels he ought to or has to do it. Try can always be traced to want or ought or both. On the other hand, one may very well want to do something or feel one ought to do it, without actually trying. One can want something without knowing how to get it or knowing that one cannot get it. One can also refrain from trying to do something one ought to do and as a consequence suffer more or less from bad conscience.

Can is determined both by the *difficulty* of the task and by *ability* (including knowledge and skills) of the person. He can perform the task if his ability surpasses the degree of difficulty involved.

In situations where we assume that the person is trying, we predict the act or problem-solution from a judgment of his ability and of the difficulty of the problem. We evaluate a person's abilities by comparing his performance with that of others in the same situation. The difficulty of a problem is evaluated by observing how often persons of a given category solve it, compared with how often they solve other types of problems. The ability-concept is based on comparison of persons under equal conditions, whereas the difficulty-concept is based on comparison of situations, given the same or comparable groups of persons. From a global evaluation of ability and difficulty we predict whether or not the problem will be solved, degree of exertion, time taken, type of solution, etc.

From the observation that a certain problem is solved or not, and information about abilities and/or task-difficulty, a number of inferences can be drawn: solution means can and tries. This rule has two main exceptions: solution, low ability, and difficult task mean luck, solution and no trying mean unintended result. Solution and low ability (e.g.

100

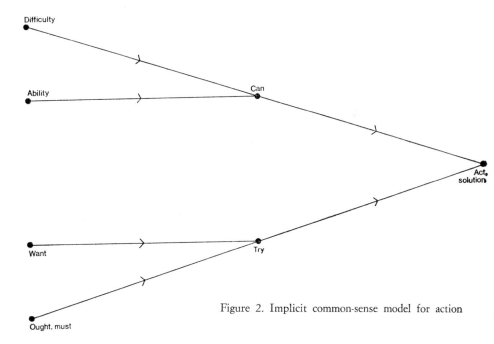

Figure 2. Implicit common-sense model for action

in children) mean easy problem. Solution and difficult task means high ability. Solution, but symptoms of exertion, means difficult task for person, i.e. a task close to his capacity level. No solution despite high ability and easy task means does not try. No solution and tries mean cannot (because of too low ability and/or too difficult task).

Can is usually general, but it can also be situation — or time-bound. He can row the boat across when the wind is westerly, when he is sober, etc. In everyday life we are also aware of typical mechanisms for neutralizing failure:

1. In the sour grapes fable the fox maintains his self-esteem by pretending that he does not want the grapes, rather than admitting that he cannot reach them.

2. The converse displacement may be observed, e.g. when a child is asked to do something well within his ability and answers: 'It is too difficult'. Here the absence of action is explained by cannot instead of the true will not, the latter being apt to be met by coercion and punishment.

Another mechanism related to can is to impress others with one's self-assurance. Normally, self-assurance increases with increasing ability and by posing as self-assured one may try to create the image of being a person with high abilities.

Wish-fulfillment and pleasure

In common-sense psychology it is an axiom that if a person wants X and gets X, then the person will be satisfied. This relation is assumed to be absolutely valid and apparent exceptions are interpreted in one of three ways.

A person wants a juicy tasty apple, buys an apple, but experiences no satisfaction. The following explanations are possible:

a) The apple was not as he wanted it, i.e. the goal was not reached.

b) He really didn't want an apple in the first place, or the wish vanished in the meantime.

c) He really was satisfied, but other matters pushed the experience into the background (a headache, an unpleasant thought, etc.).

It has already been mentioned that many of our actions are not determined by personal wishes, but by what one is supposed to do or must do. Everyday psychology also assumes some pleasure in succeeding dictated by ought and must.

An important variant of ought and must is what is labeled a *need*. A person may need a doctor, a change of environment, a hobby, a wife (husband), etc. He may be quite unaware of such needs. When a person becomes aware of or accepts as genuine such a need, this becomes a strong determinant of his actions and results in some, at least momentary, satisfaction when the need is eliminated.

Fiction frequently deals at great length with more or less subtle conflicts between personal wants on the one hand and duties and responsibilities on the other. In some of the simplest types of fiction such as many paperback westerns, love-stories, and science fiction there are conflicts *between* persons with simple, but opposed, wants (entirely good heroes v. totally bad scoundrels). Intermediate level fiction introduces simple conflicts within the same person, and in the masterpieces of literature one may find described very subtle and complicated networks of conflicting wishes and obligations.

Fiction writers, being under the obligation to be entertaining, are frequently concerned with what may be labeled 'paradoxical' pleasures and sufferings. Among these are pleasures derived from the forbiddenness of forbidden things (kleptomania, adultery, desecration, use of four-letter words, etc.). The opposite of this in a certain sense is the emptiness and disappointment which may be involved in being virtuous and successful or which may follow the achievement of a goal (post-coital and post-marital depression, the unhappiness of being rich, famous, or powerful, etc.). Other popular themes are the pleasure derived from

102

abstaining from pleasure (the lust involved in ascetism or puritanism) and the pleasure derived from suffering (enjoying one's sorrow, or deprivation). The latter relates closely to the more interpersonally defined masochism (enjoying pleasure inflicted by others) the converse of which is sadism (enjoying the infliction of suffering on others). In general, and in a very simplified way, the entertainment involved in the above themes may derive in part from the fact that they challenge or complicate the simple wish-fulfillment-pleasure axiom, which otherwise is taken for granted in everyday life.

The *distance* between a person's present situation and the fulfillment of a wish is a very important psychological dimension. It is not primarily a function of spatial distance, but rather a function of time, exertion, and probability. Wish-fulfillment is more distant the farther in the future it is, the more the effort and work required, and the less the likelihood of achievement.

By means of the distance concept one may classify some emotional and intellectual processes and observe some parallels between them (see Figure 3).

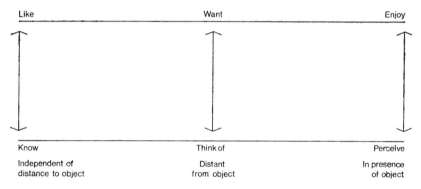

Figure 3. Some parallels between emotional and cognitive functions as they relate to psychological distance

The diagram shown in Figure 3 points in the direction of a central problem. Can affective and cognitive processes exist independently of each other or are they merely different aspects of the same underlying processes? Common sense appears to indicate a basic assymmetry here, at least as long as conscious phenomena are concerned. It appears to be a contradiction to assert that one can like or dislike something one does not know, that one can want something without thinking of it, and that one can enjoy something without perceiving it. On the other hand, it is not contradictory to state that one knows something, thinks of something, or perceives something in a completely neutral way. However, it is commonly assumed that neutrality is unstable and hard to achieve, and that it is, perhaps, always only approximate. Nevertheless, its existence is not doubted. If we choose to conceptualize neutrality as a zero region on a like-dislike dimension, then it too may be seen as a feeling tone and then it becomes necessarily true not only that to every feeling there corresponds a cognition, but also that to every cognition there corresponds a feeling.

'Almost there' is an important special case of distance. If one is close to the goal or if one is close to something one wants to avoid, the wish gets more intense. Also, disappointment is much stronger when one is almost there and yet does not reach the goal, than when the goal always has remained distant. There is something special about one's experience when one holds no. 13055 in a lottery and the main winning number is 13056.

Many emotional states are linked with psychological distance and with changes in psychological distance. One talks about *hope* when the chances are seen as good, *confidence* when one is certain of reaching the goal, *worry* and *anxiety* when one is uncertain, *disappointment* when something goes contrary to expectation, *depression* and *despair* when important goals remain forever out of reach, etc. Terminology in this area is rich and confusing, words are used in a more or less variable sense, and different languages have more or less different classifications.

One may influence and control others by providing them with various kinds of information about the distance to their goal. A person may be induced to work harder or less hard by being told that the task is impossible, difficult, or easy, that the goal is in sight or not, etc. One can *tempt* a person by giving him the impression that the goal is almost within his reach, and make him *suffer* by keeping the goal out of reach. Examples of the latter would be letting a prisoner *nearly* escape, or the story of Tantalus, who stood in water up to his neck surrounded by branches with delicious fruits, but who was not allowed to drink and eat. When a person enjoys a thing or a situation one may attribute the pleasure to the thing or to the person (or perhaps to both). Common sense seems to involve the following assumption: We regard the things as causing our own pleasures, and also the pleasures of other people, when they coincide with our own. When another person differs from us in his evaluation of something, we tend to attribute his experience to personal characteristics rather than to the thing.

Let us first consider the main rule: We feel that our experiences are caused by the object, because, when we have the experience the object is present, and when we don't have the experience, the object is absent. Consequently we say 'the movie is exciting', 'the music is good', 'the food is excellent'. We also expect others to experience the same as we do, and when they don't, we may get disappointed and irritated and sometimes try to convince them that our evaluation is the correct one. If we do not succeed, we usually explain the difference in experience by assuming some idiosyncracy in the other. Less frequently, we think that we ourselves are deviant. We tend to think that the other one did not experience the thing as we did because of his lack of education, his insensitivity, his temporary mood, his lack of a sense of humor, etc. When we observe a person drink from a bottle of cod liver oil with every indication of pleasure, most of us attribute the pleasure to a peculiarity of the person rather than to the oil.

People often seem to have difficulty in taking into account both the person and the object at the same time. Either one discusses whether or not a piece of art is good (art being dealt with as an objective phenomenon), or one concludes that whether or not something is good is entirely a matter of personal taste (art being treated as a subjective phenomenon). A possible intermediate position would be that, although the experience of art has a very considerable subjective, i.e. individual element, it is also true that there is some degree of consensus among observers within a given culture or tradition as to what is a masterpiece and what is not. Therefore, art also has an objective, i.e. intersubjective element.

Finally, some elementary principles relating to pleasure will be mentioned:

1. Satisfaction leads one to like something and to wish for it. Narcotics peddlers frequently give the drug free to their clients the first time and let the price remain low until the wish has become strong and stabilized.

2. By giving a person things he wants, one may make him like oneself, and/or make him feel under an obligation to return the favor in some way.

3. One may let a person enjoy something in order to please his friends or in order to irritate his enemies.

4. Since the experience of pleasure is normally attributed to the thing, one may show a person that someone else is enjoying it, and thereby make him want to enjoy it too. This technique is well known to parents as a means of inducing a reluctant child to taste some food or to take some medicine.

5. One may give a person something he will enjoy, in order to help him overcome depressed feelings, or in order to make him generally more pleasant to be with, more disposed to do other people favors, etc.

Like and dislike

Likes and dislikes in all degrees from love via neutrality to hate represent a central theme in common-sense psychology. Like and dislike are relatively stable phenomena, which may often remain unchanged for months and years, in contradistinction to wishes and enjoyment, which are highly variable.

In everyday life, there is a widespread tendency to assume that one cannot have different feelings for different parts of the same whole, without experiencing conflict and tension, and without doing something to correct the situation. In other words, there is a distinction between situations where our feeling for other persons and for things are balanced and situations where they are not.

Heider (1958, pp. 176-177) gives the following example: 101 subjects, consisting of high school and college students and other adults were given the following description of a situation and were asked to write down the most probable outcome. 'Bob thinks Jim very stupid and a first-class bore. One day Bob reads some poetry he likes so well that he takes the trouble to track down the author in order to shake his hand. He finds that Jim wrote the poems'. Since Jim and his poems are experienced as belonging together, the dislike for Jim and the liking of the poems creates an imbalanced situation. The subjects resolved this in the following ways: (1) Forty-six per cent changed the negative author to a positive person, e.g., 'He grudgingly changes his mind about Jim'. In this way both entities become positive and balance was achieved. (2) Twenty-nine per cent changed the value of the poetry, e.g., 'He decides the poems are lousy'. In this way balance was achieved by transforming the unit into one which was consistently negative. (3) Five per cent challenged the unit formation itself, e.g., 'Bob would probably question Jim's authorship of the poems'. (4) Two subjects altered the unit by differentiating the author in such a way that the unit comprised only the positive part of the author and the admired poetry, e.g., 'He then thinks Jim is smart in some lines but dumb in others'. (5) The rest of the subjects did not resolve the disharmony, but some were definitely aware that the situation represented a conflict. 'Bob is confused and does not know what to do. He finally briefly mentions his liking of the poems to Jim without much warmth'.

In general, the formation of units or wholes (belongingness) involves a person and things produced or owned by him, or belonging to the same category as he does. Persons belonging to the same family, profession, religion, ethnic group, nationality, etc. may be seen as parts of the same unit. The grouping of elements into units, however, is relative to the surrounding circumstances. This is illustrated in the following question (Heider, p. 179): 'A Kansan boasts about the Empire State Building. Where is this most likely to happen, in Topeka, New York, Paris, or Chicago? The obvious answer is: In Paris. Boasting implies that the person who does the boasting and the object about which he boasts form a unit'. The only place where such unit formation is likely to occur in the given case is outside the United States.

The tendency to balance means that we are inclined to perceive a person as having mostly positive or mostly negative traits, which means a simplification and an emphasis on the unitary character of persons. Compare this with the discussion of our tendency to typification in Chapter VII, pp. 126-129.

Perceived similarity with oneself creates a tendency to like a person. Conversely, if a person is perceived as different from oneself, there is a tendency to dislike him. The balance system involves three elements, I like myself — we are similar (belong to same category or unit) — I like him. In special cases where we don't like ourselves, another outcome may be expected. If a person is an alcoholic and hates himself for it, his response to another person who drinks may on occasion be very hostile. In this case the triad may be: I dislike myself (as an alcoholic) — he and I are similar — I dislike him.

Members of the same family are usually seen as belonging together. If we like the parents we have a tendency to like their children, and when we dislike the parents we are apt to discover unsympathetic traits in their children. On the other hand, it is true that we, on occasion, are impressed with the differences between members or parts of a unit. In this case we may tend to perceive man and wife as *contrasts* or opposites. Common-sense psychology is not empty in this respect, even though it sometimes predicts assimilation and sometimes contrast. The point is that there is departure from objectivity and a tendency to selective distortion, one way or the other. Husbands and wives typically rate themselves and their partners similarly on many traits. However, this assumed similarity is more pronounced in happily married than in unhappily married couples. Furthermore, one may expect that people who are in open conflict, such as many separated or divorced persons, will tend to emphasize differences rather than similarities in their perception of each other.

In common-sense psychology there are many and partly conflicting views on the role of contact versus separation for peoples' mutual feelings. Prolonged and intimate contact may lead to intensification of feelings, both increasing sympathy and increasing hostility, but also to increasing indifference. Common sense attributes these effects to the nature of the rewards and conflicts that are forthcoming, as the interaction reveals more and more of the participants' traits or dispositions. Young couples have often been advised to attempt to get to know each other as well as possible before making any decisions. Again, the value of this advice may depend very much on the social structure involved. In societies where the role of man and wife (wives) is highly structured and defined, the effects of prolonged intimacy may be quite different from that in our contemporary Western society, where marriage roles are becoming increasingly diffuse. Such things as possibility and ease of obtaining a divorce may strongly influence the way partners interpret and respond to their experiences.

With respect to the effect of separation, common sense seems to suggest that it will lead to a decline in the intensity of feelings in the long run, whereas short separations may have the opposite effect. There is a proverb in many languages to the effect that 'time will heal every wound'. Obviously, many other factors will influence the outcome, notably the depth and extent of the initial feelings, the degree to which the liked or disliked person was involved in the person's daily life, plans, etc. Another set of factors are the events and the kind of life that occur during the separation. It is commonplace to assume that a rich and/or demanding and satisfactory life may lead to a more rapid decline in feelings for an unattainable person than an empty, undemanding, and unsatisfactory life. Particularly in the erotic sphere, surroundings with numerous attractive potential partners are believed to enhance the chances for earlier feelings to be displaced by new ones, whereas life in a monastery or equivalent places such as a military base in the Antarctic, will tend to maintain and even intensify feelings of attraction for the already existing reference person. Again, writers of fiction have described cases of paradoxical stability of love or hate under conditions which normally would have tended to annihilate them. Fiction emphasizes such phenomena as desperate and 'unexplainable' love of apparently completely unworthy persons (Maugham's *Of Human Bondage*) and the persistence of hatred in the face of pure love and inexhaustible kindness.

Again, one's attitude toward fiction must remain a double one. On the one hand, fiction may contain apparently genuine, i.e. psychologically correct descriptions, on the other hand, it may contain descriptions which are fascinating and entertaining precisely because they approach or transcend the boundaries of what is likely to occur.

The tendency to balance and unity in one's feeling is well known in everyday life. Yet we also know that people get bored and have a craving for the unknown and exciting. The prototype of this are the numerous stories of how a person comes to a Christian-type Heaven, and after a while gets so thoroughly bored that he asks for a transfer to Hell instead. In technologically advanced cultures it is a recognized social problem how people are to spend their free time. Another example of the tendency to imbalance is the case where people who are very different are mutually attracted and enjoy each other's company.

In all cultures *love* has (in some sense of the term) been assigned a fundamental role in human life. We all know so much about love in its various manifestations that it is almost impossible to say anything nontrivial. There is no doubt that this concept or rather cluster of concepts refers to one of the basic dimensions in mental life. In western cultures the concept goes back to Plato and to the biblical tradition 'but the greatest of these is love'. The Platonic tradition distinguishes between several forms of love, physical, erotic love being the lowest, then followed by love of persons and pieces of nature and art, then love of more abstract kinds of beauty and order, like institutions, laws, mathematics, etc., and finally a kind of supreme love of Beauty and Order itself. The Platonic tradition was merged with the Christian, and the highest form of love became the love of God.

It has also been characteristic of Christian cultures, on the one hand to continue to use words like love very widely, yet making a very sharp distinction between the 'higher' forms of love such as love of God and love of one's neighbors and fellow-men, or one's country, and the 'lower' forms of 'carnal', erotic love. Among the things common to all variants of love is that they involve positive and very strong feelings.

The discussion here will be limited, admittedly somewhat arbitrarily, to a few comments on the love that exists between parents and children, and on the complex theme of jealousy.

Child-parent love

It is taken for granted in daily life that parents love their children and that children love their parents. An indirect reflection of this it that fiction so frequently contains descriptions of cases where parents are indifferent to or hate their children and vice versa, and this moves us in a very deep and somehow shattering way. We all know that the love of parents for their children is somehow different from the love children have for their parents. The love of the parents has three salient ingredients.

First, it is loaded with moral obligation of an absolute character. Most parents feel responsible for their children and obliged to take care of them and love them whatever happens. If they think they have failed in this, they will feel guilt in a very painful way. This is not to say that parental love does not have other components, but merely that it occurs within a framework of strong obligation. The very thought of one not loving one's children may be almost unthinkable.

Secondly, the parents' self-image and aspirations are more or less heavily invested in their children. The parents want to have children with such and such characteristics, and may experience sorrow, pain, or irritation when the children deviate from the aspirations.

Finally, parental love tends to be relatively undemanding and unselfish, since it is recognized that a child cannot love one back in an adult way. Yet parents are always looking for signs of love in their children; they may falsely interpret childish behavior as indicating love, and both in real life and in fiction there are countless accounts of adult disappointment, when the adolescent fails to give the expected signs of love and appreciation 'in exchange for 15 years of self-sacrifice'. Common sense generally recognizes that children's capacity for love in the adult sense increases as they grow older, and that they have at first primarily a tremendous demand for safety and consolation. Yet, it is probably true that the common-sense psychology of children's love, and their mental life in general, have never attained the general sophistication of the common-sense psychology of adults. For one thing many adults, particularly men and unmarried people, never have had extensive enough encounters with children to get to know them intuitively. Furthermore, the axiom that 'after all, we are all pretty much alike' (Bakan, 1968), which greatly facilitates adult interaction and mutual understanding, does not apply to the same extent to children. Children are different from adults and the difference is greater, the smaller the child. Interacting with the infant may in some sense be fairly easy, because it is so primitive and uncomplicated, but as the child passes into toddlerhood and starts to talk, matters become more complicated. The preschool child and the young schoolchild are quite complex persons, and yet they are in many ways different from adults. Ordinary common-sense psychology does not always work very well with them. This is the reason why child psychology, in a certain sense, is the branch of scientific psychology which, together with psychopathology, where the same considerations apply, has advanced knowledge most, relative to what everyone already knew intuitively.

Jealousy

In order to illustrate a relatively complex theme within our common-sense knowledge of likes and dislikes, let us briefly recapitulate what we all know about *jealousy*.

The typical setting for jealousy is a triad where the jealous person feels that his partner is in love with (interested in, attracted to) a third person. Most of us know what it feels like to be jealous, and we know that it is intensely unpleasant, often involves all kinds of bodily sensations, and aggression, depression, disappointment, withdrawal, etc. in varying proportions.

In triads we know there is a strong tendency toward balance. If two persons (A and B) like each other and B also likes a third person C, one may then expect that A would also like C. In the case of jealousy this is clearly not the case. On the contrary, strong negative feelings are evoked and, paradoxically enough, frequently most strongly against one's partner, and less strongly toward the third person. However, if one's feelings toward one's partner had become totally extinct or totally negative, there would be no more jealousy, but only withdrawal and dissolution of the partnership. The distinguishing characteristic of jealousy is that one feels aggressive and hateful toward one's partner, while at the same time maintaining a strong positive emotional tie.

We all know that jealousy is incompatible with warmth and love-making. The jealous person is cold, hateful, and withdrawn into himself, and his positive feelings are suppressed. This doubleness of jealousy involves deep personal feelings, and is very hard to bear for any long period. It can lead to violent emotional outbursts, 'crimes passionelles', psychotic breakdowns, depressions, etc.

The jealous person has a very complicated relation to the third person involved, especially when he does not know him well. He may be afraid to get to know him because he may turn out to be a charming person, thereby confirming his partner's impression and making the situation appear more threatening. On the other hand, a negative impression of the third person will contradict his partner's impression and thereby set him further apart from the partner (as liking different types of people). Thirdly, getting to know the third person in a balanced and grown up way is incompatible with the very childish state in which the jealous person is situated. He does not want to be objective and open, he does not *want* to understand. Against the three preceding tendencies stands the strong rival *curiosity,* the wish to know as much as possible about the rival, how dangerous he is, what the chances are that the romance will come to pass, etc. The net result is that the jealous person may have a very vague and confusing conception of the rival, and a multiply ambivalent attitude toward gathering information about him.

The jealous person's adjustment to uncertainty is especially revealing as far as degree of emotional disturbance is concerned. When the jealousy is not directly confirmed, but only based on a number of ambiguous and incomplete cues, it may lead to fantasies and suspicions in an otherwise normal person that are reminiscent of what is usually called paranoiac states. Everything is perceived as having an alternative hidden meaning. The jealous person may even display paradoxical wishes of having the suspicions confirmed, because even the worst truth is seen as preferable to continued uncertainty. Even in the case of wholly or partly unjustified jealousy it may be very hard to escape from one's suspicions; although they are capable of unambiguous verification, they are very hard to falsify unambiguously. The reason for this is that, in this type of situation, one's partner may very well be interested in keeping a secret of his emotional attachments and affairs. If one's partner is keeping things secret this would lead to overt behavior that is approximately identical to the behavior of a completely innocent person. In the case where the partner is aware of the jealousy, it becomes even more probable that he will be careful to assume an innocent attitude, even in minor details. This creates optimal conditions for suspicious fantasies, and the situation becomes even worse because most people are reminded of the times they themselves have been successfully deceitful. 'I have deceived people, everyone I know has deceived people, why shouldn't my partner also do it to me'.

Jealousy is experienced as a state, a departure from normal, within which one is imprisoned against one's will. It is almost completely resistant to attempts at detached intellectual analysis or attempts to 'pull oneself together'. It obviously is a *childish* state, and reveals a childish dependence between adults that may not normally be visible. The childishness is also revealed in the oversimplified and rigid structure of jealous thought, and in the difficulties of taking the point of view of one's partner or the point of view of the third person. Also, the jealous person cannot easily detach himself from the situation, and finds little comfort in the thought that the 'romance' is almost certain to pass after a while. The *here-and-now* perspective dominates.

In summary, jealousy reveals an implicit demand for absolute monopoly on the feelings of one's partner.

Norms and values

Many of our acts are determined by what ought to be done rather than by what we personally want to do. We try to keep our promises and appointments. We frequently tell the truth, even if it leads to unpleasant consequences. We don't put the knife in our mouth while eating. We don't steal, even when we think we will not be discovered, etc. We all have definite and frequently convergent ideas about what ought to be done, what is responsible or just, and about what people are entitled to in given situations.

It is characteristic of ought that it is *impersonal*. In language this is reflected in the use of terms such as 'one' (ought to), and 'it' (ought to). The moral rule that, e.g., parents ought to love each one of their children equally strongly, is felt as a requirement in general, i.e., it does not emanate from any particular source and it applies to all people who have more than one child.

Norms and values can be related to supernatural entities and to subjective experiences such as one's conscience. They may also derive from institutions such as written laws and regulations. In principle, they are independent of persons and of particular circumstances. Justice should be done equally to friend and enemy. This does not mean that we are not influenced in moral questions by our own wishes and points of view, but it means that one *ought not* to let such matters have an influence. Moral principles are independent and objective.

The rules for what is right and wrong in any given situation make up what may be called the *moral reality*. This is known to vary from one society to another. It is just as important for us to know and adapt to this reality as it is to know and adapt to the physical reality. We can only live together with our fellow beings if we, by and large, follow the rules. We must keep our promises and appointments, tell the truth (if we can), cooperate in a just distribution of rights and duties, etc.

In everyday life one frequently talks about moral and esthetic values. The relationship between a value and ought to is parallel to the relationship between like and wish. The experience that something ought to be or ought not to be done arises when a moral value becomes relevant and when it is not fulfilled, not conformed with. This is similar to when a personal goal is distant and a wish arises. Like and value are both relatively stable dispositions, which may not always be represented in action. They differ in that like is egocentric (relates to the person himself) whereas values are objective, in the sense of being impersonal, independent of persons.

How do we know that a given act is guided by moral principles rather than personal wishes? There are two strong indications of this: 1) If the person does something that we know he personally dislikes, but which is morally correct. 2) If the person refrains from doing something immoral that we know he personally likes. In both the preceding situations the person must not be under any kind of threat or pressure.

As in the case of like-dislike, norms lead to considerations about balance. People with different value systems provoke each other, and have difficulties in interacting, or at least have to be careful when interacting. Examples: Contacts between a conservative and a communist, between a fervent religious believer and a convinced atheist, between an active prohibitionist and a whisky-producer. The reason why violent conflicts and disputes are apt to arise from such contacts is that values are usually conceived of as general and universally valid. People do not normally think they uphold their fundamental value systems on the basis of purely subjective preferences. Differences in such matters become provocative because one cannot, as in the case of wishes and preferences, talk about things as being a matter of 'personal taste'. Values are usually seen as either true or false. Therefore, persons in severe conflict with each other over fundamental values can only maintain their inner balance by assuming that the other one is narrow- minded, stupid, uneducated, misled, possessed by the devil, morally degenerated, sick in his mind, etc. Other solutions can be reached by denying the other one the status of a complete human being by describing him as a stinking jackal or hyena, pig, s.o.b., etc., or by seeing him as a monomaniac i.e. dominated entirely by one motive (greed for money, power, pleasure, etc.).

Norms may be utilized in order to influence people and in order to defend oneself against influences. One may ask a person for a favor in a situation where he cannot say no without being rude. One may also utilize norms by doing things for another in order to place him in debt to oneself. This may give one tremendous power over another person ('I saved you from ruin'. 'I gave up my career for you sake', etc.). To make another person too heavily indebted to oneself, may, however, also have adverse side effects. A person who is thus indebted loses so much of his freedom to the donor that he may become increasingly hostile toward him. This hostility is not morally accepted and is suppressed, but may thereby become even more dangerous.

Norms may be used in self-defense, e.g. in refusing to accept gifts or obey suggestions by saying 'I cannot do it because it wouldn't be proper', 'it wouldn't be right', etc.

Three main types of influence may induce a person to transgress the rules: He may be *tempted* to do something immoral. Examples would be seduction and bribery. Breaking of norms induced by temptation are usually judged very severely.

A person may be *threatened* in order to compel him to do something immoral. The threat may involve physical violence or some kind of blackmail. Usually immoral actions performed under threat are judged mildly. It is common sense to assume that it is generally easier to resist temptation than to resist threat.

Finally, one may *command* someone to do something immoral. This may be intimately related to threats, but a command is also difficult to resist because one has a (moral) duty to obey. Such cases are highly controversial, as witnessed by well-known discussions about crimes of war (Nürnberg, My Lai, etc.).

Benefit and harm

The psychology of everyday life emphasizes at least five different aspects of acts resulting in harm or benefit to someone. 1) Who was the actor? 2) What was intended by the act? 3) Why did the person act in this way? 4) What was the actual outcome of the act? 5) How did the target person interpret the act?

The very same act will be judged in very different ways according to the outcome of the above analysis. Take some examples:

P acted in this way, but did not intend to.

P acted in this way, but O (the target person) does not know that P did it.

P acted without intending to, but O thinks is was intentional.

P did not do it, but O thinks he did.

P intended to benefit O, but the outcome was that he harmed O.

P and O may agree or disagree in judging the outcome, and they may be aware of each other's judgments or not.

One may distinguish between immediate and long-term consequences of acts. Not infrequently these consequences are in contrast, one of them involving benefit and the other harm. The actor and the target person may not know this. Examples: Young children frequently perceive the doctor as someone who tries to hurt them. Invalids frequently regard certain forms of help as disasteful, because it focuses on and emphasizes their handicap, and thereby their inferiority. In the same way as help to invalids and the underprivileged is a delicate matter, so is the giving of money. The giving of money can all too easily be interpreted as an insult.

Acts intended to benefit or harm can also be interpreted from the point of view of internal balance (see above). We can be nice to someone by telling him that he has made something good or valuable, that a friend of his has done something valuable, that his friend likes what he has done, that his enemy is unpleasant, that two of his friends like each other, etc. All this creates or maintains balanced units. Conversely, we can make a person unhappy or angry by telling him that he has done wrong, made something useless, that his friends dislike each other, that one is enthusiastic about his enemy, by attacking his heroes and ideological points of view, etc.

Aggressive acts usually stem from anger, and according to common sense a main reason is that we are threatened or hurt in our self-respect. Both in the case of good and bad acts it is necessary to reciprocate or retaliate in one way or another, in order to re-establish the interpersonal balance. Gifts and invitations have to be reciprocated, if for no other reason than because one must rid oneself of the state of indebtedness. Malicious acts are reacted to in kind, in order to show the other one that he is mistaken in believing he can do such a thing without punishment. Retaliation may also relate to moral principles and may thereby become more or less impersonal. An example of this is when parents spank their children and say: 'I am sorry I have to punish you'. Another common reaction is to point out that an act was unjust. 'How can you say something like that to me, how can you treat me like this when I have done you nothing but good?'. In this way one attempts to make the other one appear and feel evil and unreasonable. In some circumstances one may also make a point of *forgiving* the other one, with a hint that the other one's act was so unreasonable that one cannot bother to take it seriously. Oscar Wilde said: 'Always forgive your enemies: nothing annoys them so much'.

In addition to the action aspect, of benefit and harm there is also an emotional aspect, namely our feelings concerning what happens to the other one. One may roughly distinguish between four main types of emotional reaction to the lot of another person: 1) We can be happy when someone else is happy. 2) We can suffer when the other one suffers (pity). 3) We can be irritated when the other is lucky (envy). 4) We may enjoy that someone is unlucky (malicious joy).

When we share another's happiness or sorrow (1 and 2 above) we never feel the same as the person who has the primary emotion. We cannot put ourselves entirely into his situation, and irrespective of how close we are to him, his emotions remain his own. We feel happy, because he is happy, whereas he is happy because of something that happened to him. In such situations one may, frequently, observe a subtle mutual regulation of the feelings or at least of the expressions of feelings. The empathizer expresses himself a little more strongly than he feels, whereas the person who is happy or unhappy restrains himself and attempts to communicate in ways which may be understood by the other one. It should be noted in this context that the preceding types of emotional sharing are under moral control — one ought to share the joy of one's fellow beings and also to share their sorrow. On the other hand, envy and malicious joy are evil and therefore are usually covered up, except in children and in unguarded moments of spontaneous expression in adults.

Metaphors

A few of the main features of everyday psychology have now been briefly described. However, the reader may quite rightly object that, even if the description were very much enlarged and refined, it would never be possible to catch in systematic terms the subtle nuances of actual life as it is lived or as it is portrayed in the masterpieces of literature. It is frequently said that writers such as Dostojevsky are great psychologists, and that one may learn much about human nature from them.

An important difference between a literary and a scientific description is that the former contains numerous strong *metaphors,* whereas the latter attempts to avoid them. *A metaphor is the describing of a thing by stating that it is similar to another thing, but without stating exactly in what ways the two things are similar.* The similarities in literary metaphors are usually highly complex and difficult to formulate briefly. The metaphor induces a double experience of the two or more things compared and evokes multiple patterns of background ideas and feelings.

The following quotation from Knut Hamsun serves to illustrate the use of metaphors. It will also serve to remind the reader of what he knows intuitively about love, (cf. the discussion on pp. 109-111) in a way that no scientfic description could match.

> Ah, what was Love? A breeze whispering in the roses, no, a yellow phosphorescence in the blood. Love was a music hot as hell which stirs even old men's hearts to dance. It was like the daisy that opens wide to the coming of night, and it was like the anemone that closes at a breath and dies at a touch.
> Such a thing was Love.
> It might ruin its man, raise him up again and brand him anew, it might love me today, you tomorrow and him tomorrow night, so inconstant was it. But again it might hold like an unbreakable seal and burn with an unquenchable flame even to the hour of death, for so eternal was it. How then was Love?
> Oh, Love is the summer night with stars in the sky and fragrance on the earth. But why does it make the youth seek hidden paths and why does it make the greybeard stand tiptoe in his lonely chamber? Ah, Love turns the heart of man to a garden of fungus, a luxuriant and shameless garden wherein mysterious and immodest toadstools raise their heads.
> Does it not lead the friar to slink into closed gardens and glue his eyes to the windows of the sleepers at night? And does it not possess the nun with folly and darken the understanding of the princess? It casts the king's head to the ground so that his hair sweeps all the dust of the highway, and he whispers unseemly words to himself the while and laughs and puts out his tongue.
> Such was Love.
> No, no, it was again something very different and it was like nothing else in the world. It came to earth one spring night when a youth saw two eyes. He gazed and saw. He kissed a mouth, and then it was as though two lights met in his heart, a sun flashing towards a star. He fell into an embrace, and then he heard and saw no more in all the world. (Hamsun, 1929.)

Hamsun's description consists for the most part of complex metaphors. One may, to use a metaphor, talk about the degree of *life* in a metaphor. The degree of life is perhaps roughly proportional to the frequency of the expression in the language. Metaphors are continuously created and continuously die in every language. The more popular a metaphor becomes, the faster it is weakened. Hamsun used very vivid metaphors, i.e. quite unusual comparisons and sequences of words, which have the effect of arousing the reader and creating rich images.

Everyday life descriptions are replete with dead metaphors, i.e. clichés. Examples are 'the foot of the mountain' (anatomical metaphor), 'he sank into a trance' (spatial metaphor), and many sensory metaphors such as 'a cold glance', 'a warm smile', 'a light conversation', 'a smooth manner', 'a dry form of humor', etc.

All languages appear to contain metaphors, and, e.g., sensory metaphors may to some extent be common even to languages which are historically independent (see Brown, 1958).

Metaphorical descriptions of mental phenomena tend to induce strong and complex experiences. The effect is due to their very ambiguity and therefore they can only be of indirect help to the researcher (in suggesting to him problems and lines of inquiry). It has been pointed out by philosophers that scientific language and scientific models also frequently have metaphor-like properties. However, unlike the writer of fiction, the scientist works with increasingly *analytic* metaphors, i.e. he tries to spell out exactly in what ways a set of phenomena and his model of them are similar.

Between the analytic and the arbitrary

In the ancient legend, Odysseus is said to have sailed through a narrow strait with one bloodthirsty monster on each side, and so close that, in order to avoid one of them, he inevitably was forced too close to the other one. Common sense appears to leave the theoretical psychologist exactly in this position, as far as the analytic and the arbitrary are concerned.

We have already commented extensively on the self-evidence of common sense. It contains numerous principles, which, upon closer scrutiny, turn out to be analytic, i.e. to follow from the definitions of the concepts involved. The inferential rules in the analysis of perception and of action have this quality, and, likewise, the wish-fulfillment-pleasure axiom, the balance principle, and probably most of the other relationships described. This is the domain of the analytic.

However, the conceptual network of common-sense psychology alone is clearly not sufficient to guide our dealings with people. It has already been mentioned that we must also depend on our sociological common sense in order to predict and understand. Now, our sociological conceptions appear to be of another order than our psychological. The rules of how 'one' ought to behave, although involving some hierarchical structure — this rule is necessary in order to maintain that rule, etc. — are essentially arbitrary, in the sense that they can ultimately be explained only by *historical coincidences*. Sociological 'reality' does not rest on universal and eternal 'laws', but on local regularities that, in principle, can be substituted by others. The preceding means that, to a large extent, we explain and predict behavior on the basis of our knowledge of the given culture. 'This is how things are done (with us)', 'this is how people are (nowadays)'. Hence, these explanations and predictions are not derivable from any theoretical principles, but simply reflect local regularities resulting from historical coincidence.

A second source of knowledge, without which we could not function successfully, is the experience we have of particular other individuals. We get to know the individual characteristics of our family members, relatives, friends, colleagues, etc., and this makes it possible to live with them. Again, this personal knowledge reflects highly local regularities involving single individuals, which are ultimately explainable only by the coincidences that determine the genetic make-up and the life of these persons. Once more, we are confronted with the arbitrary. Thus in our daily lives we experience all events in terms of the conceptual network of common sense and of our knowledge of historically determined local regularities. At no point does there seem to be any opening for empirically testable general theories.

The history of scientific psychology can be seen as a long series of attempts to steer a course between these extremes of the analytic and the arbitrary. On the one hand, one has tried to avoid the analytic by relying heavily on empirical research, only to discover, belatedly, that one's data were more or less completely situation-bound or culture-bound, i.e., from the theoretical point of view, arbitrary. On the other hand, one has tried to escape from the empirically arbitrary by concentrating on theory-building only to discover, belatedly, that one's principles were empirically untestable, being merely reformulations of analytic common-sense axioms. In the next four chapters we will, among other things, attempt to illustrate this.

Questions after Chapter VI

1. Criticize and suggest revisions of the list of fundamental common-sense concepts given on pp. 97-99.

2. Can you suggest alternatives to the common-sense model for action presented in Figure 2?

3. Discuss further the problem of the relationship between the cognitive and affective aspect of mental processes.

4. Do you think the discussion of jealousy given in this chapter is adequate? What would a general and empirically testable theory (or hypothesis) about jealousy look like and what could it contribute?

5. Is what Hamsun says about love true or false? Try to analyze this problem as deeply as possible.

VII. Individual differences

In this and the following three chapters we will attempt to describe some aspects of the insight that psychologists have so far been able to achieve within a few central problem areas. The emphasis will be on *how* psychologists have come to think, that is, on the abstract structure of understanding, rather than on concrete findings and particular hypotheses. The reader should preferably have some elementary background in psychology, in order to profit maximally from what follows. However, the presentation will consistently be kept as nontechnical and elementary as possible.

Ordering

An important characteristic of the mind is that it introduces and searches for order in the complex events and impressions that occur. Some realms of the world are easier to order than others. Social anthropologists have shown how people all over the world have classified and named animal and plant species in great numbers, including such species as have no practical use. Animals and plants are apparently especially amenable to classification, because the species are discontinuous and because they involve many individuals who clearly belong to a given species. There are variations in appearance from one rabbit to another and from one squirrel to another, but the differences in appearance within these two species are very small, compared to the differences between any given rabbit and any given squirrel. The easy accessibility of biological classifications has been capitalized on by human thinking, as particularly witnessed by their fundamental epistemological role in so-called totemistic societies.

Conversely, the ordering, e.g., of substances proceeded fairly slowly, and was first developed in specific areas such as pottery, metallurgy, etc., where technical necessity led to the development of advanced classifications. Substances do not easily fall into very comprehensive and clearly discontinuous groups, and, hence, their ordering only accelerated after one started systematically to investigate their weights, hardness, reactions to each other in solutions, reactions to heating, pressure, etc.

Other persons represent a cognitive problem with some similarity to that of biological species, except that it involves intraspecies instead of interspecies variation. In every society, individuals are categorized according to their roles and positions, and, more specifically, according to their membership in totem-groups, clans, tribes, castes, social classes, races, occupations, etc. Society usually provides prescriptions, not only for their formal authority, rights, duties, knowledge, skills, language, etc., but also provides ample cues for the recognition of the positions in the form of clothes, haircut, paint, headdress, as well as all kinds of verbal and contextual cues. However, these sociological classifications which are ready-made and easy to acquire, by no means exhaust the differences between people. One judge differs from another judge, one farmer differs from another farmer. No two hippies or any two suburban housewives are identical, even though we may have exhausted the sociological distinctions that exist. The remaining differences, disregarding the physical ones, are *personal* or *psychological*.

In order to describe and communicate about these psychological differences, we have a vocabulary of hundreds of adjectives, as well as many adverbs, and various modifiers such as 'very', 'somewhat', 'partly', 'probably', etc. Furthermore, we can describe people in their individuality by introducing metaphors, by accumulating and juxtaposing descriptions of several ways in which they have been known to behave, etc. Therefore, we appear very well equipped to describe individual persons from a psychological point of view.

In order to reveal the implicit structure of our ordinary language descriptions of how people differ psychologically, we must try to make explicit what is meant by the general term *order* in this area. Differences between persons can be regarded as elementary or complex, discrete or continuous. An elementary difference is one which, for the given purpose, is not further analyzed. A complex or structural difference is one which is treated as involving many interrelated components. A discrete difference is one which merely involves a characteristic and its opposite or absence. Example: noisy — quiet. The same difference is treated as continuous when it is seen as involving an unlimited number or degrees, some of which are verbalized, e.g., as 'very noisy', 'medium noisy (quiet)' 'rather quiet', 'very quiet', etc. The point to be made here is that individual differences may be analyzed in a practically unlimited number of ways, and that the only restrictions are that they have to be communicated in terms of our ordinary language.

124

Let us now imagine the universe of all possible combinations of all the ways in which people may differ from each other, psychologically. We may think of individual persons as particular combinations or configurations of these differences, or as points in some kind of superspace. This universe of difference would be without order if persons were distributed randomly in the space. All kinds of persons would then be possible and equally likely (or unlikely) to occur. On the other hand, there would be progressively more order, the more unevenly people were distributed. With a relatively high degree of ordering, there would be numerous configurations of characteristics, or as we would say, personality-structures, that would not exist, and numerous others that would be very unlikely to occur. Conversely, there would be areas in the superspace that would be very densely populated with persons. In everyday language, we would say that the persons in these areas were of particular types. The more ordering of the universe of individual differences, the more *typification* would be said to occur. In a very highly ordered person-universe, frequent comments to a hypothetical description of a person would be 'There ain't no such person alive', and 'Yeah, I know the type, there are thousands of them'.

Given the problem of individual differences, i.e., of ordering people from a psychological point of view, three broad research areas may be explicitly formulated:

A. *What kind of order exists in people's conception of other people?* This is a question concerning the subjective order that exists. Some of the relevant research can be found under the heading of 'person perception' in psychological textbooks.

B. *What kind of order actually exists as far as psychological variation is concerned?* This question concerns the objective order that exists. Relevant research can be found especially under the headings of 'personality', 'abilities', and 'developmental psychology' in psychological textbooks.

C. *What correspondences and discrepancies exist in the relationship between A and B?* In other words, how well, and in what ways, does the subjective order correspond with the objective? Again, the relevant material is mostly found under the heading of 'person perception'.

Subjective ordering of people

In our daily lives we meet and get to know many people, but we do not usually attempt to formulate the resulting categorizations in general terms. However, we do reflect about ourselves and about some of the people we meet, at a concrete level, and we engage in discussions and gossip about the personalities and abilities of absent persons. Sometimes we have occasion to attempt to describe a person.

It is quite apparent from these fragments of explicit discourse that, at least when we talk about our subjective knowledge, we are strongly inclined to typify, i.e. to introduce considerable amounts of order. We use expressions such as 'I know the type', 'That is typical of these men', 'I know exactly what kind of a woman you are referring to', 'That is just how this sort of person thinks', 'How else would an impulsive red-head respond', 'That's how a paranoiac would see it', 'You can recognize the criminal in that expression', etc. Statements such as 'They are all like that' directly assert that certain characteristics are invariably present in certain populations, and, by implication, that other alternative characteristics are absent.

Inquiring about the subjective ordering of people, one must distinguish between the ordering that is implicit in one's actual dealings *with* people, and that which is implicit in one's talk *about* people. The former is very hard to study, due to the complexity of people's interaction with each other. The fleeting impressions, momentary understandings, choices of expression, shifts in attitude, etc. that occur while we interact with a person, undoubtedly reflect *how* we intuitively conceive of him, but the structure of this conception can usually only be discovered by attempting to formulate it, i.e. talk *about* the person. Hence, almost all research in this area involves probing how we think *of* people, rather than how we actually interact differentially with them.

The following method, originally developed by the late George Kelly (1955) aims directly at discovering a person's subjective ordering of people. In one variant, the subject is asked to consider, e.g., the following list: Self, Mother, Father, Brother, Sister, Spouse, Ex-flame, Pal, Ex-pal, Rejecting Person, Pitied Person, Threatening Person, Attractive Person, Accepted Teacher, Rejected Teacher, Boss, Successful Person, Happy Person, Ethical Person.

The instruction is to fill in a specific person in each of the preceding headings. If this is not possible, one should fill in a person who comes close to occupying the position indicated. No person should be placed in more than one of the positions. The subject is presented with a form of the type shown in Figure 4. The instruction is, for each triple comparison of persons indicated by circles, to write, under the heading 'Emergent Pole', *in what important way two of the three are similar and different from the third.* Under 'Implicit Pole' one writes in what way the third person is different. Then one fills in for all the persons, whether they have the characteristic indicated under 'Emergent Pole' or the one indicated under 'Implicit Pole'. One then proceeds to the next row, where another triple comparison is indicated, decides on another pair of characteristics, etc. In this way one gets one kind of approximate picture of the kind of order involved in the subject's conception of persons.

Most directly, the method yields some of the terms which the subject feels describe important similarities and differences between people. It also yields a kind of implicit description of how he sees persons who, presumably, have some importance for him. However, the method also permits us to go beyond what is directly expressed, to the subject's underlying ways of ordering people and constructs.

Through a method of systematic scanning of the protocol, column for column or row for row, described by Kelly on pp. 280-291 in his book, it is possible to discover the subject's implicit typology of constructs and persons. In other words, we can describe what psychological characteristics, to the subject, seem to go together, and what types of persons he tends to see. The core of a cluster of psychological characteristics may, to one subject be, e.g., 'intellectual, cold, insensitive' vs. 'anti-intellectual, warm and sensitive'. This means that a considerable proportion of the differences between people are seen as related to this division or typology. Similarly, a subject may, e.g. tend to see people as predominantly like his father or different from him. Such groupings may emerge in a very clear way from the data gathered by this method, yet may have been quite unknown to the subject.

Like all formalized psychological methods, Kelly's method introduces some artificiality. It forces the subject to find *brief* descriptions of complex matters, it forces him to select only *one* characteristic out of several that he may think of, it forces him to disregard the *degree* to which a characteristic is present and to draw an arbitrary line between presence and absence. Furthermore, it forces him to suppress initial reactions such as 'It depends on what you mean by . . .' and 'It depends on the particular circumstances involved', etc. Finally, it is limited to the level at which the subject talks *about* persons, rather than the level at which he deals with them directly. There are many studies indicating discrepancies between these two levels (see e.g. Rommetveit, 1960).

It is not possible here to discuss all the interesting uses and variations of Kelly's method or of other methods that have been developed, nor can we go into the empirical findings, except to mention the most general one: people do indeed introduce vast amounts of order into their experiences of people, in other words, the tendency to typification is very strong.

Objective order of people

The term 'objective' refers to how things actually 'are', independently of how they appear to any particular individual. In this case, the objective order refers to the order of the actually existing individual differences. The individual as he is seen by a subject belongs to the subjective realm. The individual, as he appears to those who know him, is an objective entity to the extent that the others (independently of each other) agree in their description of him. His objectivity, in this sense, derives from the fact that his expressions and acts have relatively unambiguous social meanings, i.e. meanings which are the same to all onlookers. When we say 'He is a gregarious, open and very friendly person with a keen sense of humor' we may mean that this is the verdict of all those who know him. In such a case, the agreement of the others need not be merely a series of parallel judgments of independent 'monads', but explicit agreement emerging partly from previous communications between them about what they think about the subject.

However, in common-sense psychology, we know that it may not always be adequate to define the person as being what others think he is. This insight is expressed in statements such as 'At home he is gregarious, open, ... etc., but with other people he tends to by shy, reticent, ... etc.', 'People think he is gregarious, open, ... etc., but really he is very shy, reticent, ... etc'.

The preceding indicates that the characteristics of a person are, to some extent, situation-bound, and that many disagreements about identity can be traced back to the fact that observations were made in different situations. Particularly, it is common sense that a person may be different when interacting with different observers, and that this may explain some of the disagreement in judgment between these observers.

Another source of disagreement between observers stems from their

Figure 4. Test form for Kelly's Role Construct Repertory Test.
Reproduced from Kelly (1955, p. 270)

	Person
1	Self
2	Mother
3	Father
4	Brother
5	Sister
6	Spouse
7	Ex-flame
8	Pal
9	Ex-pal
10	Rejecting Person
11	Pitied Person
12	Threatening Person
13	Attractive Person
14	Accepted Teacher
15	Rejected Teacher
16	Boss
17	Successful Person
18	Happy Person
19	Ethical Person

CONSTRUCTS

SORT NO.	EMERGENT POLE	IMPLICIT POLE
1	Don't believe in God	Very religious
2	Same sort of education	Complete different education
3	Not athletic	Athletic
4	Both girls	A boy
5	Parents	Idea different
6	Understand me better	Don't understand at all
7	Teach the right thing	Teach the wrong thing
8	Achieved a lot	Hasn't achieved a lot
9	Higher education	No education
10	Don't like other people	Like other people
11	More religious	Not religious
12	Believe in higher education	Not believing in too much education
13	More sociable	Not sociable
14	Both girls	Not girls
15	Both girls	Not girls
16	Both have high morals	Lower morals
17	Think alike	Think differently
18	Same age	Different ages
19	Believe the same about me	Believe differently about me
20	Both friends	Not friends
21	More understanding	Less understanding
22	Both appreciate music	Don't understand music

129

different standards or reference points. Suppose that we let different observers judge the degree of 'carefulness' of our subject on some scale. One observer may perhaps, as a reference point, think of his aunt, who apparently had led a very eventful life (there were rumours of wild orgies and rather delicate deviations in sexual and narcotic matters), but who skillfully managed to keep a highly respectable and bourgeois front all her life. Another may think of his uncle from a rural area, where people are reluctant to commit themselves in so many words. When asked whether his brother (who owned the neighboring farm) lived in the area, the uncle, after long deliberation, had answered 'maybe'. A third observer may think of a friend who is a professional racing car driver, who always keeps his car in the most meticulous order and who has only been hospitalized twice with severe injuries in a ten-year-long career. Although these hypothetical examples are extreme, they serve to illustrate the point that differences in judgments of 'carefulness' need not reflect anything more profound than variations in frames of reference. However, in a study of how much observers agree in describing a given subject, this kind of difference may easily obscure any information about how the observers actually differ in their conception of the subject.

Common-sense statements frequently indicate that people may be different from what they appear to be. This is frequently asserted by observers who for some reason, such as closeness of acquaintance or circumstances of acquaintance, think they are in a more favorable position than others to judge. 'I am his wife', 'We were together during the War', etc. However, the statements by favorably placed observers cannot be regarded as more objective than other individual statements. On the contrary, it is well known that, e.g., close relatives of a person may sometimes render descriptions that not only deviate drastically from what other, more detached, people think, but also from what the psychologist comes to regard as the truth. For numerous illustrations of this and related points, see e.g. Laing (1967).

The highest standard of objectivity in descriptions of individual differences is provided by the psychologist, to the extent that his results survive the ordeal of the critical game, i.e. to the extent that they fulfill reasonably strict methodological requirements. The psychologist's interpretations of data gathered by various controlled methods and subjected to various kinds of cross-checks, represent our closest approximations to a knowledge of who the subject really is. One important characteristic of the psychologist's knowledge is that not only is the interpretation reasonably consistent with the available evidence, but it can sometimes also serve to explain some of the variability in how other people see the subject in different situations and contexts. Hence, in what follows, the objective order of individual differences is taken to be the one that has so far been discovered by psychologists. However, it should never be regarded as more than a temporary approximation, since our knowledge of individual differences is all the time changed by the results of new research and in the light of new interpretations.

Psychologists describe individual differences in terms of *variables*. A variable is a characteristic that may be present in varying degrees. Sometimes variables are conceived of as dichotomous, i.e. as having only two values, typically either two opposites (good-evil, black-white) or presence vs. absence (member vs. non-member of union, has children-childless).

However, most variables in the study of individual differences have been conceived of as being *continuous*, which means having indefinitely many degrees or values.

The most general finding in studies of continuous variables is that the observed values tend to be distributed approximately according to the *normal*, bell-shaped curve (see Figure 5 a).

It may by gathered from Figure 5 that most persons have intermediate values on the given variable and that the number with extreme values is very small. There is nothing mysterious about why we so often get approximations to the bell-shaped curve. It can be shown statistically that this curve emerges whenever there are a very great number of mutually unrelated causes or determinants of a variable. This is typically true of psychological characteristics which are a cumulative function of innumerable factors, genetic, biological, and psychological, that have influenced the person during his life history. Deviations from the normal curve occur whenever we introduce external constraints on the measurement. An example would be a study of the time taken to solve a given problem. If the problem is made very easy, a very high number of persons will solve it with the maximum speed possible, namely at their reaction time limit. The consequence is a highly skewed distribution of the type shown in Fig. 5 b.

Returning to the problem of describing individual differences we note that there exist an infinitive number of variables that could be selected. One must, therefore, discuss the criteria for selection. Let us take, as an arbitrary chosen example of a possible variable, the length of time persons wash their hands when in a lavatory. It is quite possible that one could discover a certain degree of consistency in individual performance from time to time, and reliable individual differences. The reason why this variable, despite its possibly excellent psychometric

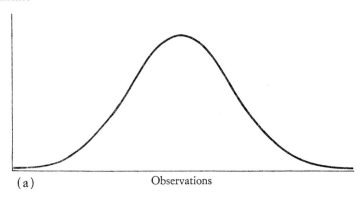

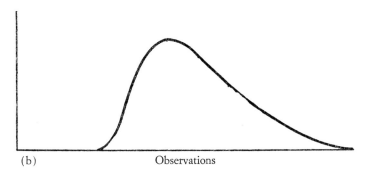

Figure 5. Normal curve (a) and highly skewed curve (b)

characteristics, is not proposed as an important descriptive measure, is clearly that it is so restricted in scope.

Traits

Given an estimate of an individual's average washing time, one can only predict how he will perform during future visits to lavatories. In order for a variable to become theoretically and practically interesting it must be defined in a relatively general way and encompass many different types of situations. When a variable allegedly has these desirable characteristics it may be called a *trait* or a *personality* trait. Let us expand our first example and introduce a trait labeled *'need for personal cleanliness'*. A trait generally has the following three characteristics:

132

a) It cannot be directly estimated from any single type of measure. It may at first glance appear as if this particular example, which is somewhat atypical, may allow for a direct measure via the person's actually observed physical cleanliness. However, the reader is reminded that if we observe the person while being hauled out of East River or returning from a two week's trek in the wilderness our conclusions might be erroneous. This is also the case if the person arrives at an appointment with the psychologist and expects to be subjected to a physical examination.

b) The trait 'need for physical cleanliness' is logically related to a number of more specific measures such as, e.g., 'frequency of changing shirts', 'frequency of changing underwear', 'frequency of showering', 'consumption of deodorants', 'frequency and length of toothbrushing sessions', etc.

c) The trait is also logically related to an indefinite number of more general traits such as 'general orderliness', 'concern about others' opinion', etc.

The logical structure of a network of traits is shown in Figure 6.

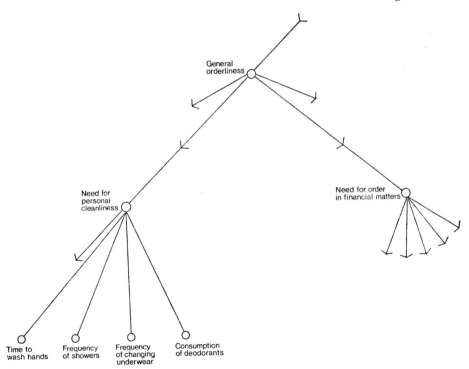

Figure 6. Example of logical structure of network of personality traits.

Such a network should not be taken to have an absolute or privileged status. An indefinite number of alternatively organized trait-systems may be proposed, one may increase the number of trait levels involved or eliminate some that exist, etc. The only fundamental requirement common to all such attempts is that the measurable variables should correlate with each other. In the given case, there is no use for the construct of need for personal cleanliness unless at least some, but preferably most of the measurable variables are positively intercorrelated.

People who take long time to wash their hands should tend to shower often, change underwear often, and have a relatively high consumption of deodorants, etc. It should be noted that the correlation between measures need not always be positive. Some higher order constructs may be devised that logically require alternative manifestations of the type either/or (see Else Frenkel Brunswik, 1954, p. 302). This may then imply a negative correlation between measures. Finally, it should be noted that there may exist other types of order than correlative and these should not be excluded. However, it remains true that, typically, we expect positive correlations.

Psychologists have always tried to construe very general traits, intended to explain considerable proportions of existing individual differences in wide areas. However, there often seems to be an inverse relationship between explanatory power and scope of application. The more general the trait the less it appears to explain and the more specific the trait the more it appears to explain. In order to understand this general trend, it should first be recognized that *the performance of a person in any particular situation is always a function of many factors, several of which are irrelevant to the theoretical purpose involved.* Thus, frequency of showers is not only a function of the person's need for personal cleanliness, but also of the availability of shower facilities, the rules of his work, the particular outdoor or indoor climate in which he works and lives, the level of physical exercise involved, personal tendency to transpiration, etc. This means that no particular measure is ever a pure estimate of a higher order trait, it is always contaminated by irrelevant factors. Now, it very frequently turns out that many of these irrelevant factors are common to relatively restricted areas. In the example used above, all the irrelevant factors mentioned, with the possible exception of shower facilities, are likely to be equally influential in determining the measures of frequency of change of shirts and underwear, consumption of deodorants, etc.

This means that the correlation between these measures may become much higher than it would have been on the basis of the need for personal cleanliness alone. In order to illustrate the same thing once more, let us consider the group of measures related to the need for order in financial matters. Among these may be, degree of keeping up to date on one's bank account, average time before paying one's bills, frequency of overstepping deadlines, extent of attempts to estimate current expenditure in various areas by collecting stubs and keeping records, extent of planning and budgeting in advance, etc. All these measures are influenced by other factors in addition to a constant personal need for order in financial matters. Examples of such other factors would be, wife's attitude to money, security and regularity of one's income, inflation, prospects of old age pension and insurance, etc. Many of these factors may tend to affect the various measures in a similar way, thus increasing the correlation between them.

The next step in our chain of reasoning is to note that, in our two examples and probably in most cases, the irrelevant common factors in one area are different from and often unrelated to the irrelevant common factors in another area. For example, climate on the one hand and inflation in the economy on the other hand are hardly related. This has the consequence that the correlation between the single measures relating to need for personal cleanliness and the single measures relating to need for order in financial matters will be very much lower than the correlations *within* these areas. However, if any correlation remains at all, it will, for instance, support the higher order construct of 'general orderliness'.

In general, we can now see that broadening the scope of an hypothetical trait means that the data will tend to contain successively more unrelated variation and that the empirical correlations will tend to become lower. The net effect is that a general trait will tend to be supported only by a very small proportion of the variation. This is not very surprising, since one would have expected common-sense psychology, even though it may be relatively inefficient and susceptible to distortions (cf. chapter II, pp. 33-38) to have incorporated any obviously useful typology.

The preceding does not mean that one should give up the attempts to search for order in objective individual differences. It only means that one should be aware that the search goes on in an ocean of unrelated information and that the identification of useful higher order traits is only possible with prolonged empirical efforts within a highly sophisticated statistical and methodological framework.

As an example of what has been achieved so far, the findings of the Swedish psychologist Rubenowitz (1963) will be mentioned. On the basis of a very wide ranging set of different measures, and taking all kinds of statistical and methodological precautions, he has been able to present fairly convincing evidence of the existence of a general trait of *flexibility-rigidity*. In Figure 7 is shown the main structure of the assumed trait.

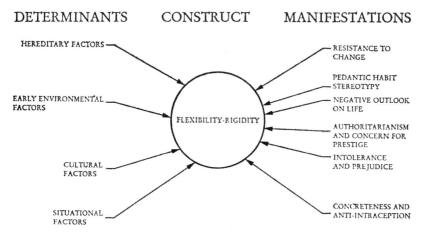

Figure 7. A diagrammatic representation of the relation between the hypothesized flexibility-rigidity construct and the possible determinants and manifestations. Reproduced from Rubenowitz, 1963, p. 230.

In his conclusions, Rubenowitz at one point makes the following careful statement, which may serve to illustrate both the contents of his findings and the limitations associated with them:

Thus, *other things being equal,* an extremely rigid person can be expected to hold an authoritarian subservient attitude in relation to a variety of authority figures — parents, leaders, parties, supernatural power, social and institutional norms, etc. — he can be expected to show intolerance to people holding a different opinion to his own, and he can be expected to have a somewhat compulsive need for order and a disinclination to compromise. One can further, among other things, expect a condemnatory attitude toward unconventional art, an affectively colored irrational attitude toward politics, and a harsh, forbidding attitude on questions of upbringing.

However, this clear-cut picture seldom or never appears in real life; in most situations other factors besides flexibility contribute to the variance in attitude and behavior. Of these, intelligence appears to play a prominent role. (Rubenowitz, 1963, pp. 233-234.)

The following should be emphasized in the above quotation. First, Rubenowitz makes a point of emphasizing that the statement is only

136

valid when other things are equal, i.e. when all the irrelevant variation is held constant. Second, this statement is a description of an *extremely* rigid person. Recalling what we have said about the normal curve in the distribution over variables, it becomes apparent that this applies only to very few persons, most people being situated somewhere in the middle of the flexibility-rigidity scale. Third, even then, Rubenowitz uses the formulation 'can be expected', indicating that we are dealing with probabilities rather than with certainties. Fourth, he emphasizes that this picture seldom or never appears in real life, because of the masking effect of other factors.

In order to complete the balanced skeptical picture one must have, even of methodologically sound achievements, the reader should also be reminded of our conclusion in Chapter II, p. 41, that statistical significance does not mean theoretical or practical significance. Even though Rubenowitz has found statistically significant factor loadings in expected patterns, they *may* be interpreted in other ways than as reflecting flexibility-rigidity as defined by him, and they account for so little of the general variation that their practical usefulness is doubtful.

So far, nothing that psychologists have discovered in the way of objective order in individual differences, contradicts a skeptical outlook on typification in this area. The practitioner should continue to attempt to keep his mind open to the new, unexpected, and unique in each new person that he encounters, rather than succumb to the temptation to typify. For relevant evidence, see Vernon (1963).

Correspondence between the subjective and the objective order

Psychologists, and laymen, have always been very much interested in the problem of estimating the *veridicality* or correctness of subjective impressions and conceptions, in other words, in the degree of correspondence between the subjective and the objective. Gradually, there has emerged some insight into the logic of this problem, which is formally equivalent to the general problem of estimating the correspondence between predictions (whether based on subjective estimates or objective measures) and outcomes. The general paradigm is illustrated in Figure 8, for the case of one variable with a limited number of values, here set to 5.

Suppose that we have a set of subjective estimates of the degree of, e.g., rigidity of 100 persons, and that the estimates are distributed as shown to the left in Figure 8. Suppose, furthermore, that the distribu-

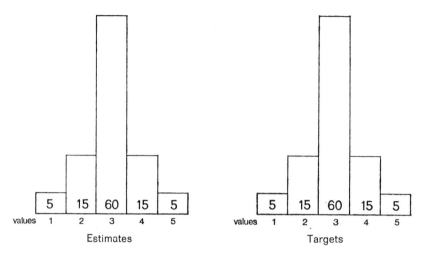

Figure 8. Hypothetical example for comparison between subjective estimates and objective measures of individual differences in one variable. Explanation and discussion in text.

tion of these persons on objectively measured rigidity is as shown to the right in Figure 8. The two distributions are purposively made identical, in order to simplify the example as well as in order to emphasize the complete independence of measures of co-variation or correspondence from distribution as such. The relationship between these two identically distributed variables may be anything from perfectly regular to entirely random. In the first case one may predict with perfect certainty from the estimate to the left to the corresponding target to the right. In the last case, knowledge of the estimate does not improve one's chances of being correct beyond the base-rates, i.e. knowledge of the distribution to the right. Theoretically, and sometimes also in reality, we may also observe performances significantly *below* chance level, i.e. based on some kind of systematic misinterpretation.

How, then, are we to measure the degree of success of the subjective estimates? One obvious, but very unfortunate solution, which has also been used in psychological research, is to count the number of 'hits' vs. the number of 'misses'. To the statistically untrained mind this may appear as a reasonable measure of how good the correspondence is. Another, even worse, procedure is to count not only the 'hits', but also the 'near-hits', and contrast them with 'misses' on the grounds that the 'near-hits' are 'approximately' correct estimates.

The reason why these measures, presented alone, are entirely inadequate is, of course, that they ignore what could be expected on the basis of chance alone, given the two distributions. The shape of the distributions determines the probability of 'hits', 'near-hits', and 'misses' on the basis of pure chance, and these probabilities should be the reference points for estimating degree of success of correspondence.

The basic logic is this: The probability of a given objective target value, e.g. 3, is .60. The probability that the subjective estimate will be 3 is also .60, and, hence, the probability of getting a 'hit' on 3 by pure chance is .36. In other words, with the given sample of 100 persons, we can expect to get 36 'hits' on value 3, on the basis of chance alone. Similarly, the expected frequency of 'hits' for values 2 and 4 is $.15 \times .15 = .0225$ for each and the corresponding expectation for values 1 and 5 is $.05 \times .05 = .0025$ for each. Altogether this leads us to expect 41 'hits' out of 100 possible by pure chance, i.e. in the case that the estimates and the target measures are entirely unrelated.

In a similar way we may calculate the frequency of 'near-hits' to be expected by chance. The student should verify his understanding of this by attempting the calculation, keeping in mind that a 'near-hit' is defined as 'estimates that hit a neighboring scale value to the correct one'. When 3 is correct, 2 and 4 are 'near-hits', etc. The outcome is that we may expect 39 'near-hits', i.e. a total of 80 'hits' + 'near-hits' out of 100 possible. This is sufficiently impressive to lead people insufficiently trained in statistical reasoning to believe that the subjective estimates or objective predictive instruments used are highly successful, even when performance does not exceed the pure chance level.

The dependence of the measures of 'hits' and 'near-hits' on the shape of the marginal distributions can be illustrated by the example of a distribution of subjective estimates concentrated on the value 3. This means that the person who estimates chooses to judge every one of the 100 persons as intermediate (3) in rigidity. The outcome of this strategy would be to raise the probability of 'hits' to .60 and the probability of 'hits' + 'near-hits' to .90, even though there is still only a chance relationship between the estimates and the targets. The reader interested in the further ramifications of this line of reasoning is referred to a classical paper by Meehl and Rosen (1955). It should also be noted that the strategy of counting the 'hits' in the given example, corresponds to counting the $+A+B$'s and $-A-B$'s in the 2×2 distribution used in Chapter II. This would have yielded 50 out of 80 or 62.5% 'hits' with a chance relationship. Again, there is a failure to take into account the base rates and the resulting chance probabilities.

In summary, the psychologist, who frequently operates in situations where large numbers of unrelated factors are influential, must constantly be on guard against the illusion of seeing order when there is none.

Abilities

As described in Chapter VI, pp. 100-101, one of the two main conditions of action, according to common-sense psychology is *can*. Can is a function of the difficulty of the task and the ability of the person. If a person P fails in task A and succeeds in task B, then A is more difficult than B, at least for P. If P fails in task A, whereas person Q succeeds, then Q has greater ability than P, at least with respect to task A. More generally, the difficulty of a task is often implicitly defined by the performance of a given group of persons in this task relative to the performance of the same group in other tasks. Similarly, the ability of a person is often implicitly defined by his performance in a given group of tasks relative to the performance of other persons in the same group of tasks.

The preceding relativistic definitions lead to certain logical difficulties in the case of changing abilities. This is particularly evident in studies of children. If the same task is given twice to a group of children with an interval of, let us say, one year, one may typically observe that, on the second occasion, more children pass than one year earlier. Although the difficulty of the task relative to other tasks, and the ability of a given child relative to the other children, may not have changed, we are, nevertheless, compelled to admit that, in an absolute sense the task has become easier to the group, or, which amounts to the same, the ability of the children has become higher. Both the relative and the absolute perspectives are useful, but one should take care not to confuse them.

In the area of intelligence testing, with which the reader may have at least some superficial familiarity, IQ (Intelligence Quotient) is an example of a relative measure of ability, which, therefore, often tends to be approximately constant as the child grows. IQ is defined as Mental Age (calculated from test scores)/Chronological Age × 100. On the other hand, MA (mental age) is an example of an absolute measure which almost invariably increases over age. For many practical purposes it may be particularly relevant to know what the child's ability is compared with other children, but for theoretical purposes, e.g. of analyzing the nature of abilities, one may often want to concentrate on absolute performance.

Ability and difficulty are two determinants of a person's performance on a task, but, from the point of view of psychology, they pose only one theoretical problem, namely that of the nature of the ability. The person *has* an ability to a certain degree, whereas the task requires this same ability to a certain (higher, identical, or lower) degree. Analysis of the task helps us specify the nature of the required abilities.

Abilities are dimensions along which individuals differ, and, hence, the general logic of traits also applies to abilities. An ability may be defined as a member of the subclass of traits that describe what a person *can* do. The reason why we devote a special section to abilities is mainly that they have been so extensively studied by psychologists. This has permitted the development of some particularly advanced theoretical and practical understanding, which may complement what has been said about traits in general.

Among the terms that we daily use in specifying ability are speed, strength, coordination, endurance, persistence, rigidity, flexibility, creativity, skill, knowledge, and intelligence. Some of these terms usually refer primarily to physical characteristics (strength, coordination, endurance), some include try-components (persistence, rigidity, flexibility, creativity); speed and skill may refer both to physical and cognitive performance, and knowledge and intelligence are mainly of a cognitive nature.

Most of the types of ability mentioned here are clearly recognized as modifiable. One can be trained to increase speed, strength, coordination, endurance, one can induce attitudes fostering persistence, rigidity, flexibility, and creativity. One acquires skill and knowledge. Common sense recognizes that there are limits both with respect to the rate and extent of this modifiability and frequently regards these limits as in some vague sense innate.

Intelligence (giftedness, brightness) seems to come in a rather special position among the abilities since it is usually seen as essentially invariant in adults, and hence may be expected to yield more general predictions than the modifiable traits. Statements such as 'during the months that followed he became much more intelligent', definitely sound as if they were taken from a science fiction novel. In this section we shall exclusively be concerned with intellectual abilities since these have been most extensively analyzed.

However, before turning to the general logic of defining and testing intellectual abilities, it should be briefly mentioned that ordinary language and common-sense psychology recognize different levels of abilities, just as they generally recognize different trait levels. We talk about musical talent, dramatic talent, drawing talent, mathematical talent, linguistic talent, etc., and even of talents or knack for more specific types of tasks such as 'remembering phone numbers', 'mental arithmetic', 'grammatical analysis', etc. On the other hand, there is the general dimension of 'brightness — stupidity', which is felt to apply to a person's performance in general, although sometimes with the exception of particular areas. 'She is a very bright person, but she has no talent for mathematics', 'he is generally very bright, but he is hopeless when it comes to understanding literature, drama, and especially poetry'.

There exist two different major traditions of psychological research on abilities, namely the experimental tradition and the test tradition.

The experimental tradition

In this tradition one has attempted to analyze abilities by varying characteristics of tasks under strictly controlled conditions. The logic of this research is as follows: if tasks A and B differ only in one respect t, and if there is a difference in the subjects' performance on these tasks, then this difference in performance may be attributed to t. If B is the more difficult task we may then infer that the reason why some subjects pass A but fail in B or why children learn to pass A before they learn to pass B, but where the opposites of these cases do not occur, is a difference in ability having to do with t.

Before we turn to a discussion of the power and problems of the experimental method in connection with some actual research data, we must expand somewhat on the logic of analyzing data in this field.

A central concept is that of a *perfectly homogeneous distribution*. A perfectly homogeneous distribution may be defined as one in which there are no deviations from the two-dimensional pattern established by ranking the tasks according to number of persons who do solve them, and by ranking the persons according to number of tasks they solve. A hypothetical example of such a distribution which includes 6 tasks and 8 persons is given in Table 3.

Table 3. Example of a perfectly homogeneous distribution

Tasks								
6	+	—	—	—	—	—	—	—
5	+	—	—	—	—	—	—	—
4	+	+	+	—	—	—	—	—
3	+	+	+	—	—	—	—	—
2	+	+	+	+	—	—	—	—
1	+	+	+	+	+	+	—	—
Persons	1	2	3	4	5	6	7	8

In Table 3 the depicted distribution has a maximum of order, since all the data are consistent with the assumption that the tasks and the persons differ in only one dimension. Thus the persons may be regarded as differing only in one relevant ability, and the tasks may be regarded as relevantly different only in how much of this ability they require. The amount of ability of a given person is indicated by the most difficult task passed by him or the least difficult task failed by him. Conversely, the degree of difficulty of a given task is indicated by the ability of the most able person that fails it, or by the ability of the least able person that passes it. The reader should check his understanding of the preceding by attempting to count how many of the +'s and —'s may, singly, be given the opposite sign without destroying the perfectly homogeneous distribution. Altogether 12 such changes are possible.

Experimental research on abilities attempts to construct theories on the basis of which one can construct sets of tasks that yield approximately perfect homogeneous distribution. The minimum number of tasks involved in such an undertaking is two. A perfectly homogeneous distribution yields only two types of 2×2 tables for pairs of tasks. If the more difficult task is called A and the easier task B, one gets no instances of + on A *and* — on B, but all the three remaining combinations are permissible. If A and B are exactly equal in difficulty, one should, ideally, get no instances of + A — B and no instances of — A + B, i.e. two zero cells. The reader should scan some pairs of tasks in Table 3 in order to verify this for himself. In, for example, the pair of tasks 2 and 3, 3 being more difficult, there are no subjects who pass 3 and fail 2, whereas all the three remaining possibilities are represented.

In order to concretize what has been said above about the experimental study of abilities, two very simple actual examples will be presented. Both are taken from a study of 160 children between the ages 4 and 11, conducted by the present author in Boulder, Colorado (Smedslund, 1964). The reader should try to get a clear picture of what was actually said and done in this study, in order to understand the kind of data from which Table 4 was extracted, and in order to profit from the subsequent descussion.

ITEM I: CLASS INCLUSION

Subitem Ia:
Thirteen red pieces of linoleum, ten round (diameter ¾ in) and three square (side ¾ in). Six white pieces, three round (diameter ¾ in) and three square (side ¾ in). The pieces were arranged in a mixed irregular

distribution on a square piece of black linoleum (9 by 9 in). An identical piece of linoleum was used as cover.

The subject was corrected every time he failed to give the right answer to one of the preparatory questions, 1 to 9 below. Then the question was repeated until the correction was remembered.

Preparatory questions:

(Experimenter points at a red round piece.)

1. What color is this?
2. What shape does it have?

(Experimenter points at a white square piece.)

3. What color is this?
4. What shape does it have?
5. Can you place all the white ones over here (corner of the support)?

(Experimenter removes all the white pieces and points at the remaining red ones.)

6. Are all these red?
7. Are there more round ones or more square ones here?

(Objects covered, experimenter points at cover.)

8. Are all the pieces under here red?
9. Are there more round ones or more square ones?

Test questions:
10. Are there more red ones or more round ones?
11. How do you know that?

(Object uncovered.)

12. Now, look at them. Are there more red ones or more round ones?
13. How do you know that? (This question was frequently omitted when the responses to 10, 11, and 12 were correct.)

Subitem Ib:
The materials and procedure of this second subitem may be obtained by substituting the term 'red' for the term 'white' and vice versa, and the term 'square' for the term 'round' and vice versa, in the description of subitem Ia. The questions corresponding to questions 1 to 4 in Ia were omitted in Ib. Square supports and covers were used in both subitems.

ITEM II: MULTIPLICATION OF CLASSES

Subitem IIa:

A fourfold table with each cell 4 by 4 in, drawn on a white square piece of linoleum (side 9 in). Three black square pieces of linoleum (side 3⅞ in) covered three cells in the fourfold table. The lower right cell was uncovered and empty. (Throughout this paper, all directions are defined relative to the experimenter's point of view). Under the covers in the three other cells were hidden the following collections of objects: in the upper right cell, three star-shaped yellow figures of linoleum (regular four-pointed stars, ¾ in in longest extension), in the upper left cell three star-shaped green figures (same size), and in the lower left cell, three round green figures (¾ in in diameter). All the possible combinations of the three shapes, star, square, and round, and three colors, yellow, green, and blue, were displayed in an irregular arrangement on a white square support (side 3 in). The round and the square objects had sides of ¾ in. The support was placed immediately to the right of the fourfold table, and the nine objects will be referred to as the comparison set.

The subject was corrected every time he failed to give the right answer to one of the preparatory questions, 1 to 16 below. Then the question was repeated until the correction was remembered, once or a specified number of times in succession:

Preparatory questions:

(Upper right cell uncovered, experimenter points at objects in this cell.)
1. What color do these have?
2. What shape do they have?
(Experimenter points at comparison set.)
3. Can you see one more just like them, over here?
(Upper right cell covered, experimenter points at it, and then at comparison set.)
4. Can you see one just like these, over here?
5. Question 4 was repeated at least three times and until three successive correct answers were received. Before each repetition, the support of the comparison set was rotated to a new position, so that the child had to search for the object identical to those in the upper right cell. The procedure with respect to the upper right cell was then exactly repeated with respect to the upper left cell, and the lower left cell (questions 6 to 15).

16. Questions 4, 9, and 14 repeated once in succession. Questions 9 and 14 were identical to 4, but referred to, respectively, the upper left and the lower left cell. In case of errors, the sequence of questions was repeated until correct twice in succession. Every false response was corrected by uncovering the respective cell.

Test questions:

17. Now you know what is in all those three (experimenter points at all three covered cells). But we haven't placed anything here (lower right cell). Which one of these (comparison set) belongs here (should be here)?
18. Why do you think this one (child's choice) belongs here?
(All cells uncovered, lower right cell empty.)
19. Show me the one (in the comparison set) you think belongs here (lower right cell).
20. Why do you think this one (child's choice) belongs here?
(This question was frequently omitted when responses to 17, 18, and 19 were correct.)

Subitem IIb:

Same fourfold table-covers, and support for comparison set as in IIa. The lower right cell uncovered and empty. Under the covers in the other three cells were hidden the following collections of objects: in the upper right cell, three blue, square figures of linoleum (side ¾ in), in the upper left cell, three red, square figures (same material, same size), and in the lower left cell three red quarter moons (same material, longest linear extension 1 in). The comparison set contained all the possible combinations of three shapes, square, round, and moon shape, and three colors, yellow, red, and blue. The round figures in the comparison set had a diameter of ¾ in, and the square and moon-shaped figures had the same dimensions as those in the cells.

The procedure was identical to that of subitem IIa.

ITEM VI: TRANSITIVITY OF LENGTH

Subitem VIa:

Three wooden sticks ($^5/_{16}$ by $^5/_{16}$ in in cross section), two of them black (lengths 12 ⅛ and 11 ⅞ in), and one blue (length 12 in). Four V-shaped figures of black cardboard, intended to induce a Mueller-Lyer

146

illusion. The arms formed an angle of approximately 50 degrees. The length of the arms was 5 ¾ in, they were ⅜ in wide, and the cardboard was approximately $1/_{16}$ in thick.

When the Mueller-Lyer (M-L) figures were used, each black stick was placed on top of two figures, with its ends a little outside the apex of the figures. The longer stick was always placed on two figures with their arms pointing inwards, and the shorter stick on figures with arms pointing outwards. This created a perceptual illusion which reversed the actual size relationship (see also Smedslund, 1969).

The subject was corrected every time he failed to give the right answer to one of the preparatory questions, 1 to 6 below.

Preparatory questions:

(Black sticks placed close together, longer stick to the right, ends nearest experimenter coinciding.)

1. Which one of these two is longer?

(Black sticks placed 20 in from each other. M-L figures under the sticks, longer stick to the right.)

2. Which one of the two looks longer? Don't count these (M-L figures), only the sticks! That's a very easy question!

(Distance between sticks 20 in, M-L figures, longer stick to the left, blue stick compared with longer stick, ends toward the experimenter coinciding.)

3. Which one of these two is longer?

blue stick compared with longer stick, ends toward the experimenter

4. Which one of these two is longer?

(Blue stick placed between the two others.)

5. Do you remember which one was longer, this one (longer stick) or this one (blue stick)?

6. Do you remember which one was longer, this one (shorter stick) or this one (blue stick)?

(If the answer to 6 was wrong, both 5 and 6 were repeated.)

Test questions:

(Blue stick removed from table, but held visible in the experimenter's hand.)

7. Which one is longer of these two (longer and shorter black sticks)?

8. Why do you think so?

Subitem VIb:

The materials were identical to those in VIa. The procedure was also the same, except that question 1 in VIa was not repeated and that the longer stick was placed first to the left (in the question corresponding to 2 in VIa) and then to the right (in the questions corresponding to 3 to 8 in VIa.)

ITEM VII: CONSERVATION OF LENGTH

Subitem VIIa:
The same black sticks and M-L figures as in item VI were used.

Preparatory questions:
(Sticks placed on M-L figures, longer stick to the right.)
1. First a very easy question. Which one of these two *looks* longer? Don't count these (M-L figures), only the sticks!
(In two or three cases the subject did not respond according to the M-L illusion. In these cases it was sufficient for the experimenter to ask, with doubt in his voice, 'Do you really think that one *looks* longer?' in order to bring about a reversal of judgement.)
(Both sticks held upright and close together, with lower ends on the table.)
2. Which one is longer now?
(Sticks laid slowly down again on their respective M-L figures.)
3. Do you remember which one was longer when they were upright?
(If the answer was incorrect, both sticks were held upright again, and the procedure was repeated from question 2.)

Test questions:
4. Which one is longer now?
5. Why do you think so?

Subitem VIIb:
Same materials and same procedure as in VIIa, except that no question corresponding to 1 was given and that the longer stick was placed to the left (Smedslund, 1964, pp. 8-11, 14-16).

The relations between results on the item-pairs I-II and VI-VII are presented in Table 4. The numbers to the left should be understood as follows: 80 children passed both I and II, 44 failed both, 35 passed I but failed II, and one child passed II, but failed I. Similarly for the numbers to the right.

Table 4. Interitem relations between II (multiplication of classes) and I (class inclusion) and between VI (transitivity of length) and VII (conservation of length). Taken from Smedslund (1964, p. 22)

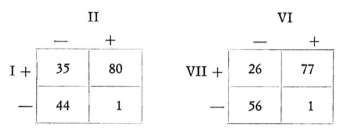

In both the examples in Table 4 the approximation to perfect homogeneity is so close that one has little difficulty in regarding the single deviations as the result of diagnostic error.

In the case of the tests of transitivity and conservation of length (VI and VII) the differences in objects used, perceptual conditions and instructions, etc. were minimal, and essentially they differed only in the intellectual structure of the task. This means that the difference in structure can also be regarded as the main determinant of the difference in results and the following interpretation is almost unavoidable: The transitive inference pattern 'A$>$B$_1$, B$_2>$C, therefore A$>$B' is valid, only when B$_1$ = B$_2$, i.e., when B is regarded as unchanged from one position to another (conservation). This means that transitivity of length presupposes conservation of length, and is also more complex than conservation. Other things equal, one must therefore expect the acquisition of conservation invariably to precede the acquisition of transitivity.

The statement that transitivity presupposes conservation, but also other things, may be regarded as strictly necessary, which means that it cannot be otherwise. One may, then, justifiably, wonder why it is necessary and of interest to conduct empirical research on such questions. The answer is that the empirical studies have at least three important functions. The first one is simply to check whether or not the procedures are actually successful in equalizing irrelevant conditions, and permitting us to study the selected variable(s), here differences in intellectual task structure. If the data had *not* yielded approximations to perfect homogeneity, we would have known that all sources of irrelevant variation had not been eliminated. Secondly, empirical studies are necessary in order to decide which ones of several logically possible alternatives are actually realized. An example illustrating the latter type of diagnostic research will be given below. A third important function of empirical research is to provide starting points and supports for theoretical analysis. For example, in the study described here, the close logical tie between conservation and transitivity was not clearly seen before it was suggested by the extremely regular data. Let us now briefly consider the findings in Table 4 concerning the relationship between II (multiplication of classes) and I (class inclusion). Here, the data are much more theoretically ambiguous. There is again a close approximation to a perfectly homogeneous distribution, which means that the irrelevant differences between the two situations, in objects used, perceptual conditions, and instructions, did not have any noticeably disturbing influence. However, the structural differences between the tasks are much more unclear than in the case of transitivity and conservation. It is not immediately clear that multiplication of classes should presuppose class inclusion. The two tasks both require that two independent attributes of the objects are kept in mind simultaneously. It may also be argued that multiplication of classes is more demanding since it requires the construction of a new object that is not there, whereas class inclusion in a sense only demands a simple comparison of two known facts. However, a choice between various alternative conceptions of how subjects solve these tasks cannot be effected without further empirical research.

An excerpt from some studies of arithmetic calculation in adult subjects (Smedslund, 1968, summarized in Smedslund, 1969, pp. 244-245) may serve as an example of a somewhat more advanced type of diagnostic research.

The subjects were instructed that each task would begin with two equal quantities (V=H) and that the experimenter would read aloud trials of operations like $+V—V—H$ (where $+V$ meant one unit added to V, and $—H$ meant one unit subtracted from H, etc.). The task was to state, as fast as possible, which one of the two quantities was bigger (or smaller) after each given triad of operations. Each subject was given a number of different items, and his reaction times were recorded by means of a stop-watch. The diagnostic problem here was to infer *how* a subject processed the given information to reach a conclusion.

Direct interrogation led to very little useful information. The rapid mental processes involved seemed to be largely unconscious and when a subject made a testable statement about his own performance he was often wrong. One subject said that items like $+V—H+H$ were particularly easy, although his reaction times to this item type were actually very long. Another subject said that items of the type $+V+V—H$ were particularly easy, although items of this type had never been given to him! The constructive and unreliable nature of the subjects' few and incomplete memories was therefore evident.

The following entirely objective diagnostic procedure was eventually devised. First, the validity of the *transformation hypothesis* was ascertained. The transformation hypothesis states that when an outcome is coded in the form 'more in V(H)' and the instruction is to tell which quantity has less, the subject must use some time and effort to transform 'more in V(H)' into 'less in H(V)'. Conversely, an outcome in form 'less in H(V)' must be transformed into 'more in V(H)' when the instruction is to tell which one has more. The transformation hypothesis had been strongly supported in a previous study with 5- and 6-year-old children, where the number of errors was the dependent variable.

The transformation hypothesis was tested with adults both at the group level and individually with three subjects. The results of the latter more methodologically interesting study will be briefly reported here. Three subjects were given a set of 96 items (each containing three operations) a total of four times, twice with a 'more'-instruction and twice with a 'less'-instruction. The data thus consisted of $4 \times 96 = 384$ reaction times for each subject.

One-third of the items contained an identity, that is, two plus operations or two minus operations with the same locus. Examples: $+V+V-H$, $-H+H+H$, $-V+V+V$. Regardless of the sequence in which any of these items is processed, it will invariably yield a conclusion in the form 'more in ...' (or 'less in ...'). $+V+V+H$ can be processed as $(+V+V)+H$ or as $(+V+H)+V$. In both cases it will yield a 'more' conclusion, and, consequently, it should be processed faster with a 'more' than with a 'less' instruction. An item such as $-H+H-H$, invariably yields a 'less' conclusion, and, hence, should be processed faster with a 'less' than with a 'more' instruction. Similar predictions can be made for all the items containing an identity. The predictions from the transformation hypothesis were confirmed in 77, 85, and 79%, respectively, of the comparisons for the three subjects.

Having tentatively established the validity of the transformation hypothesis, one may proceed to make inferences about how the subjects process the one-third of the items which do not contain identities and do not begin with an asymmetry (two elements with different operation and different locus such as $+V-H-V$ and $-H+V+H$). Initial asymmetries are known to prolong processing time and tend to overshadow or distort all other effects. Examples of items in the remaining group are $+V+H-H$ and $-V+V+H$. Each of them can theoretically be processed in three different ways, depending on which two elements are first combined. If the subject prefers symmetries or merely the first two elements, item $+V+H-H$ will be processed as $(+V+H)-H$ ($+V$ and $+H$ cancel each other and $-H$ remains), it will yield a 'less' conclusion, and should be processed faster with the 'less' instruction than with the 'more' instruction. On the other hand, the prediction is reversed if the subject prefers to process inversions first, that is $(+H-H)+V$. The alternative $(+V-H)+H$ is unlikely to occur because of the difficulty of the asymmetries. A similar line of reasoning can be applied to the whole group of items, and one can check the predictions against the actually obtained reaction times.

The hypothesis about a preference for processing the first two elements first was supported by 78, 72, and 71%, respectively, of the comparisons for the three subjects, whereas predictions from the hypotheses of preference for inversions and for symmetries received only chance level support. A final check on the given hypotheses was conducted by comparing items with identical first two elements and different signs of the third element (initial identities and asymmetries were excluded), given the 'more' and the 'less' instructions. The joint prediction from the transformation hypothesis and the hypothesis of preference for processing the first two elements first was supported in 88, 81, and 94%, respectively, of the comparisons. Although the examples are fairly trivial, they do illustrate the possibility of making systematic inferences about *how* subjects are processing information.

In conclusion, the experimental study of abilities attempts to develop methods for diagnosing exactly *how* tasks are solved, and consequently to delimit exactly in what ways people differ in ability. Of particular promise and importance is the understanding that we can get of the nature of the difference between older and younger children from the structure of the tasks they can and cannot solve.

The test tradition

This tradition in the study of abilities has grown out of practically oriented work. The first useful intelligence test was constructed by Binet and Simon in 1905 and shortly thereafter the concept of IQ (Intelligence Quotient) was introduced (see p. 140). A description of what the tests are like can be found in any introductory textbook. Psychologists have gradually developed a highly sophisticated understanding of the problems involved in the construction of adequate tests and this technology is one of the undisputed advances of our discipline. The purpose here, however, is neither to describe in detail the process of test-construction, nor to survey existing tests and findings. Instead, an attempt will be made to indicate briefly the basic logic of testing and to analyze certain aspects of its social function.

A test is a device for estimating the extent to which some characteristic (trait, ability) is present in individuals. The intelligence tests were primarily developed for predicting children's ability to do well in school. The logic underlying the selection of items in a test is simply that they should form a *representative sample* from the universe of tasks about which one wishes to say something. In the case of a scholastic aptitude test the universe may simply consist of those tasks that confront the child in school. In the case of a test of let us say numerical ability, the universe consists of all tasks involving manipulation of numbers.

The term 'representative' means that the probability of being included in the test items should be the same for all parts of the universe involved. For example, a test intended to predict general school performance should not contain only or predominantly the kind of tasks encountered in Written Composition or only or predominantly the kind of tasks encountered in Arithmetic, etc. Any deviation from representativeness may lower the test's usefulness. Suppose that a child excels in Written Composition and is low in Arithmetic. A test containing mostly items of the type encountered in Written Composition would then tend to overestimate the child's expected average school performance, whereas it would tend to underestimate the average performance of a child low on Written Composition and high in Arithmetic. The importance of the method of securing representativeness will be discussed below in connection with the problem of test validity.

Some tests are constructed on the basis of, or in conjunction with, theories. In such cases the test items are supposed to form a representative sample of the abstract universe defined by the theory, rather than of any concrete area of activities. A classical example of this is Raven's Progressive Matrices (Raven, 1965), an intelligence test composed of items consisting of complex perceptual figures to be compared. The test was construed under the influence of Sperman's intelligence theory, which emphasizes reasoning with analogies (A relates to B as C relates to?) Such analogy reasoning is required by the Raven items.

The number of items in a test must not be too few, because then chance effects could strongly influence the outcome. Representativeness would also be harder to achieve, since important task-variants would have to be left unrepresented. On the other hand, the number of items should not be too high, mainly because the test would become impractical to administer and because there is usually a diminishing return when the number of items exceeds certain limits. This diminishing return is simply a function of the increasing similarity of additional items to the already selected ones. Obviously as the psychological difference between items diminishes additional items will give progressively less new information.

Finally, items that all or nearly all subjects in the relevant population pass or fail are uninteresting, since, everyone responding in the same way, they cannot yield any information about individual differences.

The degree of adequacy of a given test has two aspects. One is the degree to which the test results are susceptible to disturbance by irrelevant random factors. This is the *accuracy* of the test, and can be estimated by three different main procedures. One is the *test-retest* method and involves study of the extent to which a repeated testing of the same persons yields the same result. A second is the *parallel-forms* method and involves study of the extent to which two supposedly equivalent forms of the same test yield the same result. Finally, there is the *split-half* method in which the given test is divided into two by taking every other item and in which the outcomes of the two half-tests are compared. In all three procedures one gets a correlation coefficient which is an estimate of the accuracy of the test as a measuring instrument.

The other aspect of test adequacy is the extent to which the test measures what it is supposed to measure. This is the *validity* of the test. Obviously one may have a highly accurate test which measures something completely different from what it is supposed to. On the other hand, a highly inaccurate test cannot by definition have much validity. In other words, accuracy is a necessary but not sufficient condition for validity.

The estimation of validity depends on the way in which the test has been constructed. If the test has been constructed by a direct sampling from a well-defined concrete universe, it is said to have content or *face validity*. An example of this would be a test of Arithmetic ability in 4th grade, where one has simply taken every n'th item in every chapter of the textbook in Arithmetic for the 4th grade. In this case the logic of the procedure itself almost ensures validity.

On the other hand, validity becomes more of a problem to the extent that the test is not constructed by direct sampling procedures from concrete universes, but on the basis of assumptions and hunches as to what is typical and what attributes are relevant in abstractly defined task universes. Thus a test of spatial ability may be constructed on the basis of assumptions about what aspects of spatial tasks are most important and of what kind of tasks are typical, in life in general. The test may turn out to have a satisfactory accuracy, as tested by any of the three methods mentioned above, yet its validity may remain uncertain. One way of estimating the validity would, e.g., be to study the relationship of the test results with the children's performances in Drawing and Geometry in school. Before this is done, a good thing is to ensure that the estimates of Drawing performance and Geometry themselves have satisfactory accuracy. If the correlations between the three measures turn out to be reasonably high one may say that the test has some *practical usefulness* for predictive purposes. Actually, it may not be satisfactory to talk about the validity of a test as such, since it can be used for many different purposes and conceivably within many conceptual frameworks. Validity will then vary according to purpose and framework. A test may have practical validity for such and such a purpose (present or future), whereas we may also talk about the validity of the construct involved (in this case spatial ability). However, the meaning of the term validity has now shifted from predictive emphasis (degree to which a test is measuring or forecasting what it is supposed to measure or forecast) to existential emphasis (is it justifiable to posit such a thing as a spatial ability?). The latter is often called construct validity.

Here we encounter again the general problem of traits, discussed on pp. 131-137. Obviously, support for the construct of spatial ability (or any other type of ability) must normally rest on the establishment of significant positive correlations between different estimates. One difficulty here is, as already mentioned, that the more different the tests, the more irrelevant variation tends to be introduced and the lower the correlations tend to become. Finally, when the number of tests devised exceeds two, there occurs an intriguing logical and statistical problem. Suppose that we have devised and administered a test (T) of spatial ability to a group of children and that, in addition, we have secured accurate estimates of the same children's performance in Drawing (D) and Geometry (G) in school. Suppose furthermore that all three correlations turn out to be positive and quite substantial. As is shown in Figure 9 there still remains an important ambiguity with respect to the extent to which this finding supports the construct of spatial ability.

It is quite possible that what is common to D and G is different from what is common to G and T, and that this again is different from what is common to D and T (alternative A.) On the other hand, it is possible that a part of the variation is common to all three variables and therefore can be attributed (tentatively) to an underlying factor such as spatial ability. The same problem exists, with additional complications for sets

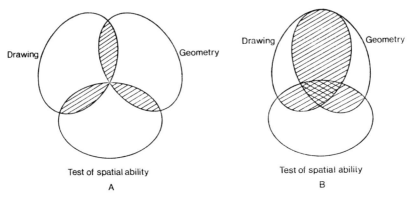

Figure 9. Two alternative relationships between three positively correlated variables. A. No common underlying factor. B. Common underlying factor.

of four and more variables. A number of methods have been devised in this area of *multivariate statistics* both to estimate the size and significance of various sources of variation and to discover possible underlying factors. All researchers and theoreticians in the area of individual differences today must have a thorough understanding of the basic logic of these methods.

Some of the outcomes of half a century of research in the area of human abilities are summarized e.g. in Anastasi (1958) and Cronbach (1960). Although the data typically contain fairly substantial correlations and some amount of order, it is hard to draw any clear conclusions with respect to such questions as how many human abilities there are, and how they are to be defined. The most immediate reason for this can be explained with reference to Figure 9 as follows: How shall one define the factor of spatial ability supposedly revealed by the common variation in case B? An almost indefinite number of specific hypotheses can explain the findings, and these hypotheses can only be tested by varying the tasks in T, D, and G in various ways and noting the outcome. This means that one must turn to experimental methods in order further to delimit the factors. However, when this is done it is typically the case that the originally established commonality turns out to be a function of very complicated patterns of variables. In a sense every step in the direction of more detailed inquiry further complicates the picture. Using an analogy with the microscope, one might say that when magnification is increased, what earlier appeared simple now appears complex. Even though the entire matter remains highly controversial and the evidence equivocal, the following type of interpretation of the structure of abilities may be gaining adherents.

Basically the performance of a person in a given task is determined by a very high number of factors, many of which tend to vary quite haphazardly. Thus, whether or not a person remembers a given syllable in a memory test depends among many other things on whether he was attentive at the moment it was presented, whether he chanced to hit upon a useful context to support memorization, whether he happened to store this in a way that made retrieval easy, whether he is attentive when he is called upon to reproduce, etc. Each of the preceding factors is again influenced by a number of other unrelated determinants, etc. However, despite this high amount of relatively random variability, the structure of the events which historically and concomitantly determine a given performance are by no means entirely random. Ability to solve mathematical problems depends on the solution of other mathematical problems, etc. Typically there may develop generalized attitudes towards what happens in the mathematics lessons and this leads to generalized patterns of rapid vs. slow, genuine vs. superficial acquisition of mathematics. This again will be reflected in test-patterns in a tendency for understanding of certain types of mathematics to be correlated with understanding of other types of mathematics, etc. Unitary abilities can therefore be expected to be approximated to the extent that there exist historically and/or logically related activities. As an example, one may expect some unitary ability to copy objects by drawing them, in our culture, since we tend to practice drawing by copying all kinds of objects. On the other hand, in a culture where drawing occurs only in the copying of certain highly limited stylized patterns one may only expect a very specific drawing ability related to these patterns, whereas performance in other drawing tasks may be less unitary. In other words, ability may be linked to aspects of culturally defined unitary activities. This theory of abilities also presupposes that the innate and maturationally unfolding capacities of individuals are from the beginning highly differentiated, i.e. that nature does not operate with a few large chunks of variability but rather with extremely numerous and extremely small units of variability. The outcome of the preceding would be to conclude that there can be no definite, eternally and universally valid answer to the question of what are the basic human abilities. Rather one would have to confine oneself to diagnosing those abilities that exist under given sociocultural circumstances at any given period of time. This would lead to a social science rather than a natural science perspective on the structure of abilities. The student is urged to consider this suggestion in the light of the evidence offered by textbooks and reviews. Is it plausible? If not, what are the alternatives?

The social function of ability tests

Whatever it is that they measure, ability tests have received official recognition as useful instruments for sorting people and for facilitating decisions about their future placement in society. In order to evaluate their potential social functions let us consider the set of data given in Table 5. These data are illustrative of a trend that has been found in numerous studies.

Table 5. Relationship between socioeconomic status, IQ, and (in parentheses) percentage later continuing to college in the 6th grade of an American high school. Data compiled from Havighurst et al. (1962)

Socioeconomic status (SES)

		High		Low	
IQ	High	51	(71%)	57	(23%)
	Low	33	(18%)	96	(5%)

First of all, the table shows again the well-established fact that the intelligence tests measure something that is strongly related to socioeconomic status and that they support the old proverb 'rich is bright — poor is stupid'. Nearly ⅔ of those high in SES are high in IQ, whereas nearly ⅔ of those low in SES are low in IQ, even though they have up to that point had the same number of years in school.

Second, the percentages in parentheses show that even when matched not only on preceding schooling but also on IQ, the children with high SES are much more likely to continue to college than children with low SES. Many studies have shown that this difference, although frequently a function of mere economic opportunity, persists even when the material opportunities (loans, access to nearby university, etc.) are literally equalized.

The preceding shows that the abilities measured by intelligence tests tend to be higher in the higher socioeconomic echelons, and furthermore that there are factors which tend to minimize the number of transitions between higher and lower status. Since higher education today is practically indispensable for future high SES it is clear that there is a high tendency for offspring to maintain their parents' SES.

Third, the widespread use af ability tests as screening devices means that they contribute to the maintenance of predominantly high IQ's among those high in SES.

Finally, the preceding should be considered in connection with the observation that the intelligence tests were originally devised to predict performance in the school system and that e.g. among a set of more than 4,000 validity coefficients, practically every one is with grades in school (see Bennett, Seashore and Wesman, 1955). There is little evidence that performance on intelligence tests relates in any very substantial way to performance in the world outside the educational institutions. This includes performance in actual complex work situations, ability to survive in the ghetto, ability to understand other people, ability to teach, ability to handle administrative or interpersonal situations, ability to live with one's family, ability to treat children adequately, ability to create opportunities for enjoying oneself, sense of humor, ability to solve emotional problems, to create art, to find meaning, to enrich other people's lives, etc. etc. An example of relevant research is given by Thorndike and Hagen (1959). They report around 10,000 correlations between aptitude test scores and measures of vocational success and found no more statistically significant ones than could be expected by chance. These findings can be interpreted in various ways, but on face value they seem to indicate absence of relationship.

As far as is known, intelligence tests and performance in the educational system may form a huge, relatively closed world, closely associated with socioeconomic status, but unrelated to many important aspects of living in general. Perhaps intelligence tests largely measure adaptation to the peculiar form of intellectual living (going to school) that has such a high prestige in Western culture. Perhaps we have absolutized this high prestige tradition to such an extent that we recognize neither the ritualism of many performances included, nor the complexity and human value of all those performances that are not related to school grades. In order to get a better perspective on the preceding let us turn for a moment to pure fiction.

A fable of colors

Once upon a time there was a society in which color discrimination and color classification were more highly valued than any other human characteristics. In the higher echelons the language was filled with color metaphors and all kinds of oblique allusions to color distinctions. In the lower echelons language and thinking were much less geared to color. As this society proceeded to develop in its own particular ways, a man named Cinet designed a color discrimination and classification test which made it possible to sort people according to their ability. The resulting unified measure was called 'color quotient' (CQ) and was calculated from color age divided by chronological age multiplied by 100. The school system of this society was heavily infested with color discrimination training (in the lower grades), and color classification exercises. In the higher grades there was much concern with the understanding of color metaphors and with the logic of hypothetical color systems (with no concrete basis). All higher level occupations included performances supposedly requiring a relatively high CQ. The terminology of doctors and pharmacists could only be understood after extensive training in color classification, the print in the lawbooks varied delicately and meaningfully in hue and business was conducted with the help of color-symbol computers. In brief, the well-to-do men and women in power in this society were able to exercise their important function only because of their exceptional color discrimination and their knack for manipulating and recombining higher order color symbols and metaphors.

Cinet and his followers, the cycologists, performed an important function in this society. They helped to screen people for admission to higher educational institutions and to discover and treat retarded children and adults who were so backward in color discrimination and classification that they could only occupy very lowly positions or had to be kept in institutions. There was, at one time, a violent discussion about whether or not it was really humane to keep alive those unfortunates who were completely color blind and who, consequently, were functioning at an entirely subhuman level.

The student is encouraged to think about this piece of fiction and to consider the possibility that our construct of intelligence may perhaps be the product of a particular sociocultural context, and closely related to the existence of a certain kind of formal educational system. The plausibility of this idea is enhanced by the fact that intelligence as we have conceived of it appears to be peculiarly unrelated to much that goes on in people's lives outside schools and colleges.

Speculation and conclusions can proceed in many directions from the above and we will deliberately refrain from elaborating on these topics. The sophistication in the test construction is a genuine and lasting advance. Yet no psychologist should bury himself in the technology of testing without considering the wider drama in which the tests play an important role.

Questions after Chapter VII

1. Try the REP-test procedure on yourself. What did you learn and what are your comments?

2. Are you really convinced that the search for general traits is futile? Do you have any objections to the discussion of traits in this chapter?

3. Try to analyze for yourself the relationship between conservation and transitivity of length, and the role of empirical studies in discovering and supporting the interpretations. Do you think your conclusions from this case can be generalized to all psychological research?

4. Try to make clear to yourself the difference between accuracy and validity and the constraints that exist in the relationship between these two measures.

5. In what ways do you think the fable of color is a valid analogy to intelligence testing and in what ways is it not?

VIII. General psychology: Psychophysics

In the preceding chapter some of the insights gained in studying individual differences were described. However, the mainstream of psychology has always been more concerned with what is common to people than with their differences. Psychology has been conceived of as the study of human nature, or, in other words, as the study of the universally and eternally valid laws or principles that govern mental processes. Within this theoretical perspective, experimental psychology has developed, beginning with rather artificial, but very scientific looking, models, and then gradually with increasing realization of the particular intricacies which are inherent in the subject matter of psychology. This realization of the nature of the technical and theoretical problems in experimental psychology is another of the major achievements which set professional psychologists somewhat apart from laymen. In this and the two following chapters the development of insight will be briefly described with particular reference to three traditional fields, namely, *psychophysics, learning,* and *motivation.* Anticipating the conclusion, it may be pointed out that many of the methodological and conceptual/theoretical insights gained in these and in other fields may have lasting value, even if one rejects or severely limits the range of applicability of the premise that there exists a universal and eternal human nature.

Fechner

Psychophysics was the branch of experimental psychology that was first established, and its founder was Gustav Theodor Fechner (1801-1887). Like many German scientists of his time, he had a broad and many-faceted education and corresponding interests. He first studied medicine and took his Doctor's degree in this field, but then got interested in physics and mathematics, and among other things did some important experimental studies of electricity. When thirty-three years old he became Professor of Physics in Leipzig. After a prolonged nervous illness that made him unable to work for 12 years, he developed a strong interest in a mystical philosophy of nature. He felt that the whole universe was a unit and that all things have life and consciousness. In the context of this philosophical outlook, he felt that it would be important to demonstrate that so-called mental and so-called physical phenomena were lawfully related. He labeled this problem-area *psychophysics,* and made a distinction between *internal* and *external* psychophysics. Internal psychophysics was the study of the relationship between conscious experiences and processes in the nervous system, which were at this time little known and difficult to study. He therefore decided to concentrate on external psychophysics, which was the study of the relationship between physical stimulation of the sense organs and the corresponding subjective experience. In accordance with his natural science training, he thought that all observation should involve *measurement,* and it was therefore natural that he selected for study the *intensity* of the physical stimulation and the *intensity* of the corresponding subjective experience. Stimulus-intensity was readily measurable by physical methods, and the main problem was how to measure the intensity of experience in such a way that a mathematical function of the two variables could be determined.

Early in his work, he came across some experiments conducted by the physiologist Ernst Heinrich Weber about 25 years earlier, which indicated that the just noticeable difference between two stimuli is directly proportional to the absolute stimulus-intensity. Weber's results could be expressed in the following formula (where ΔS is the smallest possible change in stimulus intensity that yields a noticeable change in the subjective, i.e. experienced, intensity, S is the absolute stimulus intensity, and K is a constant):

$$\frac{\Delta S}{S} = K$$

Concretely, this means that if the stimulus involved is weak, even a very slight change will be noticeable, whereas only a considerable change is noticeable if the stimulus is strong. If one candle is burning in a room, the addition of another candle means a very distinct change in the subjectively experienced illumination. On the other hand, if one thousand candles are burning, the addition of one will not be noticeable. If the difference in weight between 100 and 110 g is just noticeable, then one must compare a weight of 200 g with one of 220 in order to sense the difference.

Fechner made the, as we shall see later, highly controversial assumption that the different just noticeable differences (j.n.d.'s) at different stimulus-intensities are subjectively equal and thus represent a kind of unit. If this is true, one may measure the intensity of a subjective experience by how many j.n.d.'s it is from zero, i.e. the weakest absolute stimulus-intensity that can be noticed. Instead of the clumsy direct method of measurement, one may then use a reformulation of Weber's law, which gives the lawful relationship between stimulus-intensity and subjective intensity. Fechner's formula, disregarding some constants which were to be separately determined for each sensory modality and each set of experimental conditions, may be formulated as follows: (O = subjective intensity and S = stimulus-intensity):

$$O = \log S$$

With this formula Fechner thought he had described a way of measuring subjective experiences. The central problem now was to determine empirical difference thresholds, i.e. the magnitudes of the j.n.d.'s under given conditions. Only then could one specify the formula in concrete situations and use it for predictive purposes. In order to achieve this, Fechner developed his famous psychophysical methods, which represent his most important contributions to psychology. He very early recognized that a threshold is a *statistical* concept. Sometimes a person notices a given physical difference in intensity and sometimes not, i.e. the threshold is a fluctuating magnitude. It must therefore be defined as the physical difference that is noticed by the person in a certain percentage of the exposures, typically 75%. Fechner devised three main procedures, which for many years remained fundamental in all psychological measurement: 1. *The method of limits* consists in varying the intensity of one of two physical stimuli A and B (e.g. lights or sounds), from A clearly stronger than B to A clearly weaker than B, and recording the points where the person's judgment changes from A>B to A=B, and from A=B to A<B. Then A's intensity is changed gradually from A clearly weaker than B to A clearly stronger than B, recording again the points where judgment changes from A<B to A=B and from A=B to A>B. This is repeated many times with the same person, and then with other persons, and as a result one can compute a measure of one j.n.d. for the given stimulus intensity of B. 2. *The method of constant stimuli* consists in presenting a constant stimulus A successively together with many different intensities of another stimulus B (in unsystematic sequences) and recording the person's judgments (A>B, A=B, A<B) (see also pp. 166-167). 3. *The method of adjustment* consists in presenting a stimulus A with a certain intensity and letting the person repeatedly try to adjust the intensity of another stimulus B to A so that he experi-

ences the two stimuli as equal. Here the measure of a j.n.d. is derived from the distribution of the estimates around the true value.

After the appearance of Fechner's important book *Elemente der Psychophysik* in 1860, psychophysics developed rapidly. New variants and improvements of the methods were devised and the statistical analysis became more refined. Fechner's problem grew out of his metaphysical speculations about cosmic unity, but his success undoubtedly was due to his experimental and mathematical background. The psychophysical methods permitted one aspect of mental phenomena, namely sensation, to be investigated in the laboratory, and this laid the foundation for an experimental psychology.

Stimulus detection

Let us now turn to some of the basic problems as they are envisaged by psychophysics today. The earlier workers in the field spoke of *the absolute threshold* as the lowest stimulus-intensity that can be apprehended by the subject. Ideally, one might expect this to be a definite value that could be measured once and for all. This would mean that each time a stimulus with intensity above the threshold is presented, the subject should detect it and that each time a stimulus below the threshold is presented, the subject should not detect it. Actually one always finds curves of the type illustrated in Figure 10. This type of curve means that the probability (relative frequency) of detection is an S-shaped function of the intensity of the stimulus. The stimulus-intensity which leads to detection half of the times (probability = .50) may then be defined as the threshold, although this is clearly somewhat arbitrary.

In earlier days there was a tendency to regard the absolute threshold or at least the threshold function as an approximate constant, i.e. as a pure psychophysical relationship which would permit accurate prediction from physical stimulus-intensity to probability of detection and vice versa. However, there are some inherent difficulties in this simple picture, which have gradually led to a very much revised and extended interpretation of the processes involved.

Let us consider more closely the actual procedure in a threshold experiment. The subject may be told that stimuli of varying intensities are going to be presented, one at a time, and that he is to say 'yes' each time he detects the stimulus and 'no' each time he cannot detect it. Now, one may ask, what is to prevent the subject from saying 'yes' every time, or most of the time, knowing that there is always a stimulus presented. Subjects need not be downright dishonest, since in these tasks one is

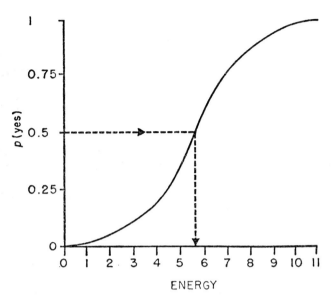

Figure 10. Probability of detection of stimulus as a function of physical stimulus-intensity.

nearly always uncertain as to whether or not one has perceived anything. Consequently, one's wish to get a high score may very well lead one to say 'yes' rather than 'no' in case of doubt, especially since one knows that there is a stimulus. Even to extremely weak stimuli one occasionally gets 'yes' responses, and one may very well wonder whether this reveals genuine detection or something else. This problem was very early recognized and one first attempted to control it by inserting a few 'catch'-trials in every experiment. In these trials no stimulus was presented and subjects who said 'yes' were warned, and, if they continued, discarded from consideration. However, since it was quite apparent that, usually, no intentional dishonesty was involved, the problem was not really solved by the insertion of the catch-trials. It was necessary to investigate the phenomenon systematically, since it clearly influenced the threshold values.

It should be noted that at this point interest has been shifted from a pure psychophysical relationship to a psychological problem, namely the determinants of saying 'yes' and 'no' under identical external stimulus conditions. One obvious possibility has been implicit in the preceding discussion, namely that the subject's belief that there is always a stimulus present makes him more inclined to say 'yes'. How will the subject's tendency to say 'yes' when there is no stimulus to be affected by variations in how often he expects a stimulus to be presented? This can be investigated in experiments where a constant stimulus-intensity, e.g. somewhat above the 50% threshold, is employed, and where the stimulus presentation probability is varied. In Table 6 are given a set of results for stimulus presentation probabilities of .90 and .10.

Table 6. Response probabilities for stimulus presentation probabilities of .90 and .10. Same stimulus-intensity in both cases. Modified from Galanter, 1962, p. 102.

Stimulus presentation probability = .90				Stimulus presentation probability = .10			
		Response				Response	
		Yes	No			Yes	No
Stimulus	Pres.	0.97	0.03	Stimulus	Pres.	0.28	0.72
	Abs.	0.62	0.38		Abs.	0.04	0.96

Results of the type presented in Table 6 show that the subjective likelihood of an actual stimulus being presented is indeed a very potent determinant of the distribution of 'yes' vs. 'no' responses. It should be noted that this likelihood can be manipulated not only by global probabilities in randomized sequences, but also by any kind of patterning of the presentations. Thus, if there is a consistent sequence such as (perceptible) stimulus — no (perceptible) stimulus — stimulus — no stimulus — ..., the subject's expectancies will build up and have the same decisive influence on the threshold function.

On the basis of the preceding we may, then, conclude that there is no particular absolute threshold, but that the detection curve is a function both of stimulus intensy *and* of the expectancies the subject has built up. Since the building up of expectancies is a process of learning, it may be noted that even the simplest possible psychophysical experiment is 'contaminated' by learning effects. It should be added that the threshold function not only depends on the final stabilized expectancies as such, but actually *changes* during the period when the expectancies are in the process of being built up and consolidated.

However, the factors influencing the threshold function are not exhausted by including the subject's cognition of the frequency and temporal structure of the events involved. Two other major factors can easily be shown to be operative. One of them is clearly implied in the question of why the subject should be 'dishonest', and in the reasonable hypothesis that he may wish to get 'high' scores. It is clearly a precondition for doing this kind of experiment that subjects try to be honest and that they try to do their best, i.e. try to detect the stimulus. In terms of the common-sense model of action, the psychophysical threshold study is clearly a study of what the subject *can* do, and hence presupposes that he tries. However, the preceding is not a sufficient analysis of the experiment as far as try is concerned. One must also consider the actual consequences of the various possible outcomes in terms of the over-all motivation. If the subject says 'yes' and there is an actual stimulus, the subject is obviously rewarded since this is what he tries to achieve. Similarly, although perhaps not so strongly, he is rewarded if he says 'no' and is told that there is no actual stimulus. On the other hand, he experiences simple failure if he says 'no' when an actual stimulus is said to be present. Finally, he experiences both failure and possible embarrassment if he says 'yes' and is informed that there is no actual stimulus.

The mentioned possibilities form what is usually called the *payoff matrix* for the given stimulus detection situation, and one may surmise that the values of the outcomes may have an important influence on the relative frequency of 'yes' and 'no' given the same stimulus presentation expectations and the same stimulus-intensity. Experiments have been performed on this question using payoff matrices where the subject wins or loses small amounts of money, different for the different outcome-types. The finding is that the value of the gains or losses does indeed influence the frequency of the response categories in exactly the same way as we have already shown for stimulus presentation probability. Thus increasing the value of the reward for correctly saying 'yes' increases the probability of saying 'yes', etc. and one can establish exact correspondences such that, e.g., a certain decrease in likelihood of stimulus presentation is exactly offset by a corresponding increase in value of the reward.

It should be noted that the traditional threshold determination experiment is not a situation where there is no payoff matrix, but rather it is a situation with an *undetermined* payoff matrix. We may then conclude that *values* and hence what traditionally has been called the subject's *motivation* is an important factor entering the psychophysical experiment and determining the recorded values of the detection threshold. Analogously to the case of expectancies, it may be added that the values and hence the payoff matrix may change during the experiment itself. An example would be the case of a subject who gets so thoroughly embarrassed by being caught saying 'yes' when there is no stimulus, that he changes his entire strategy. While formerly he tried as hard as possible to maximize the number of successful detections of a stimulus by saying 'yes', he may now try equally hard to minimize the number of cases of mistaken 'yes' by being extremely careful about saying 'yes'.

A third potent and rather obvious determinant of the detection curve is the concomitant stimulus-field in which the investigated stimulus is imbedded. In the preceding we have proceeded as if the subject was, at the time of investigation, only confronted with one stimulus variable. This is clearly an untenable position. In the case of visual stimuli, there is a background illumination and a background patterning, and similarly for audition there is background 'noise' and background patterned sounds. Similarly for the other senses. To be sure, one has often studied stimulus detection under conditions of absolute darkness or absolute silence (leaving only an unavoidable 'subjective' experience of light and the sound of the blood streaming through the vessels in the ear, the heartbeat, etc.). But this leads to results that are only valid under these extreme conditions, that are practically never realized in normal life, and, consequently, the findings may have limited value.

Finally, it should be noted that the values and expectancies of subjects are always influenced by fluctuations in the cultural situation which lie outside the scope of the single detection experiments, and, therefore, may make replications of a study very difficult. Thus, in a period when psychologists turn to ever more subtle ways of deceiving their subjects, students may become increasingly suspicious and consequently may not build up expectancies in the same trusting way as they did in more idyllic times. Similarly, inflation may reduce the value of the 10 cent and 5 cent rewards used in a given study, and in order to replicate it, one may have to perform laborious and perhaps rather circular tests in order to find the value equivalents in latter-day small change. It may, therefore, be concluded that the dream of an elegant and definite absolute threshold has faded, and instead one has discovered that one is (after all) still dealing with ever-changing expectancies and motives, and with a tendency to be influenced by the remainder of the stimulus field. With this in mind, let us now proceed to the next complication in the psychophysical experiment, namely the problem of stimulus recognition.

Stimulus recognition

Whereas detection is deciding whether or not there is a stimulus, recognition is deciding *what* the stimulus is, i.e. identifying it.

What factors can determine the ease with which we recognize a stimulus, presupposing that it is clearly detectable? An obvious common-sense hypothesis is that recognition becomes more difficult the more similar the stimulus involved is to other stimuli. However, suppose that the alternatives to be recognized are indeed easily discriminable from each other. Can there be anything else that determines the recognizability of a stimulus given clear detectability and clear discriminability? The answer is yes, but in order to formulate this insight in a clear and generally valid manner, it becomes necessary to make a short excursion into the field of *information theory*. This theory was originally developed in the field of telecommunications and engineering, but has been generalized and has found widespread applications in many scientific branches including psychology. *Information* is the opposite of *uncertainty,* and both concepts have retained much of the meaning they had in everyday language. The higher the number of alternative things that may happen in a given situation, the higher the uncertainty. If four different kinds of events may happen in a situation, it involves more uncertainty than a situation where only two kinds of events may happen. Conversely, when one event out of four possible happens, it carries more information (= reduces more uncertainty) than when one event out of two possible happens. The more uneven the probability distribution for the alternatives are, the less is the total uncertainty. If the alternatives are A and B, the uncertainty is less when the probabilities of A and of B are respectively .90 and .10, than when they are .50 and .50. In the former case, it is highly probable that A and not B will materialize, whereas in the latter case one can have no preferred expectancy as to what will happen.

The concept of information (uncertainty) can be quantified and one may, under certain circumstances, *measure* how much information must be digested in order to solve given tasks. The unit for measuring information is called a *bit*. The exact mathematical formulation will not be given here, but an approximate idea of what a bit means can be gained from the following concrete example (Figure 11):

Suppose we have an 8×8 diagram of the type given in Figure 11, and suppose further that we think of one of the cells. Another person is given the task of finding this cell by asking questions, which are only to be answered by 'yes' and 'no'. This is a situation where the number

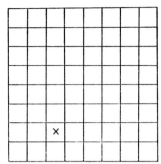

Figure 11. Diagram for illustration of information measurement.

of alternatives is known, namely 64, and we may further assume that these alternatives are equally probable for the person who is given the task. (In reality the subjective probabilities are almost always unequally distributed.)

A bit can (incompletely) be defined as the amount of information given when the number of alternative and equiprobable alternatives is divided by two. Thus if the first question is 'is the cell to the right of a vertical line dividing the diagram in two equal parts?' the answer, in this case 'yes', provides one bit of information, since half of the alternatives are excluded. For each new question that divides the remaining alternatives exactly in two, one bit of information will be extracted, and it can be seen that by this strategy one can always find any given cell in the diagram by means of 6 bits of information. The reader should verify this for himself, and also consider what happens if he adopts other strategies, not dividing the number of alternatives by two.

The concept of information has been introduced in the discussion of recognition, because it has been shown that it is a powerful determinant of recognizability of stimuli. The following principle summarizes widely confirmed empirical findings: *Recognizability of individual stimuli is severely limited by the amount of information they carry.* If a set of stimuli differ only in one dimension (sound intensity, pitch, brightness of light, etc.) the limit for errorless recognition lies around a little less than 3 bits. This means that we can errorlessly recognize stimuli in one-dimensional sets with up to approximately 7 members. This is true regardless of how widely the stimuli are spread out along the dimension. If the number of members of the set increases above 7, we start to make errors. It should be added that the number 7 refers to the number of categories to be recognized and not to the number of actual stimuli.

172

We can errorlessly categorize any number of unidimensionally varying stimuli in about seven groups (Miller, 1956).

Here we have hit upon a research finding of great generality that was not clearly anticipated by common sense. The reason for this is obviously that recognition of stimuli varying only in one dimension practically never occurs outside the laboratory. If we let the stimuli to be recognized vary in two, three, and more dimensions, the amount of information that can be processed increases, i.e. we can recognize more categories. However, the increase in capacity is less than the sum of the information in the dimensions taken separately, and as the number of dimensions increases the increase in the number of categories that can be recognized becomes progressively smaller. The absolute upper limit for stimuli of any complexity has been estimated to be about ten or eleven bits, or equivalent to around one to two thousand equiprobable stimulus-categories.

When we turn to stimuli with unequal probabilities, the recognition task become much easier and this accords with our daily experience of almost unlimited ability to recognize individual objects and events. For further readings of increasing technicality the student is referred to Neisser (1967), Attneave (1959), and Garner (1962).

Let us now for a moment turn to a concrete recognition task. If we tell a person that he is to recognize which of the twenty-six letters of the alphabet is flashed briefly on a screen, he will, if the presentations are brief enough, make a certain number of errors. If, however, we tell him to recognize which of the first five letters of the alphabet is to be flashed on the screen, his accuracy per letter increases strongly, as could be expected from the preceding. Concretely, this means that he is more often correct in recognizing say the letter 'A' when he believes that one of the five first letters is flashed than when he believes that one of the twenty-six letters is flashed. This makes sense. However, we can also do the experiment in another way. First, we apparently flash one of the twenty-six letters on the screen, while actually we flash one of the first five. We then ask the subject which of the first five it was. Now he could not have anticipated the number of alternatives to be given. Yet it turns out that his accuracy per letter is still nearly (but not quite) as high as when he is told in advance that he is to choose between only five letters. With both procedures the most important thing seems to be the number of categories or response alternatives. There are many more interesting problems and results in the study of recognition but this will have to do as a sample.

The preceding discussion leads to the following conclusion: Whether or not a given detectable event will be correctly recognized by a subject depends on the set of alternatives involved. In other words, recognition is influenced by those other events that, from the subject's point of view, *could* have happened, but did not. Once again, it is clear that one cannot maintain a belief in some kind of invariant linkage between the positively given physical stimulus and the subject's experience.

Stimulus discrimination

In the introduction to this chapter it has already been mentioned how Weber and Fechner introduced the study of discrimination and how the concept of difference threshold and that of 'one just noticeable difference' (j.n.d.) became established. Using Fechner's method of constant stimuli, in which one standard stimulus is compared successively with a number of both stronger and weaker other (comparison) stimuli, one gets a threshold function of the type shown in Figure 12.

From data of the type presented in Figure 12 one calculates the differential threshold or one j.n.d. as half the difference between the points where 75 percent and 25 percent of the judgments are in one direction. In the given example this means $(Y—X)/2$. In the introduction we also mentioned Weber's famous law, which states that the size of the just noticeable difference is directly proportional to the absolute stimulus intensity. Despite certain modifications, Weber's law remains essentially valid as an approximative description of the way our sense organs function, and it can be verified at a purely physiological level.

However, it should be noticed that Weber's law, no less than most other simple principles, really has an 'other things equal' qualification tagged on. This qualification primarily refers to the same major psychological determinants as were shown to be influential in the case of stimulus detection, namely learning, motivation, and background stimulation. In typical studies measuring the difference threshold, the relative frequency of presentation of the different standard-comparison pairs has been equal and the sequence of presentations has been carefully randomized. However, it is clear that if the frequencies were biased, e.g. if the comparison stimulus were greater than the standard in 75 instead of in 50 percent of the presentations, the j.n.d. would surely be strongly modified. Similarly, this could be achieved by introducing some kind of sequential structuring in the presentations, such as regular simple alternation between having the comparison stimulus stronger than and weaker than the standard.

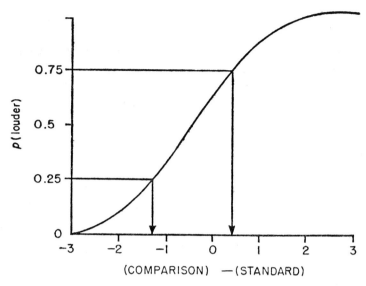

Figure 12. Difference threshold function. Probability of judging a stimulus as stronger (louder, higher, brighter... etc.) than another as a function of their physical difference.

The potential effect of variations in motivation is also clear. It has been observed that if naive and unpracticed observers are put on payoff schedules that reward them for correct judgments and punish them for wrong, the just noticeable difference may decrease to one half of its original value. No doubt all kinds of variations in the payoff matrix (such as differential reward of judgments of stronger and weaker, etc.), would lead to change in the difference threshold function. It is also well known that for instance the discrimination between the chromatic colors, without prolonged training in the laboratory, is strongly influenced by cultural differences, reflected in the different color vocabularies, (Brown, 1965, Conklin, 1955).

The third main factor influencing discrimination, namely that of background stimulation, has always been rigidly controlled in the laboratory, but, both theoretically and in connection with applied problems, it is of great importance. As an example, one may want to know how well pitch is discriminated under various conditions of background noise, etc. After having observed the same kind of problem in the study of discrimination as in the study of detection, we are ready to consider a fourth major problem in psychophysics, namely that of scaling.

The problem of scaling

As we have seen (pp. 164-165) Fechner attempted to scale subjective appearances of stimuli by assuming a) that Weber's law was valid, i.e that the size of a j.n.d for any given stimulus intensity is a constant fraction of that intensity, and b) that the different j.n.d.'s were subjectively equal. Weber's law was empirically supported, but the assumption of the subjective equality of the j.n.d.'s was hard to test. Consequently, one looked for other more direct methods of estimating subjective appearances, and the first experimental technique for doing so was devised toward the end of the nineteenth century. It is called the *category scaling method*. The subject is presented with stimuli one at a time and is asked to judge their relative magnitude by placing them in a given set of categories. The set may consist, e.g., of the first seven integers and the subject is told to place the weakest stimuli in category 1 and the strongest in category 7. He is shown examples of these stimuli so that he knows which the weakest and strongest are. The subject is furthermore told that he is to distribute the other stimuli among the categories in such a way that the intervals between the categories are subjectively equal. This means that the subjective difference between, e.g., categories 1 and 2 should be the same as the subjective difference between 4 and 5, etc. Some fifteen to twenty stimuli are then presented to the subject, one at a time, and the subject assigns a category name to each one. This is repeated several times and the average of the category values assigned to each stimulus is taken as the category scale value of the stimulus. This is a reliable method, as revealed by the stability of the findings over repetitions. When category scales are plotted against physical stimulus intensities, one gets roughly the kind of logarithmic relationship that could be expected from Fechner's theory.

However, there also exist other methods of scaling, notably the direct magnitude scales devised by S. S. Stevens and coworkers, and later by G. Ekman and coworkers. In a typical case the subject is, e.g., given a stimulus with the assigned numerical value of 10 and is asked to assign the value 20 to a stimulus with the double subjective magnitude, 5 to a stimulus with half the subjective magnitude, 15 to a stimulus with 50% higher subjective magnitude, etc. These ratio estimates are just as reliable as the category estimates, but yield different empirical results. More specifically, the relationship between stimulus-intensity and subjective estimate now turns out to be a so-called *power-function*, i.e. of the type $O = k.S^n$, where O is the estimate, S is the physical magnitude, and k and n are constants.

176

The discrepancy between the two kinds of scales has led to much research, and, among other things, it has, in some situations, been found that the results of the category scaling method, but not to the same extent those of the magnitude estimation methods, are disturbed if the physical stimulus magnitudes are unequally distributed. More specifically, when the stimuli are concentrated mostly among the highest magnitudes the categories are displaced towards the higher magnitudes, and the opposite effect is found when the presented stimuli are concentrated in the lower range of magnitudes given.

The effect may, intuitively, appear to derive from a tendency to prefer approximately equal frequencies in each category. Corresponding findings with the magnitude estimation method show no comparable distortion. However, later more intensive research on data from individual subjects rather than on group averages, has also shown disturbing bias effects in ratio-scaling (see Poulton, 1968).

There is no place here for a continued description of the intricate problems confronting psychologists in the area of psychophysics. However, let us mention one final set of observations that appear to be of particular theoretical importance. Ekman and his coworkers in Stockholm have done a series of studies of the relationship between subjective variables. In one of these studies (Eisler & Ekman, 1959), subjects first estimated the pitch of a set of signals, and then, in a second part of the study estimated the degree of similarity between all the different pairs of signals. It turned out that there was a very simple and stable relationship between subjective pitch and subjective similarity of pitches. Specifically, subjective similarity between two experiences differing in only one dimension corresponds to the ratio of the lowest scale value of this dimension to the arithmetic mean of the two given scale values. Ekman points out that relationships between subjective variables are generally much simpler than psychophysical relationships (among other things the former lack empirical constants to be determined), and also that these simple relationships would have remained undiscovered if one had felt obliged to retain physical measurement as one pole of the comparisons.

The preceding brief survey of a few topics in the area of psychophysics may be ended with the following conclusions:

1. A great number of simple functional relationships have been found to hold true under prevalent laboratory conditions.

2. A high level of sophistication has been achieved in the construction of detection, recognition, and discrimination functions and of scales. This problem insight and technological skill have undoubtedly been of great value to the psychologist for many theoretical and practical

177

purposes far beyond the original area of psychophysics. For example, Thurstone (in the 1930's) applied the method of category scaling to the measurement of intensity of attitudes, thereby laying the foundations for an important branch of social psychology. In fields of applied psychology such as studies of work conditions and of traffic, psychophysical methods may be important in determining optimal arrangements for instrument panels, signal lamps, headlights, buzzers, general illumination, background noise, etc.

3. In psychophysical studies, as in all dealings with people, the all-pervasive influence of learning, motivation, and background stimulation must be recognized and controlled. Furthermore, the modern scaling methods presuppose complex cognitive abilities in the subjects, and, hence, may be expected to be influenced by such factors as level of mental development and educational and cultural background.

4. Physical stimulus attributes are only one of several categories of determinants of how the world appears to the subject. Their influence is not generally and strictly predictable, but can be foreseen only after continuous readjustment of the functions for each new constellation of 'other things equal'.

Questions after Chapter VIII

1. Are you convinced that there is no real and relatively constant detection threshold? Could it be that such a real threshold is merely distorted and overshadowed by the effects of learning, motivation and the perceptual field?

2. Exactly why is one more often correct in recognizing a given letter when one believes that one of five letters is presented, than when one believes that one of twenty-six letters is presented? Could it possibly be otherwise or do we have here another example of a truism (tautology)?

3. What cognitive abilities are involved in magnitude scaling?

IX. General psychology: Learning

Whereas psychophysics originated in a search for *static* laws connecting the physical and the mental, the psychology of learning has been a continuous search for laws describing how people *change* as a result of their experiences. People seem to have become what they are largely as a result of their earlier experiences and they can only be changed by being provided with new experiences. Therefore, the practical and theoretical importance of the phenomena of learning has been apparent to psychologists for a long time. An additional attractiveness of the area particularly for theoreticians derives from the fact that the outlines of some obvious learning principles are clearly discernible in our common-sense understanding of people. Among these are the use of rewards and punishments to shape behavior, the principle of association by contiguity, and the idea that practice makes perfect. After learning phenomena were first made accessible to experimental study, there began a surge of empirical studies stretching over more than two thirds of a century. Also, there have been a series of efforts to create general psychological theories based on learning principles. Lately there has occurred a decline in the amount of research directed toward general theories, and there has been a widespread sobering up with respect to what can reasonably be achieved in the isolated study of learning. The purpose of this chapter is to try to formulate some of the insights gained in the field both with respect to theory and practical application. In order to do this we will first briefly review the work of some of the pioneers in the field before and around the turn of the century, and, after that, describe some of the kinds of principles that were formulated in the golden age of learning theories, roughly between 1930 and 1950. Then, a critique of learning theories in general will be presented, and finally, an attempt will be made to formulate what may be some of the lasting positive contributions of the research in this area.

Ebbinghaus

Hermann Ebbinghaus (1850-1909) was awarded a doctorate in philosophy in 1873 and then continued his studies in several places in Germany. He also spent three years in France and England. While in Paris he got hold of a copy of Fechner's *Elemente der Psychophysik*, which made a deep impression on him. He wanted to enlarge the scope of experimental psychology to include also the so-called 'higher mental processes' and of these he selected memory as being particularly promising. Some of the earlier associationistic philosophers had regarded memory as a phenomenon involving degrees of completeness or clarity and thereby as potentially measurable. Especially they had emphasized the frequency of repetition as an important determinant of how much is remembered. Ebbinghaus thus formulated the question *how can one measure memory* (in analogy to Fechner's how can one measure sensation) and he arrived at an original and elegant solution.

In order to study how associations are formed and are retained over time, it was necessary to have a material nearly completely free from previous associations. If certain items are already associated with each other to an unknown degree, one cannot determine the exact effect of repetitions on learning and memory. Ebbinghaus solved the problem by constructing syllables from two consonants with an intervening vowel, such as NIT, KEB, ZAR, and excluding all those that had a meaning in the German language. In this way he arrived at a material of more than two thousand *nonsense syllables,* of which he made lists to be learned and remembered. He served as his own subject and learned lists of nonsense syllables by reading them again and again at a constant speed. As measures of work required to learn, amount learned, and memory, he used respectively the number of repeated readings of a list, the number of syllables correctly remembered, and the important method of savings. The method of savings involved determination of how many repetitions were necessary to relearn an earlier learned list to perfection. This number was then subtracted from the number of repetitions required to learn the list the first time, and in this way one got an estimate of how much saving was involved in the second relearning.

Like Fechner, Ebbinghaus soon discovered that his various measures were *statistical* rather than exact magnitudes. Even when all syllables were meaningless, speed of presentation was constant, and the person identical (Ebbinghaus himself), different 10-syllable lists required different numbers of repetitions and the relearning after equal intervals also required a variable number of repetitions. The results consequently had to be given as *averages* of more or less wide *distributions* of measures, and thus statistical analysis also in this area became an integral part of psychological experiments from the very beginning.

One of the first problems Ebbinghaus posed concerned the relationship between the length of a list and the number of repetitions required to learn it by heart to perfection. He found that he could learn lists of 7 or 8 syllables with one reading. This was the first experimental determination of the so-called *memory span* which has come to be regarded as an important entity in theoretical psychology. It apparently reflects the same absolute limitation of the capacity to absorb information as we have already described in the discussion of recognition (p. 173). Ebbinghaus also found that as he increased the length of the list, the number of necessary repetitions increased very rapidly.

Starting from the notion that learning and memory were continuous magnitudes, another question was about the effect of so-called *overlearning* on memory measured by the method of savings. Overlearning means that one continues to repeat a list after one has learned to reproduce it without errors. Ebbinghaus found that the more overlearning he used the better was his retention.

Another question which Ebbinghaus sought to answer was how forgetting occurs as a function of time. The result was a very simple curve: forgetting was very rapid in the first few minutes after the learning, very slow in the first few hours, and practically nonexistent over longer intervals (days and weeks). This curve made at least as much impression on readers as Fechner's formula had made earlier, and it further strengthened the belief that psychology could become an exact quantitative science.

Ebbinghaus also studied the effect on speed of learning and on retention of reading a list repeatedly and continuously and of reading it with pauses between the repetitions. This variable has come to be known as the one of *massed v. distributed practice*. Ebbinghaus concluded that he learned faster, i.e. with fewer repetitions, when he inserted pauses between repetitions than when he practiced without breaks.

Finally, it should be mentioned that he compared learning and memory of nonsense syllables with learning and memory of meaningful material of various sorts. He found that the meaningful material (words, prose passages, poetry) is learned much faster and is remembered much better than the meaningless. Ebbinghaus was the first one who was able to study learning experimentally and to show how the effect of experience on the mind could be studied with quantitative methods under controlled conditions. In 1885 Ebbinghaus published his results in a small monograph with the title *Über das Gedächtnis.* This elegant and clearly written work, packed with new data, was very widely read and rapidly led to an explosive development in the study of learning and memory.

Thorndike

Edward Lee Thorndike (1874-1949) studied for some years with William James at Harvard. His first research interests were in animal psychology, which up to then had not been the scene of systematic experiments. One of Thorndike's earliest projects as a student was a systematic study of intelligence in chickens. His landlady objected to the presence of the chickens in his room, and since there was no laboratory at the university he was allowed to keep them in the basement of William James' house. Later Thorndike moved to Columbia University, and his thesis, entitled *Animal Intelligence: An Experimental Study of Associative Processes in Animals,* was published in 1898. Thorndike had, among other things, constructed 15 different problem boxes for cats. The cat was placed in the box and could only escape by pulling a cord, pushing a button, stepping on a certain place, etc. As an additional incentive to escape, food was provided outside the box. Thorndike observed the cat's behavior when it tried to escape and recorded how long a time it needed for each repeated trial. He noted that, in the beginning, the cat tried all kinds of behaviors such as pushing, scratching, biting, etc. Finally it gave the correct response by accident and was able to escape. On the next trial there would typically again be a number of 'random' and irrelevant behaviors, but on the average the solution time was shorter in the second trial, still shorter in the third, etc. until the cat was able to make the correct movement immediately upon being placed in the box. Thorndike labeled this process 'learning by trial-and-error' and explained it as a result of the rewarding effect of escaping and getting food. The satisfaction following immediately upon the correct movements led, according to Thorndike, to an automatic strengthening of the tendency to make these movements, whereas the lack of reward after the other movements led to a weakening of these.

Thorndike was an associationist, or as he said, a 'connectionist'. He once formulated his general view as follows:

If I attempt to analyze a man's entire mind, I find connections of varying strength between (a) situations, elements of situations, and compounds of situations and (b) responses, readinesses to respond, facilitations, inhibitions, and directions of responses. If all these could be completely inventoried, telling what the man would think and do and what would satisfy and annoy him, in every conceivable situation, it seems to me that nothing would be left out ... Learning is connecting. The mind is man's connection-system. (Thorndike, 1931.)

Thorndike first proposed the following two laws to account for the formation of connection. *The Law of Exercise:* The more often a given situation is followed by a particular response, the stronger will be the associative bond between them. In other words, repetition makes perfect. *The Law of Effect:* If a response leads to a satisfying state of affairs, it will tend to be repeated when the situation arises again. Superficially these two laws seem to make good sense — it is well known in everyday life that repetition and reward can serve to shape behavior and control learning. Yet there are serious problems with them, and Thorndike himself showed that the first law is not valid and that the second law is problematic in so far as its negative (punishment) aspect is concerned. The classic demonstration of the futility of the Law of Exercise is to blindfold the subject and ask him to draw lines just as long as a model line he has just been shown. As long as the subject is not allowed to compare the length of the lines he has drawn with the length of the model, he obviously cannot make any improvement even with hundreds of repetitions. Thus the Law of Exercise falls back on the Law of Effect, in the sense that learning can take place only when the outcome is allowed to influence the learner. Thorndike also modified the Law of Effect in so far as he tried to show that the effect of unpleasant outcomes (punishment) was not to weaken response tendencies to the same extent that pleasant outcomes strengthen them. Thorndike's experiments on punishment have been criticized and it has been shown later that the effects of punishment are highly complex and depend on many factors.

Thorndike was an associationist but his psychology combined this with a psychology of feelings and motives. Reward and punishment were seen as crucial in every learning process. Thorndike became very much occupied with educational psychology and was highly influential in this area. The task in educating children was to teach them to make certain connections between situations and responses and this could be done by an appropriate distribution of rewards and punishments. These words are here taken in a very wide sense. For Thorndike reward usually meant such things as an affirmation, a nod or an 'Mm' by the teacher, and punishment would be a correction, head-shaking, or a stern glance.

Pavlov

The Russian physiologist Ivan Petrovich Pavlov (1849-1936) was awarded the Nobel Prize in 1904 for his experimental studies of the digestive glands. The success of these studies mainly derived from the new techniques he used. The traditional method was to operate upon the animal (under anesthesia) in order to lay bare the glands and study their function. However, the anesthesia and the operation had a tendency to inhibit the very processes one was interested in observing. Pavlov solved this problem by inserting a tube from the organ under investigation to the surface of the body, in such a way that the secretion could be gathered, measured, and analyzed. When the wound was healed and the animal restituted, one could then proceed to study the secretion of a healthy animal under normal conditions.

In 1897 Pavlov published his main work on the function of the digestive glands. In this work he mentioned certain irregularities in the glandular function which seemed to have psychic causes. He observed that the salivary glands began to secrete even before the animal was fed, e.g. when the man who usually fed the animal came into the room. Pavlov was very long in doubt about whether or not these psychic secretions, as he called them, could be experimentally investigated and whether or not this would be a fruitful project. Finally in 1902, he decided to go ahead.

His first studies were done simply by showing a piece of bread to a dog and then letting it eat it. Soon the dog started to salivate when a piece of bread was shown. If one later on started to show pieces of bread to the dog without letting him eat them, salivation gradually diminished and finally disappeared completely. Pavlov labeled the salivation in response to food in the mouth an *unconditional* (i.e. innate) response. The salivation at the sight of the food, however, was a learned response, and since the condition for its occurrence was an association between the sight of food and the experience of having food in the mouth, he labeled it a *conditional* response. (Today, the terms unconditioned and conditioned are used instead of unconditional and conditional and the modern terminology will be adopted here.) The experience of food in the mouth is called an unconditioned stimulus and the sight of food a conditioned stimulus. It soon became apparent that conditioned responses could be elicited by an almost limitless number of stimuli in the animal's surroundings, and in order to study the phenomena under maximally controlled conditions, Pavlov devised a soundproof chamber where the animal (usually a dog) was placed in a harness. The presentation of the stimuli (most frequently sounds), the feeding of the animal, and the registration of the secretion were all mechanically controlled from an adjacent room, from which one could also observe the animal unseen.

From 1902 to his death in 1936 Pavlov worked systematically to map out the factors that influenced the process of conditioning. Some of the main results may be summarized as follows:

1. The process of conditioning occurs most rapidly when the conditioned stimulus immediately precedes the unconditioned stimulus.

2. When a conditioned stimulus is well established, it may be used as an unconditioned stimulus to establish salivary secretion to a new conditioned stimulus. Example: Salivation is conditioned to a sound, then one may establish salivation e.g. to a light, if this is repeatedly presented immediately before the sound. A precondition for this process, called *higher order conditioning,* is that one continues to give food at the end.

3. If the presentation of the unconditioned stimulus (food) after the conditioned stimulus is discontinued, the conditioned salivation will gradually diminish and finally disappear. This is called experimental *extinction.* After an interval of some hours or days, one may observe that some conditioned salivation reappears, only to be rapidly re-extinguished if the unconditioned stimulus is withheld. This *spontaneous recovery* may also be called forth if a distracting irrelevant stimulus is presented in conjunction with the original conditioned stimulus.

4. Conditioning was used by Pavlov and later by others to determine psychophysical thresholds. This may be done by giving the dog food after a sound of a given frequency, but not after the sound of another frequency. In the beginning one observes salivation also to other frequencies than to the one used in the original conditioning. This Pavlov called *generalization.* After a period of systematic conditioning to one frequency and extinction to others, salivation to the latter disappears, and a *discrimination* has been established. By making the difference between the stimuli followed by food and the stimuli not followed by food smaller and smaller one may determine the threshold value below which no discrimination can be established. Here is a purely behavioral parallel to the concept of a just noticeable difference originally developed by Fechner and his followers to study subjective experiences.

5. Pavlov observed that if a dog was given a discrimination problem which could not be solved, because the difference involved was well below the discrimination threshold, it sometimes exhibited signs of a nervous breakdown. Dogs which were given food when they saw an ellipse and no food when they saw a circle, became excited and un-

controlled when they had been shown ellipses which were very nearly a circle, for some weeks. They barked, bit their harness, tried to bite the experimenter, got scared by sudden sounds, and generally exhibited unusual and disorganized behavior. This was called an *experimental neurosis* and led Pavlov to speculate that perhaps many psychiatric conditions in humans derived originally from insoluble problems in their daily lives.

All his life Pavlov was occupied with experiments on limited and well-defined problems. They led him gradually all the way from digestive processes to psychiatric problems. In his old age he became aware of the particularly complex processes underlying language, which he called 'the second signal system'. He thought this system was somehow super-imposed on the system of more elementary conditioned responses.

The Golden Age of learning theories

During the 1930's and 1940's a new generation of American experimental psychologists, trained in the traditions established by the pioneers and working mostly with animals, dominated the scene. They believed that it was possible to arrive at fairly simple and completely general theories of learning formulated in objective and quantitative terms. The theories were envisaged to consist of mathematical functions between measured independent variables such as number of repetitions of stimulus condi-tions, measures of motivation such as time since last feeding, etc., and measured dependent variables such as probability, frequency, latency, and amplitude of responses. In between the antecedent and the conse-quent variables one frequently envisaged different sorts of intervening variables or hypothetical constructs referring to processes within the organism. By means of experiments within a physicalistic and behavior-istic framework one expected to be able to discover the network of equations that would make it possible to predict learning. For a presenta-tion and comparison of the most popular theories at that time, see Hilgard (1954). Here it must suffice to present central excerpts from some of the most influential approaches in order to communicate some flavor of the world of yesterday.

First, two of the postulates in Clark L. Hull's theory (Hilgard, 1956 p. 128):

Postulate 3. Primary reinforcement. When a response (R) is closely associated with a stimulus trace (s) and this stimulus-response conjunction is associated with a rapid decrease in drive-produced stimuli (S_D) there will result an increase in the tendency for that stimulus trace (s) to evoke that response (R).

The rapid decrease in the goal stimulus (S_G) is also reinforcing.

186

(Hilgard, p. 131):

Postulate 4. Habit strength (sHr) as a function of reinforcement. Habit strength (the tendency for a stimulus trace to evoke an associated response) increases as a positive growth function of the number of trials, provided that trials are evenly spaced, reinforcement occurs on every trial, and everything else remains constant.

The exact form of the curve is given as $sHr = 1 - 10^{-aN}$, where N is the number of trials and a is a constant $= .03$.

Another example is taken from Voeks' formalization of E. R. Guthrie's theory (Hilgard, 1956, p. 70):

Postulate 1. Principle of Association.

(a) Any stimulus-pattern which once accompanies a response, and/or immediately precedes it (by ½ second or less), becomes a full-strength direct cue for that response. (b) This is the only way in which stimulus-patterns not now cues for a particular response can become direct cues for that response.

Postulate 2: Principle of Postremity.

(a) A stimulus which has accompanied or immediately preceded two or more incompatible responses is a conditioned stimulus for only the last response made while that stimulus was present. (b) This is the only way in which a stimulus now a cue for a particular response can cease being a cue for that response.

Finally, one example will be given from McCorquodale and Meehl's formalization of E. C. Tolman's theory: (Estes et al. 1954, pp. 237-238).

Mnemonization. — The occurrence of the sequence $S_1 - R_1 - S_2$ (the adjacent members being in close temporal contiguity) results in an increment in the strength of an expectancy $(S_1R_1S_2)$. The strength increases as a decelerated function of the number of occurrences of the sequence. The growth rate is an increasing function of the absolute value of the valence of S_2. If the termination by S_2 of the sequence $S_1 - R_1$ is random with respect to non-defining properties of S_1, the asymptote of strength is $\leq$ the relative frequency P of S, following $S_1 - R_1$ (i.e. a pure number). How far this asymptote is below P is a decelerated function of the delay between the inception of R_1 and the occurrence of S_2.

The preceding excerpts should give an impression of the kind of theorizing resorted to in those not so distant years. It was taken for granted that, given the external physical situation and some immediate antecedents, one could successfully and generally predict learning (conceptualized as changes in behavior). It appears reasonable to see this as a repetition, at a more complex level, of the similar efforts of the psychophysicists to predict from external stimuli to experience. The analogy becomes even more plausible when we note that in learning, as in psychophysics, there has been a sobering up due to a belated recognition of factors and circumstances that are quite familiar from our daily lives and in common-sense thinking. There has been in all fields of psychology a gradual return from a premature and dissociated 'science play' to a reconsideration of what we all know in advance about mental phenomena.

Critique of learning theories

The critique to be presented will be directed simultaneously at all the classical learning theories originating in the thirties, forties, and fifties, since they all involved a behavioristic/physicalistic conceptual framework. The group of theories dealing with cognitive and affective incompatibility will be treated separately (see p. 197). The following concrete situation will be used to introduce the arguments: The subject is placed in front of a wall with a certain number of small drawers. The fronts of the drawers have more or less discriminable designs, one for each drawer.

The subject looks at the drawers, then selects one, pulls it open, sees a raisin, eats it, and finally lets go of the drawer which closes automatically. There is no need here to analyze the different ways in which different learning theories will analyze this sequence and describe what has been learned. It suffices to note that they all predict something and that they all imply a belief that there must exist predictability. The crucial point here is, what does the subject do next? On what basis can this be predicted?

One possibility is that he regards the selected drawer (and perhaps the other drawers as well) as belonging to a kind of slot machine and that each time he pulls out a drawer he will get a raisin. In this case his tendency to open the same drawer again may be *strengthened*. Implicit in this may be a belief that there is some kind of *causal* mechanism involved, such that when you let go of the drawer and it shuts automatically, a new raisin is dropped into it, etc. However, another equally plausible prediction is that the subject's tendency to open the selected drawer will now be *weakened,* since he has eaten the raisin and does not expect any technical miracles. In this case he will act on an hypothesis of exhaustible rather than inexhaustible supply and start opening other drawers, avoiding the one first selected. If asked, he will venture the prediction that the first selected drawer is now empty. Finally, it is possible that he (if he is a research-wise psychology student) believes the drawers are part of a randomization machine (especially if someone has whispered this in his ear). In this case his tendency to open the same drawer may *not be changed in any systematic way.* If new supplies of raisins are seen as randomly distributed in the system, he may have no definite expectancy of finding or not finding another one upon reopening the drawer. Contiguous events that do not become associated are abundant in daily life. If your doorbell sounds immediately after you have started to munch a delicious apple, you do not learn to associate apple eating with doorbells. Likewise, if, once in a while, you hear a siren on the street while sipping your coffee, this leads to no particular future expectancy. Events are associated only if they are conceived as potentially 'belonging' together (cf. the discussion of common sense, p. 107).

The preceding comments may be summarized in the following conclusion: The temporal contiguity of external events as such, even taken for granted that they are followed by proper reinforcement (see below) does not permit prediction of local learning effects, i.e. the strengthening or weakening of response tendencies or expectancies. Predictions are only possible when we know how the events are experienced by the subject. In other words, we cannot know what a subject has learned from the experience of event sequences unless we know his perception, cognition, and evaluation of these events. This again is typically not predictable from physical properties of the stimuli.

Another distinction that was frequently ignored by the learning theorists is between memory of events and later behavior. Our subject may very well answer 'yes' to the question 'did you find a raisin in the drawer?' In other words, independently of local changes in tendency to respond or expect, there may be learning in the sense of retention and interpretation of past events. This retention, although having no particular local consequences, may be useful, e.g. in the search for patterns in the distribution of raisins — 'a raisin in every other drawer', etc. More generally, most human subjects distinguish between past, present, and future events and the effects of their experiences may be different in these different modalities.

The Law of Belonging

Let us now consider for a while the general statement that *only to the extent that events are conceived as potentially belonging together can they become associated in our experience.* Belonging is a descriptive common-sense category that was adopted and elaborated by Thorndike and by the Gestalt psychologists and essentially means that events are experienced as forming a whole, as being parts of the same whole. But this means that they are associated with each other in the sense of tending to evoke expectancies and images of each other. Obviously, we have here something very close to circularity as far as learning is concerned, and in so far as belonging cannot be independently estimated. However, before proceeding to discuss this, let us add that belonging can also be and perhaps usually is the *result* of learning. If one learns that two categories of events tend to occur together, this means precisely that they are, after that, seen as belonging together.

In order to reach a more definite conclusion with respect to the relationship between belonging as a precondition for and as an outcome of learning it may be helpful to consider a concrete example.

Suppose that you switch on the lights in your living room and that, at the same time, your door bell rings faintly. You go to the door, but no one is there. You infer that some kids have been playing a practical joke or that someone made a mistake and went away. The episode is dismissed and no particular expectancies are formed, but the events are retained in memory. Two hours later you switch off the lights in your living room and again your doorbell rings faintly. You walk to the door and find no one there. Twice is too much and a suspicion dawns on you. Next, you switch on the living room lights and again the door bell rings. For good measure you switch the lights off with another ensuing ring, and you start cursing the electrician who had been in such a hurry.

In this example, repeated contiguity created belonging. Yet, it could only do so rapidly because you already had a vague conception of induction currents, etc., and because you remembered that the electrician had been there that day, etc. If there is no previous tendency to belonging, repeated coincidences of event categories may conceivably remain undetected forever. In an experiment by the author (Smedslund, 1961), subjects were asked to estimate numbers on the back side of cards by looking at certain complexly varied stimulus configurations. Subjects tried hard for up to 4800 stimulus presentations without discovering the fairly simple relationships involved. Proof that the task did not overtax human capacity was given by the informal observation that subjects who where *told* what to look for, rapidly became fairly adept at estimating the numbers. In this highly artificial situation none of the tendencies to experience belonging happened to coincide with what was to be learned.

Conclusion: We seem to be forced into a rather paradoxical position. On the one hand, the relationship between belonging and learning is probably tautological in the sense that it cannot be otherwise and that it cannot be empirically falsified. On the other hand, the relationship is useful since knowing something about the kind of belongings that are likely to and possibly can occur to the subject, helps predict learning. Strictly speaking, we do not know empirically that it helps, but rather it follows logically that it should. We are *'projecting implications into the future'*. If we know that a subject can group red objects together and can recognize how they are similar when grouped by others, and that he can do the same with respect to round objects, we expect that he will be able to learn that in a given universe all red objects are round and vice versa. Conversely, if the subject is unable to group 'diatrope' objects together, and cannot recognize what they have in common as distinct from other objects when they are assembled by others, and when he is similarly unable to recognize 'proxypede' objects, then we expect that he will not learn that in a given universe all diatrope objects are proxypede and vice versa. If he learns after all, we simply conclude that our premises must have been, or have turned, wrong. The learning of an association between two categories logically presupposes recognition of these categories. Thus we find that there exists a kind of logic of change.

The Law of Effect

Having discussed the contiguity part of learning theories we shall now consider the effect or reinforcement part. A great many theorists, of which we have mentioned Thorndike and Hull, have regarded some versions of the Law of Effect as the basic principle of learning. The law states that the tendency of behavior to recur is influenced by the immediately succeeding events. One usually distinguishes between three main types of effects, namely positive reinforcement (reward), negative reinforcement (punishment), and nonreinforcement (extinction).

We have already noted that the law of effect cannot be generally valid. The subject in our initial example with the drawers may be pleased by eating the raisin (positive reinforcement) and may continue to want raisins, yet the tendency to look into the same drawer may not be strengthened. In order to obtain the strengthening effect we must manipulate the subject's general cognition of the situation, e.g. by telling him that he is dealing with a slot machine. Another difficulty which must be circumvented is that we cannot know from the physical properties of raisins that the subject will like them. More generally, what is a reinforcer to a given subject is largely a matter of *historical* circumstances, some of which may be shared by everyone or almost everyone in a given culture or subculture, whereas others may be peculiar to this individual. In order to be certain that a demonstration of the Law of Effect will work one should ask the subject whether or not he likes raisins. If the answer is that he detests them but that he loves salted peanuts, then one should put salted peanuts in the drawers. In conclusion, the Law of Effect works only given very specific cognitive and motivational preconditions.

The Skinner box, devised by the best-known contemporary proponent of the Law of Effect, B. F. Skinner, neatly illustrates the preceding. It consists of a darkened sound-resisting box containing only a brass lever, which, if pressed, delivers a pellet of food, which falls with a clearly audible sound. Since the box contains nothing else, there is only one strategy open to the rat, namely to press the lever repeatedly. This takes care of the cognitive precondition. The food pellets are of a type that are attractive to virtually all members of the rat species investigated, and they are so small that a hungry rat does not get satiated by one or a few pellets. Hence the motivation precondition is guaranteed, and as a consequence the law of effect works.

Here is one of Skinner's descriptions, using a pigeon as subject:

An effective classrom demonstration of the Law of Effect may be arranged in the following way. A pigeon, reduced to 80 per cent of its ad lib weight, is habituated to a small semi-circular amphitheatre and is fed there for several days from a food hopper, which the experimenter presents by closing a hand switch. The demonstration consists of establishing a selected response by suitable reinforcement with food. For example, by sighting across the amphitheatre at a scale on the opposite wall, it is possible to present the hopper whenever the top of the pigeon's head rises above a given mark. Higher and higher marks are chosen until, within a few minutes, the pigeon is walking about the cage with its head held as high as possible. In another demonstration the bird is conditioned to strike a marble placed on the floor of the amphitheatre. This may be done in a few minutes by reinforcing successive steps. Food is presented first when the bird is merely moving near the marble, later when it looks down in the direction of the marble, later still when it moves its head toward the marble, and finally when it pecks it. Anyone who has seen such a demonstration knows that the Law of Effect is no theory. It simply specifies a procedure for altering the probability of a chosen response. (Skinner, 1950, p. 200)

Although this quotation does not explicitly discuss the preconditions, they are nevertheless present. The demonstration may require 'laboratory-wise' pigeons of certain strains, and, anyhow, is carefully tailored to the cognitive capacities and inclinations of the given species. The motivation precondition is ensured by the weight-reduction and by the smallness of the food pellets delivered. What, then, is the scientific status of the Law of Effect?

The logical structure of the Law of Effect may be formulated as follows: If an action A in situation S is followed by a certain event B, and B is a reinforcer (positive), then the probability of A in S increases. A reinforcer is defined as an event which increases the probability of preceding actions. As formulated in the two preceding statements it is clear that the Law of Effect is circular and empirically empty.

The possible circularity of the Law has been a matter of dispute ever since the time of Thorndike (Postman, 1947), and there has been no clear consensus, probably because it is simultaneously felt to be circular *and* useful.

Some twenty years ago Meehl (1950) attempted to rescue the Law by the following argument: A reinforcer is that part of a situation that causes increments in a response tendency. A learnable response is any response that can be modified as a function of exposure to a situation. A trans-situational reinforcer is a reinforcer that affects all learnable responses. Given these definitions, Meehl formulated the following two laws which in his opinion were non-circular:

'All reinforcers are trans-situational (The Weak Law of Effect)' and 'Every increment in strength involves a trans-situational reinforcer (The Strong Law of Effect)' (Meehl, 1950, p. 73).

Meehl's arguments seem to have two flaws which make them invalid. Let us first consider the Weak Law. If a reinforcer X is *not* trans-situational, it means that it is effective e.g. in a situation Y, but not in a situation Z. But this also means that there must be aspects of situation Y, other than X, which are not present in Z, and which explain the difference in outcome. However, these must by definition be included in the delimitation of the reinforcer. To give a concrete example, if soaked food-pellets lead to learning, whereas dry pellets do not, this means that the state of being soaked is part of the definition of the reinforcer. Hence, it is incorrect to say that food-pellets are not trans-situational reinforcers. Rather one must say that soaked food-pellets are reinforcers, and the very criterion of this being a true definition of the reinforcer, lies in the fact that it continues to be valid when other aspects of the situation are varied. Hence, a reinforcer must by definition be trans-situational. If it is not, it is, by definition, not properly described. This consideration seems to deprive the Weak Law of Effect of any empirical content.

The Strong Law of Effect was formulated as follows. 'Every increment in strength involves a trans-situational reinforcer.' The argument that this also is empty runs as follows: Every increment in strength 'as a function of behavior in exposure to a situation' (Meehl, 1950, p. 73) is presumably *caused* by something in that situation (keeping the argument within Meehl's physicalistic-behavioristic terminology). However, whatever is causing the increment by definition is a reinforcer, and we have already pointed out that every reinforcer must be trans-situational.

Hence the effort of Meehl to save the Law of Effect appears to have failed.

It remains to explain why we have such a strong experience of usefulness in connection with this Law. The answer can only be that the Law reflects the way in which we *must* think about (conceptualize) mental change. If A has once *led to* B and the subject *remembers* this and *believes* that this is still true, and the subject *wants* B, then the subject will do A again. The 'procedure' for altering response probability that Skinner talks about (see quotation, p. 192) simply consists in making as certain as possible that all the premises for change are present. Then we simply 'project the implications into the future', i.e. rely on the logic of change. From this point of view, the psychology of learning is concerned with how we can give the subject optimal possibilities and optimal reasons for change in a given direction, which, in other words, means increasing the probability that he *can* do it and that he will *try* to do it. Applying the Law of Effect means imagining a set of conditions under which the sought-for behavior would necessarily occur, and then simply trying to bring about these conditions. Our common sense (cf. Chapters V and VI) provides the specification of the conditions.

Theories of transfer

Ever since the beginning of the study of learning, the problem of transfer has been a central concern, both theoretically and practically. How does a given learning process affect performance in other areas, how does it affect other later learning processes, and how is it, itself, affected by other previous learning processes?

Pavlov noted that if a response such as salivation was conditioned to a stimulus, e.g. sound of a certain pitch, the animal also responded with salivation to sounds of other pitches. The amount of salivation tended to decrease as the difference between the original and the new pitch increased. Hull included a similar principle in his general theory, assuming that habit strength decreases as a regular function of stimulus difference measured in j.n.d.'s or log units. In general, the independent variable in all theories of transfer has been some measure of *psychological similarity*.

In what follows, we will disregard all the complications involved in such distinctions as between positive and negative effects, retroactive and proactive effects, stimulus similarity and response similarity, mediated transfer, etc., and simply confine the discussion to the general phenomenon of transfer as such.

Similarity is typically measured by having a group of judges, other than the subjects in the transfer study proper, calibrate the learning materials by means of some psychophysical scaling method. The outcome of the transfer study (various measures of number of errors, trials to perfection, etc.) is then related to the similarity scale, and empirical functions are described. At first sight, this may appear as completely straightforward empirical research. However, there are several underlying assumptions which must be made explicit before one can conclude anything about the status of these studies. First, the use of an independent group of judges for establishing a similarity scale presupposes that the judges are a representative sample from the same population as the experimental subjects. In other words, it is presupposed that the experimental subjects themselves would have generated the same similarity scale if they had been asked to. Otherwise the study would make no sense. The reason why an independent group of judges is used is simply to avoid possible complicating familiarization and learning effects in the subjects.

Actually, then, a transfer study investigates the relation between the subjective similarity between two sets of materials and the degree to which there is facilitation or interference between the processes of learning these two sets. In order to clarify the discussion, an hypothetical and simplified, but concrete example is given in Figure 13.

Condition I		Condition II	
TAR — GEB		TAR — GEB	
TIR — LOK		TID — LOK	

Figure 13. Simple interference paradigm.

We suppose that the paired associates given are imbedded in lists of paired associates to be learned. The subject's task is (in condition I) to say 'GEB' when he sees 'TAR' and to say 'LOK' when he sees 'TIR', etc. Let us assume that the distance on the subjective similarity scale between TAR and TIR is clearly smaller than the distance between TAR and TID, but that the (stimulus-response) distances between TIR and LOK and between TID and LOK are the same. Given these, and perhaps some other, in this connection, trivial assumptions, transfer theories will predict that there will be more interference between the learning of the two paired associates in conditions I than in condition II.

The status of this prediction depends on the meaning of the terms 'similarity' and 'interference'. The highest possible degree of similarity is obviously *identity,* which means that no discrimination can occur. In attempting to identify two things with perfectly identical appearances one will be in error 50 per cent of the time. As similarity decreases the things become easier to discriminate and hence the percentage of errors decreases. The term 'interference' in our example concretely refers to the number of errors in identification made during the process of learning, such as answering 'LOK' when being shown 'TAR' in cond. I, etc. Obviously we have here, once again, a relationship which is *basically circular.* We predict the actual relative number of errors from estimates implying (logically) the relative number of errors to be expected. The form of the relationship obtained depends on a number of circumstances such as the kind of materials used, the particular way in which measures are obtained, etc. Furthermore, the logic involved is not as simple as it may appear at first glance. Predictions vary not only with variations in stimulus similarity as in the given example, but also with varying response similarity, stimulus-response similarity, and with interactions of these, etc. The first comprehensive summary of the relations involved was given by Osgood (1949) and depicted in his famous 'transfer and retro-action surface'. A paper by Martin (1965) synthesizes many later developments and further complications.

However, it remains true that the insights have been gained by elaborating the implicit logic of similarity rather than by the discovery of empirical laws. The empirical research probably has functioned a) as an aid to thinking and a check that nothing has been overlooked, and b) as a check on the validity of the techniques employed. The basic assumptions of transfer theories are not testable, and failure to obtain expected results is always attributed to faulty techniques and designs. The impression that the transfer theories are meaningful and useful reflects the structure of our common-sense conceptual framework. Similarity (and its opposite, difference) is a dimension which we, unavoidably, use in describing how things are related in appearance. The so-called theories of transfer simply spell out and demonstrate the implications of this concept in the area of learning.

Dissonance theory

Given a wide definition of learning as mental change as a function of experience, there remains one influential type of psychological theory to be discussed. This type of theory regards change as principally a function of the compatibility between different part-processes in a person (whether these be cognitions or feelings). In this category belong among others, Festinger's (1957) cognitive *dissonance* theory, Heider's (1958) *balance* theory, Osgood and Tannenbaum's (1955) theory of *congruence,* and Piaget's theory of *equilibration* in mental development (Piaget and Inhelder, 1966). According to all these theories (and variants of them) mental change results not only from experience of contiguities or reinforcements, but also from incompatibilities induced by the experienced situations.

Here cognitive dissonance theory is selected for discussion. The theory deals with *cognitions* (beliefs, meanings, information). Examples: (1) 'Smoking is dangerous', (2) 'I smoke', (3) 'My new car is too expensive for me to maintain', (4) 'I made a mistake buying it'. The relationships between the cognitive elements can be of three kinds, *consonance, dissonance,* and *irrelevance.* Elements (3) and (4) above are consonant, (1) and (2) are dissonant, and the remaining relationships, (1) and (3), (1) and (4), and (2) and (4), are irrelevant. The similarity between these categories and those proposed on p. 82 should be recognized. Consonance corresponds exactly to equivalence and implication, dissonance to contradiction, and irrelevance is common to the two classifications.

The basic assumption in Festinger's theory is that people cannot tolerate cognitive dissonance and will strive to reduce it. Hence dissonance is a basic condition for change. The theory also allows for different degrees of dissonance. Dissonance is stronger (incites more strongly to change in the direction of consonance) the more *important* the elements involved are in the person's life. Thus a dissonance in one's conception of one's wife tends to be stronger than a similar dissonance in one's conception of the milkman. Dissonance is stronger the greater the ratio of dissonant to consonant elements, in other words, the greater the proportion of dissonant elements evoked in the given situation. This means that, given an initial simple dissonance such as (a) 'I am against the war in Vietnam' and (b) 'I am participating as a soldier in the war', the activation of the element 'I don't shoot at the enemy', consonant with (a) reduces the all-over dissonance and hence may act as a partial consolation. A third factor influencing degree of dissonance is the extent of cognitive overlap or *similarity* between the elements involved. Example: a decision to choose one of two cars is likely to cause less dissonance then a decision to choose a car over a boat, the reason being that the two cars are more similar than the car and the boat.

The numerous interesting refinements and implications of dissonance theory cannot be dealt with here. For general reviews of this kind of theory, see Brown (1965), Insko (1967), and Kiesler, Collins and Miller (1969).

At the end of this chapter we will mention some positive empirical contributions inspired by dissonance theory. However, here the task is to present a critical analysis. Most contemporary critics have taken their point of departure in a requirement that a theory should enable one to proceed in a mechanical way from given antecedent conditions via theoretical assumptions to prediction of concrete experimental outcomes. It has been generally concluded that cognitive dissonance theory is more or less inadequate for this purpose (like all other existing psychological theories). The independent, intervening, and dependent variables are so generally and vaguely defined that the linkage to specific and concrete observations is mostly a matter of intuitive preference. A symptom of this has been the occurrence of several public debates where different experimenters have drawn opposite conclusions from the theory.

Instead of joining the chorus of critics who attack the theory from the perspective that it should be empirically testable, we will here take a different point of view. Consider the basic assumption of the theory, namely that if two cognitive elements are dissonant there will occur attempts at dissonance reduction. We will assert that this assumption is not empirically testable, and, furthermore that it cannot be false, within any of the two main conceptual frameworks now in use for the study of man.

Within a physicalistic/behavioristic framework man is seen as a self-regulating biological system, i.e. as a system where deviations from the system-defining values are corrected by negative feedback. Within this frame of reference the obvious way to interpret dissonance is as deviation from the system defining norms, i.e. as states incompatible with and destructive to other parts of the system. Now, it follows from the definition of a self-maintaining system that deviations are corrected by negative feedback, which diminishes them. In our interpretation this means that dissonance must be followed by attempts at dissonance reduction.

In the humanistic frame of reference adopted in this book, intentionality is accepted as a basic characteristic of mental life. This means that every mental activity has a goal (the limiting case being the goal of maintaining the activity itself). It follows from this that if person P now strives to reach goal G, and is concerned with no other goals, then he will do nothing that to him is incompatible with reaching G. If he is forced to or otherwise happens to do something that appears dissonant with reaching G, then it follows from the premise that he tries to reach

198

G, that he will try to reduce the dissonance. If there were no tendency to reduce dissonance, there could be no cognitive order, nor any behavioral order, no communication, etc.

A simplified version of the logical structure involved would be: Premise 1, O is a person (or O is an organism). Premise 2, dissonance occurs in O. From these two premises it follows necessarily that there will occur attempts at (tendencies to) dissonance reduction.

The reader who feels that the preceding, admittedly brief and superficial, arguments are not entirely convincing, should attempt to argue consistently for the opposite position, namely that one can conceive of people as we know them, *without* a tendency to reduce dissonance. This should turn out to be an impossible task.

In summary, cognitive dissonance theory is probably necessarily true, and, hence, untestable within any existing frame of reference for studying psychology. It simply represents an important consequence of our basic assumptions; it is part of the network within which we interpret mental events.

One final remark: even though it is generally true that situations which induce dissonance must lead to mental change, there remains an important qualification. Sometimes it appears as if the dissonant, the conflicting, the confusing and uncertain itself becomes a goal — the pleasure of risk-taking, of paradoxes, the pleasure of destruction and negation. For various approaches to these phenomena see Fiske and Maddi (1961), Berlyne (1965) and Goffman (1967, pp. 149-270).

Some positive contributions of learning psychology

From the preceding critique of learning theories it may appear as if students of learning have returned to common sense after having realized the futility of playing natural scientists, but without any positive insight. This is by no means the case. Actually, the prolonged efforts to understand the conditions of learning have produced many quite impressive achievements, some of them of definite practical value. Here are a few examples:

How shall one make sure something is remembered?

In our common-sense terminology this is a *can* problem, since we supposedly want to *try* to remember. We are then immediately reminded of the prominent role of the concept of *belonging* as far as the formation of associations is concerned. The task is to create wholes which incorporate the to-be-associated elements as parts. When this is done, the presentation of one of the elements is certain to bring up the whole, including the other elements to be remembered.

Some time ago the writer acquired new license plates for his car and the number was 37 20 92. Being a psychologist he then considered how to imbed these rather awkward numbers in a meaningful whole. Fairly soon he hit upon a solution: a well known popular song in Scandinavia at one point refers to a 20-year-old character named 'Kalle Petterson' and to his girl friend, a 37-year-old woman of uncertain virtue named 'Josefina'. Next, there is a well-known hero of a Norwegian comic strip named '91 Stomperud'. Common to the song and the comic strip is that they have a quite 'folksy', not very sophisticated character. From that moment the mention of the car number brought the image of 'Kalle Petterson and Josefina (reverse sequence)' and '91 Stomperud (+1)' and no forgetting occurred.

Now the reader should be ready for a little exercise of his own. The following task is adapted from Miller, Galanter and Pribram (1960, p. 135), but is just one out of innumerable possible variants that can be devised.

First memorize the following rhyme:

> one is a bun
> two is a shoe
> three is a tree
> four is a door
> five is a hive
> six are sticks
> seven is heaven
> eight is a gate
> nine is a line
> ten is a hen

This was an easy task since the number sequence is acquired earlier and the associates are rhymes. Next you should consider one at a time the following 10 numbered words (or better, make up your own list of any 10 words, each on a separate piece of paper). For each word think of some ludicrous or bizarre association (image) which links it with the corresponding word in the rhyme list. This means that you shall think of some image, context, or connection between ashtray and bun, between firewood and shoe, etc. Take the time you need. Here are the words to be remembered:

1. ashtray
2. firewood
3. picture
4. cigarette
5. table
6. matchbook
7. glass
8. lamp
9. shoe
10. phonograph

A little while after you finished you may try to answer questions such as what is number 4, what is number 7, what is number 1. The chances are that, if you have followed the instructions, you will reproduce all the ten words without error.

Some studies by Wallace, Turner and Perkins and later by others have shown that people's capacity for forming associations and retaining them is practically unlimited. Miller, Galanter and Pribram describe this study as follows (1960, pp. 136-137):

> They presented pairs of English words to their subjects, who proceeding at their own pace, formed a visual image connecting the two words. The list of paired associates was given only once. Then the subjects were given one member of each pair and asked to write the other. Starting with lists of twenty-five pairs they worked up to lists of 700 pairs of words. Up to 500 pairs, the subjects were remembering about ninety-nine per cent; at 700 pairs it dropped to ninety-five per cent. Ordinarily the subjects used about twenty-five seconds to form the association, but when they had become more experienced they could work accurately with less than five seconds per pair. The subjects were not selected for their special abilities; they were ordinary people, conveniently available for the experiment.

It is also mentioned that little was forgotten two or three days later.

It belongs to this story that experimental psychologists from Ebbinghaus on have consistently and forcefully *forbidden* their subjects to resort to any sort of mnemonic device, even including such things as rhythm of reading, stress on pronunciation, etc. Instead subjects were supposed to just 'associate' and under these conditions learning was slow and labored and forgetting fast, permitting the process to be described in terms of quantitative learning and forgetting curves.

People have always had some intuitive knowledge of how to improve remembering, but only after three quarters of a century have learning psychologists come around to formulating the principle explicitly. See also Bower (1969) and Paivio (1970).

How to extinguish excessive fears (phobias)

Psychologists interested in social learning (learning involving other persons) have achieved a number of impressive, wide-ranging, and highly useful results by analyzing systematically the basic conditions under which learning takes place. For a general overview of recent developments in the social learning tradition the reader is referred to Bandura (1969). Here we can give only one example of what has been achieved in this area:

For a long time it has been common knowledge among parents that if their child is afraid or otherwise reluctant to do something (e.g. take a new medicine), it may sometimes help if the parent or an older sibling first performs the required act joyously or at least without any signs of pain or displeasure. However, the method often fails, perhaps because of the time limits imposed by the requirements of our daily life ('we can't stand here and wait all day!'), and perhaps because the procedure is never very systematically and thoroughly analyzed.

Let us now consider this kind of problem in connection with excessive fear (phobia) of snakes. A study of this was conducted by Bandura, Blanchard and Ritter. The participants were people whose snake phobias in many cases unnecessarily restricted their lives. Some of them could not perform jobs if there was any remote possibility that they might come into contact with snakes, and others could not participate in activities such as hunting, gardening, camping, or hiking because of their fear of snakes, or avoided purchasing homes in rural areas. After an initial phase where the tendency to fear and avoid snakes as well at other characteristics of the subjects were recorded, the participants were divided into several groups with different extinction procedures. The most efficient procedure (live modeling with guided participation) was described as follows (Bandura, 1969, p. 185):

... at each step the experimenter himself performed fearless behavior and gradually led subjects into touching, stroking, and then holding the snake's body with first gloved and then bare hands, while he held the snake securely by the head and tail. If a subject was unable to touch the snake after ample demonstration, she was asked to place her hand on the experimenter's and to move her hand down gradually until it touched the snake's body. After subjects no longer felt any apprehension about touching the snake under these secure conditions, anxieties about contact with the snake's head and entwining tail were extinguished. The experimenter again performed the tasks fearlessly, and then he and the subject performed the responses jointly; as subjects became less fearful the experimenter gradually reduced his participation and control over the snake until subjects were able to hold the snake in their laps without assistance, to let the snake loose in the room and retrieve it, and to let it crawl freely over their bodies. Progress through the graded approach tasks was paced according to the subjects' apprehensiveness. When they reported being able to perform one activity with little or no fear, they were eased into a more difficult interaction.

Of the tests after the experiment Bandura reports:

Following completion of the treatment series the assessment procedures were readministered to all subjects. In order to determine the generality of extinction effects, half the subjects in each of the conditions were tested initially with the familiar brown-striped king snake and then with an unfamiliar crimson-splotched corn snake that was strikingly different in coloration; the remaining subjects were tested with the two snakes in the reverse order. The behavioral test consisted of a series of tasks requiring the subjects to approach, look at, touch, and hold a snake with bare and gloved hands; to remove the snake from its cage, let it loose in the room, and then replace it in the cage; to hold it within five inches of their faces; and finally to tolerate the snake in their laps while they held their hands passively at their sides. Immediately before and during the performance of each task subjects rated the intensity of their fear arousal on a 10-interval scale to measure extinction of affective arousal accompanying specific approach responses.

The conclusion of this study was that the procedure of live modelling combined with guided participation eliminated snake phobias in virtually all subjects (92 per cent).

This was an example of the rapidly growing number of studies within the so-called social learning or behavior therapy tradition. Despite their often awkward behavioristic terminology, a remnant from the Golden Age of learning theories, they are usually rather straightforward applications of common sense. If you are afraid of snakes because you think they are going to bite you, then an observation of a fearless model to whom nothing happens, followed by carefully graded handling of the snake should lead to decline in your fear. The study shows that it is technically feasible to carry out such an extinction, and the varying outcomes in the different experimental groups, and in other studies, make us progressively more aware of finer distinctions and considerations that need to be made.

How are people influenced in their attitudes and opinions?

The preceding examples have involved situations where the person *wants* to be a better memorizer or *wants* to get rid of his phobia and where the psychologist *helps* him to change in the desired direction. However, there are also numerous occasions where one is faced with the task of changing a person's attitudes and opinions, his likes and dislikes. In these cases, the person is to be influenced in ways that he has not himself asked for and planned. Examples would be such tasks as diminishing racial prejudice, getting people to change their food preferences (to get a more balanced diet), or getting them to buy a certain product. In many cases, the influencing of other persons may seem to be ethically problematic. However, it must be remembered that such influencing is a normal and unavoidable aspect of living and that it will go on whether one likes it or not. Furthermore, it is clear that influencing may take place for ethically defensible as well as for ethically more doubtful reasons, and that one should not condemn the study of influencing per se, because it may be misused. The brightest hopes of psychology, as well as its darkest fears, lie in this area.

In what follows, two examples will be given of techniques for changing attitudes. The first example concerns a situation where one has some power over the person to be changed, at least in so far as his overt actions are concerned.

How to get someone to like fried grasshoppers

One possibility allowed for by cognitive dissonance theory is that if a person A is forced by a person B to do something which is contrary to his attitude toward something C, then more change in A's attitude may result if B is seen as unpleasant than if he is seen as pleasant. The argument runs as follows: A will experience less dissonance doing something against his own inclination if he can feel that he is doing it for a nice person, than when he feels he is doing it for an unpleasant person. If he does it for an unpleasant person there is more dissonance and he may reduce this by changing his attitude toward C to make it more compatible with what he is doing.

Many studies have investigated this kind of prediction and one of them was conducted by Zimbardo, Weisenberg, Firestone and Levy (1965). They set out to see how the attitude toward eating an initially highly disliked food — fried grasshoppers — was influenced by whether or not the persuader was seen as pleasant or unpleasant.

The subjects were given initial tests to determine their attitude toward eating fried grasshoppers, etc. Then a plate with five fried grasshoppers on each was placed in front of each of the participants. One group of participants was confronted with a 'nice' experimenter who treated his 'assistant' in a friendly and considerate manner, and another group of participants were confronted with an unpleasant experimenter who shouted at and embarrassed his assistant in front of those present. In both cases the experimenter tried to persuade the participants to eat a grasshopper, although he emphasized that their action was entirely voluntary. About fifty percent of the participants in both groups ate at least one grasshopper. There were also control groups who were not given an inducement to eat a grasshopper, but their attitudes were measured before and after a time interval equivalent to that of the experimental groups.

The result of the study was as predicted. There was a much higher tendency for the group with the unpleasant experimenter to change in the direction of liking fried grasshoppers than was the case in the group with the pleasant experimenter.

The reader should be warned that verification of such hunches based on dissonance theory is by no means uniform. Frequently experimenters report negative or confusing outcomes, which is not surprising, since in these studies there are many other possible combinations of effects possible. For instance, a subject may reject the entire situation with disgust and conclude that he had done what he did only because he was simply forced to do it. The tendency to such general disgust could quite possibly have been more frequent in the case with the unpleasant experimenter and then the results could have become the opposite of those found. However, it is clear that the more sensitive the experimenter is to the particular kind of social reality likely to be engendered by a given concrete setting, the more successful will he be in predicting outcomes, with the help of dissonance theory and other common-sense derivations.

How to get retailers to buy in times of economic depression

Finally, let us consider an example where the persuader has practically no power over the person to be persuaded, and where the person is set *not* to let himself be influenced. As we shall see, it is, even then, possible to arrange experiences in such a way that persons tend to change in desired directions. The following is an excerpt from a report on a successful sales campaign in Uruguay, where the task was to get retailers to buy ready-made curtains and curtain and upholstery fabric, at a time when they typically did not sell much, and when they were highly reluctant to place orders.

(Zimbardo and Ebbesen, 1967, pp. 117-119):

The retailer is now expecting the salesman to return at this season of the year, and he knows from the past that the salesman wants to show him the entire collection of new styles (normally around thirty styles). But this time he is not going to buy.

The persuasion attempt that was used can be subdivided into several distinct stages within each of two parts:

Part A. In the retailer's store. During the first stage, it is necessary to change the businessman's verbal repertoire about business conditions in general. For example, he must stop saying, 'Business is bad', and start saying, 'Now is the time for business to pick up'. Then one must get him to agree to a minimal commitment to see only a few new styles in the client's showroom.

Several weeks prior to this part of the process, a salesman stops by ostensibly to chat with the store owner, engages him in small talk, and then steers the conversation to business conditions, encouraging the store owner to make evaluative statements about business conditions and practices. The salesman thanks him for the interesting discussion, and then leaves armed with a list of the opinion statements which the storekeeper has made during their discussion.

From this list, six statements are chosen, varying in the degree to which the retailer (has said he) would agree with the positions they represent. For example, Statement I below is the one he would most endorse, while he also agrees with II and III. Statements IV and V are ones he disagrees with, and the final statement, VI, is the key opinion with which he disagrees. The objective of the persuasion attempt then is to change this last opinion, and to get the retailer to say (and to agree, rather than disagree) that 'buying now is necessary'. How can this be accomplished?

Statement	Customer's initial attitude
I. It is essential to keep up to date with new developments even in hard times.	+ 3
II. Varying the merchandise helps increase sales.	+ 2
III. The customary buying season is approaching.	+ 1
IV. The government will allow prices to be increased.	− 1
V. Last year's collection sold well.	− 2
VI. Buying *now* is necessary.	− 3

The approach is interesting because the salesman encourages the storekeeper to disagree with him, to argue, and finally to reject statements made by the salesman. This works as follows. In stage two of the persuasion attempt, a different salesman visits the retailer and begins the conversation with reference to the first item. 'Times are really bad, and *I* don't think it even pays to try to see what the new style trends are.' The salesman says this as if he were trying hard to persuade the retailer to agree with his opinion. According to Brehm's theory of reactance, 'the perception that a communication is attempting to influence will tend to be seen as a threat to one's freedom to decide for oneself' (1966, p. 94). This is obviously a reverse use of manipulative intent, and is also the 'Marc Antony effect.' Accordingly, reactance is evoked by the salesman's obviously persuasive approach. In trying to reestablish his psychological freedom, the store owner rejects the influence attempt by saying that he would not go so far as all that, and that maybe it is only in idle business periods that one has the time to quietly study future trends. After the salesman gets him to elaborate and reaffirm his position on this point, he proceeds to disagree with the next statement in the prepared list. 'Well, that may be true, but anyway, it would seem best not to vary merchandise too much in a period such as this.' Again there will be reactance, with the store owner stating that, to the contrary, variety is the only thing that would give things a boost now. To this, the salesman replies that the retailer may be right, but that it doesn't matter anyway since they are not yet in the buying season. The retailer now reacts by saying that the season is definitely here. The salesman always eventually agrees with the shopkeeper after he verbalizes these opinions, thereby reinforcing the response of *disagreement.*

Now the salesman continues to disagree with statements which are only mildly disapproved of by the customer, like, 'It might be the season, but the government will *not* allow prices to be increased.' The store owner disagrees, argues against such a position, saying that the government *will* allow prices to be increased, and is reinforced in his arguments by the salesman. 'Even if you could increase prices, you couldn't sell because last year's collection did not sell well.' The retailer disagrees with this for two reasons: reactance and prior reinforcement in disagreement. Finally, the salesman moves to the statement with which the store owner initially most disagreed, 'Well, even if last year's collection sold well, buying *now* is not necessary in order to make money.' When the shop owner, now *set* to disagree, argues against this proposition also, he is in fact telling the salesman that he *ought* to buy now — exactly what the salesman wanted. His initial latitude of acceptance has been extended so that he now agrees with an extreme statement that he previously rejected (see our discussion in Chapter 4 of this attitude measurement technique of Hovland, Harvey, and Sherif, 1957).

By verbalizing these opinions, the customer tends to change his general attitude toward business and buying. He is left with the suggestion that, if he really feels the way he *says* he does, the salesman could try to arrange for a showing of only a few of the new styles. Typically, the self-convinced customer agrees to be shown new materials.

Part B. In the experimental showrom. Subsequently, the store owner is invited to come to the showroom with his wife, partner, salesman, etc. Selling is never done in the customer's store, since going to the showroom is the first act of yielding, involves some effort on the part of the customer (see Cohen, 1959, on the positive power of effort), and brings him into an unfamiliar environment which the salesman controls (reread the previously presented police confession techniques on this point).

In the first stage, the customer is given much attention and social approval of his views on a particular problem he is having in his business. The salesman looks into the eyes of the customer while agreeing with him. This intensive 'eye contact' increases liking for the source of the approval (cf. Ellsworth and Carlsmith, 1968). Then he is shown some stock in a line that has made a small profit for him, but one which he is known not to be interested in at this time. When the customer finally says he came to see Line Z, Line Z is presented vividly and graphically.

As each design is presented, the salesman scans the expression of the people in the group, looking for the one who shows most approval (e.g., head-nodding) of the design. He then asks that person for an opinion. Since the opinion is certain to be favorable, the person is asked to elaborate. As he does so, the salesman scans the faces of the other people, looking for more support. He then asks for an opinion of the next person now showing most approval. He continues until he reaches the person who initially showed most disapproval (who initially might have reacted negatively). In this way, by using the first person as a model (see Chapter 5), and by social group pressure on the last person, the salesman gets all or most of the people in the group to make a positive public statement about the design.

If the group includes a highly authoritarian owner accompanied by submissive subordinates, there will be a tendency for the subordinates to look to the boss before expressing an opinion. This is solved by seating the boss so that the subordinates cannot see his expression. The ensuing social pressure works on the boss even though it comes from subordinates, because often such a boss has a great need for social approval (cf. Crowne and Marlowe's analysis of social approval, 1960).

Many other examples of applied learning techniques could have been given. However, the main point is to recognize that our common-sense conceptual framework is rich enough to suggest to the reflective mind a practically unlimited number of procedures for changing persons in desired directions.

Questions after Chapter IX

1. Try to think of experiences that exclusively or primarily affect your conception of respectively the past, the present, the future, and the possible. What comments do you have after this exercise, particularly with respect to theoretical conceptions of learning?

2. Are you really convinced that the basic principles of respectively belonging, effect, transfer, and dissonance are circular, or do you have doubts or objections?

3. Think of and discuss various ways of ensuring that one does not forget to do things.

4. Fear of harmless snakes is clearly unrealistic and also relatively isolated from the rest of the person's life. Think of fears you have and discuss in what ways they are unrealistic vs. realistic. Discuss also the complications that may arise when extinction of a particular fear has multiple and complex consequences for the person's life in other respects.

5. When, if ever, is it ethical for a psychologist to persuade someone in devious (manipulatory) ways?

X. General psychology: Motivation

Men have probably always asked questions about motivation, not only specific ones such as 'why is he doing that?', 'what is she trying to prove?', but also general ones such as, 'what are the motives that lie behind human action?', 'what drives men to act?', etc. Attempting to provide answers to these questions, philosophers and, later, psychologists have gradually worked their way through a number of conceptual difficulties. Some highly selected aspects of this history will be briefly described here, in order to provide a background for understanding current positions. For more extensive introductions see Atkinson (1964) and Madsen (1968).

McDougall

William McDougall (1871-1938) had worked in medicine and biology, and as an anthropological field worker before he turned to psychology. He was born in England and lived there for the first part of his career, but, after the First World War, he moved to the United States.

McDougall regarded the experimental psychology prevalent around the turn of the century as unimportant and unpromising. Instead of focussing exclusively on mental contents ('ideas') and on isolated individual performances, he wanted to make psychology the study of what people actually *do* (thereby being a forerunner of behaviorism) and of their life *together* (social interaction). His program to found a behavioristic social psychology was first formulated in his textbook *An Introduction to Social Psychology* (1908) and immediately became very widely read and discussed.

McDougall was heavily influenced by Darwinism and felt that the nature of man could only be understood in a biological and phylogenetic context. More specifically, the central problem was to determine those innate behavior tendencies that are characteristic of the species Homo sapiens and that are the mainspring of all human action, social or other-

209

wise. He first labeled these innate tendencies *instincts,* and defined an instinct as a series of innately determined processes always occurring in a fixed order: (1) a predisposition to perceive in a particular way, e.g. to note food odors when one is hungry, (2) an emotional impulse (the core of the instinct), and (3) physical expression or instrumental action such as flight (in fear), attack (in anger), and approach (in attraction), etc. Given this program, the major research task was simply to determine all the instincts of man. When this was accomplished, it should become possible to explain all the variants of human action and goal seeking as derived from combinations of the instincts. In the first book McDougall presented a first list of the instincts, and soon this became a very popular occupation, most new writers publishing their own preferred version. In order to give the reader an impression of what such a list looked like, we reproduce here McDougall's list from the last of his books. It should be noted that, by this time, he had exchanged the term 'instinct' for the term 'propensity', in order to emphasize that the innate tendencies were not of the behaviorally stereotyped kind that seemed to occur in many lower animals, notably the insects. Also, the list should really be read in the context of McDougall's commentaries, which were generally in the direction of making the instincts appear plausible and in accordance with common sense. However, the list as such can be used to illustrate the kind of logical difficulties that will be discussed below (McDougall, 1932, pp. 97-98).

1. To seek (and perhaps to store) food (food-seeking propensity).
2. To reject and avoid certain noxious substances (disgust propensity).
3. To court and mate (sex propensity).
4. To flee to cover in response to violent impressions that inflict or threaten pain or injury (fear propensity).
5. To explore strange places and things (curiosity propensity).
6. To feed, protect, and shelter the young (protective and parental propensity).
7. To remain in company with fellows and, if isolated, to seek that company (gregarious propensity).
8. To domineer, to lead, to assert oneself over, or display oneself before, one's fellows (self-assertive propensity).
9. To defer, to obey, to follow, to submit in the presence of others who display superior powers (submissive propensity).
10. To resent and forcibly to break down any thwarting or resistance offered to the free exercise of any other tendency (anger propensity).
11. To cry aloud for assistance when our efforts are utterly baffled (appeal propensity).
12. To construct shelters and implements (constructive propensity).
13. To acquire, possess, and defend whatever is found useful or otherwise attractive (acquisitive propensity).

14. To laugh at the defects and failures of our fellow creatures (laughter propensity).
15. To remove, or to remove oneself from, whatever produces discomfort, as by scratching or by change of position and location (comfort propensity).
16. To lie down, rest, and sleep when tired (rest or sleep propensity).
17. To wander to new scenes (migratory propensity).
18. A group of very simple propensities serving bodily needs, such as coughing, sneezing, breathing, evacuation.

We cannot here go further into McDougall's various contributions. Let us merely note that he is generally recognized as one of the important pioneers both in the field of motivation and in the field of social psychology.

Early criticism of the instinct concept

Every constructor of a list of instincts faces the problem of how *inclusive* his categories should be. Looking at McDougall's list one might, for instance, wonder whether the submissive propensity (no. 9) is really anything more than a particular learned derivate from the fear propensity (no. 4), and that consequently no. 9 should be eliminated. Similarly, one may wonder whether the constructive propensity (no. 12) is not really a learned derivate of several or most of the other propensities, and hence should be eliminated as a separate entity. Finally, it appears possible that the migratory propensity is really only a common name for behaviors that derive partly from the food-seeking propensity (no. 1) and from the curiosity propensity (no. 5), etc. Conversely, one may wonder whether one should not distinguish in no. 16 (rest or sleep propensity) between the tendency to seek rest after physical exertion, while being wide awake, and the tendency to seek sleep, while being rested physically. Furthermore, one may wonder whether in addition to no. 13 (acquisitive propensity) there should be posited a tendency to give away one's belongings and share with others, etc. A practically infinite number of other similar questions may be raised in connection with this list and with any other lists that may be constructed.

Briefly, the decision to set the number of innate tendencies at 18 is clearly quite arbitrary. On the other hand ,it is quite clear that the reduction of every significant human action to *one* underlying drive (such as Freud's Libido) is of little value, since this does not in any way help in distinguishing between actions. The positing of hundreds or thousands of innate tendencies, linked with correspondingly limited behavior forms is equally senseless. The well-known parody of this is the positing of a thumb-twiddling instinct to account for the occurrence of thumb-twiddling, and a not-thumb-twiddling instinct to account for the absence of thumb-twiddling, etc. Thus, it appears intuitively plausible, without any more stringent analysis, that a taxonomy of innate behavioral tendencies must involve some moderate intermediate number of categories in order to be of any conceivable value.

At this point, we must raise the question, what is a useful taxonomy? The most general answer that can be given to this is that a taxonomy is useful to the extent that the assignment of an event or object to a category permits one to make inferences to other not immediately given characteristics of the event or object. An eminently useless taxonomy would be to classify people according to the last letter of their first name. Almost nothing of general interest can be inferred from the fact that a person's first name ends with e.g. an 's' or a 'b'.

On the other hand, the classification of edible fruits into such categories as 'apples', 'oranges', 'grapefruit', 'pears', etc. is highly useful, since knowing that something is, e.g., an apple permits a very high number of inferences, many of them of great practical importance.

The two preceding examples involved very easily discriminable categories. It is clear that to the extent that it becomes impossible to decide unambiguously what category is involved in a given case, the corresponding taxonomy loses its value.

During the 1920's and 1930's the critique of McDougall and of instinct theories in general grew very strong. Not only did one point out the absurdities of constructing very brief or very long lists of instincts, and the arbitrariness of the decisions involved in all list making, but it was also emphasized that the universal occurrence of learning, beginning soon after birth, so profoundly modifies people's goals that the task of finding common underlying entities appeared rather hopeless. Since man is so obviously and to such an overwhelming extent a product of his surrounding culture, the construction of lists of innate instincts came to be seen as more and more pointless and fell into disrepute.

Klineberg's analysis of the motivation problem

In a textbook on social psychology that first appeared in 1940, Otto Klineberg redefined and further clarified the problem of motivation in the following way: Even though human behavior, as evidenced by numerous anthropological field studies, is indeed highly modifiable, it still remains a fact that man's biological nature must play a crucial role in how human cultures develop and in how the individual adapts to a given culture. This would seem to be true, both with respect to the particular sensory and motor equipment of humans, the characteristic limitations in their brain capacity, and in some of their psychological needs. However, in order to determine what innate biologically determined tendencies and constraints may exist, one must go beyond the earlier unsystematic and largely intuitive attempts to construct lists. Rather one should set up systematic and objective criteria for recognizing innate tendencies and allow for variations in how resistant they may be to overriding cultural influences. Klineberg used the term *dependable* for the degree to which a motive is fundamental (can be depended on to manifest itself). He was also programmatically behavioristic in defining motives as *forms of behavior*. He used the following three criteria of dependability: (1) The existence of a continuity between a particular form of behavior in man and that of other biological species, particularly the anthropoid apes. Such a continuity between biologically similar species would seem to indicate an innate component, considering that the apes are not bearers of any human type culture. (2) The existence of a known biochemical or physiological basis for the given specific form of behavior is also evidence in the same direction. (3) Universality, or near-universality in all known human communities.

Applying these criteria, Klineberg arrived at the following explicitly tentative conclusions, classifying motives in four gross categories (Klineberg, 1940, pp. 160-161):

1. Motives which are absolutely dependable, have a definite physiological basis and admit of no exceptions. Social factors play a part in their manifestations, but do not determine their existence. These include hunger, thirst, the need for rest and sleep, the elimination of waste products from the body, and similar organic requirements; also activity drives and 'esthetic' drives.

2. Motives which have a definite physiological basis, are found in all societies, but admit of exceptions in the case of individuals. Social factors not only determine the manner of their expression, but may also in certain circumstances cause them not to appear. These include sex, post-maternal behavior, and possibly also self-preservation.

3. Motives which have an indirect physiological basis and occur with great frequency, but admit of exceptions both in groups and in individuals. These include aggressiveness, flight and probably also self-assertiveness.

4. Motives which have no known physiological basis, but which occur with some frequency either because of social factors common to the majority of human communities, or as a means to the satisfaction of practical interests. They are primarily means to an end, but may come to function as ends in themselves. These include gregariousness, the paternal motive, the prematernal motive, the filial motive, acquisitiveness, and selfsubmission.

During the three decades that have passed since the appearance of

Klineberg's book, a vast amount of new and better evidence has been accumulated through anthropological, ethological, and experimental psychological studies. Today one could therefore, given his theoretical perspective, change, reformulate, qualify, and add to Klineberg's list in many ways. However, this will not be done here, since we prefer to concentrate on developments, that, in our view, have rendered Klineberg's conceptual framework obsolete. Yet, one should not forget that, in an historical perspective, Klineberg's thinking was a step forward from McDougall's, since it introduced systematic and objective empirical criteria instead of a relatively intuitive and subjective procedure.

The difference between habit and motive: a dilemma for behaviorists

In his book Klineberg consistently describes motives as particular forms of behavior, but with no further analysis of the more detailed structure involved. One gets the impression that he and generally the earlier behaviorists thought of motives as involving or being identical with directly observable behaviors. In the decade around 1950, there began to appear a number of articles and passages in books indicating uneasiness with the conceptual status of the motivation concept. Among these were Krech (1949), Brown (1953), Kelly (1955, pp. 35-37, p. 68), and Postman (1956). The way the uneasiness was formulated varied, but in retrospect and from the point of view of this book, one major difficulty may have been the following:

Almost every author writing about motives (propensities, drives, needs, etc.) has regarded them as having the two main attributes of *strength* and *direction.* It is entirely in line with everyday language to say that if someone has a motive, he must have it to some degree, and it must involve a something that is wanted, a goal (or goal state). Now, the problem that had become apparent was that one had difficulties in distinguishing between 'habits' and 'motives'. The reason can be clarified by the following example: Observing the behavior of one of our fellow men, we note a number of recurrent regularities. Every morning he, e.g., brushes his teeth. One may then say that he has (when he was a boy) acquired the habit of brushing his teeth under certain given conditions, notably after meals. We infer the existence of the habit from the regularity with which the tooth-brushing behavior appears in given external conditions. The same man also goes regularly to his work, and we say that he has a motive to keep his job. Why do we, in every day life, say that he has such a motive? Behavioristically inclined psychologists would answer that he does everything he can to arrive at the office in time every working day — if there is no train, he will take a taxi, if there are no taxis available he will hitch-hike, if this is not feasible he will walk, etc. Furthermore, he will show motor restlessness if blocked in his progress toward the office. These are indices of the existence of a motive. But note that these apply to the tooth-brushing habit too. If the man's right hand is hurt, he will brush his teeth with his left hand, if his toothbrush is not in its usual place he will look for it, and eventually run out and buy a new one, if he is definitely blocked in his attempts to brush his teeth he will show signs of frustration, etc. Thus, we are logically forced to talk of a 'tooth-brushing-motive' too. Conversely, the daily departure for the office is elicited regularly by the same external situations (the clock showing 8.15, etc.) and is executed in the same sequence and therefore must logically be considered as a habit too.

To summarize the preceding, it was becoming clear that motives and habits, when conceived of as observable behaviors, could not be clearly and consistently distinguished. Hence, they had to be conceived of as *constructs inferred from behavior*. Since they were indiscriminable on the consequent side, both being anchored in the direction and strength of behavior tendencies, it only remained to attempt to distinguish them on the antecedent side, motive strength being a function of such factors as number of hours since feeding, whereas habit strength was seen as a function of previous frequency of reinforcement, etc. However, instead of describing the various, in our view rather unconvincing, attempts to conceptualize habit and motive in order to keep them apart as observables, we will turn to another development which, in a way, brought the concept of motivation within a purely behavioristic framework to its logical conclusion.

Egon Brunswik's hierarchical lens model

Egon Brunswik (1900-1955) was an Austrian psychologist who emigrated to the United States in 1939. He had done experimental work on perception, but gradually became increasingly concerned with the conceptual and methodological foundations of psychology. This is not the place to review his sophisticated and very general theoretical system (see Brunswik, 1952 and 1956), but we will merely concentrate on some aspects that relate directly to the problem of motivation. Brunswik was one of the first to analyze the notion of behavior in a systematic and generally valid manner and to show that it cannot be treated as a simple physical observable, but has a characteristic structure, which necessitates more complex observational procedures. This again, as we shall see, throws some light on the problem of motivation from a strictly behavioristic point of view.

If we observe a flock of birds passing us, says Brunswik, the diagnosis of *what* they are doing is not a matter of simple direct observation. Although many interpretations are unlikely, we cannot simply conclude, for instance, that the birds are 'flying southwards'. They may just as well be 'flying toward the big barn' or 'towards the hill behind the barn', etc. One cannot at the moment of the initial observation decide which one of the alternative interpretations is the true one. In other words, observations of behavior are, in this case, and, according to Brunswik, always, *ambiguous*. Only by observing the birds successively in positions where the hill, the barn, and south are in different directions can one reach a decision.

Another example of the ambiguity of behavior observations: In an experiment on avoidance conditioning, a subject's hand is placed with the palm down and one finger on a grid that gets electrically charged immediately after a buzzer is sounded. Predictably enough, the finger soon starts to jerk upwards immediately when the buzzer sounds. In this case one cannot simply conclude that the person has learned to extend his finger as observed. Proof that this is unwarranted can be found by simply turning the hand so that the palm is now upward. When the buzzer sounds, the opposite set of muscles are now immediately activated and there is finger flexion instead of extension. Obviously, the subject has learned something other and more than the simple finger movement first observed.

In general, physically defined behavior is always an *ambiguous* indicator of what is going on in the subject, and a correct diagnosis must involve determination of those variables or situations of which behavior is a *constant function*. If the birds fly toward the barn irrespective of starting point, or if the subject retracts from the grid with any part of his body and in any position, then we may infer with some justification that there are respectively approach to the barn and avoidance of the grid. Brunswik briefly and precisely characterized the structure of behavior as involving *periodically recurrent vicariously mediated equifinality*. From time to time and by variable means behavior converges on, or is a constant function of, limited classes of environmental situations or variables. As a graphical representation of behavior, Brunswik proposed the *lens model,* one version of which is depicted in Figure 14.

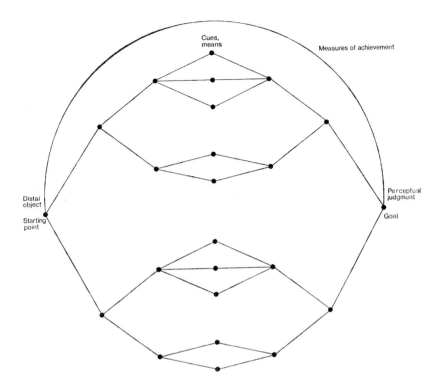

Figure 14. Brunswik's lens model.

The lens model applies both to perception and to overt behavior. In the former case, the left focus is the distal variable, such as e.g. the physical length of an object. This distal variable is causally and/or statistically linked in various ways with the stimuli that impinge on the subject's sense organs (in this case the retina). These stimuli, which Brunswik calls 'proximal', include various relevant cues such as projection of the object on the retina and a number of cues to its distance. On the basis of these cues, the organism synthesizes the information and the right hand focus is the resulting judgment behavior. The wide arch spanning the entire model indicates measures of the degree of achievement or stabilization of organism-environment relationships.

In the case of overt goal directed behavior, the left focus is the initial situation for a goal directed sequence. Various combinations of alternative means are applied, that eventually converge on the goal situation to the right. Again the arch above the figure measures the degree of achievement. It should be noted that the entire model is based on a

217

statistical point of view; it summarizes tendencies over many repetitions. As an example in the case of overt behavior, the reader may consider the case of arriving at the office at 9 o'clock sharp every working day (right focus). The person typically manages to do this despite all the major and minor vicissitudes of life, not only train strikes and snow storms, but also such delaying circumstances as removing stains from one's trousers, not being able to find a certain tie, having to repair a leaking faucet, being awakened 20 minutes late, etc.

It should be noted that hierarchical organization is a typical feature of all these processes. Each part of the process of getting to the office in time, getting dressed, brushing one's teeth, having breakfast, catching the train, etc., has a similar internal structure. Also, they are all subordinated to higher order processes. Thus if getting to the office ceases to be a goal, the desperate hurry for a given train ceases, if one is informed that the firm is broke and one will not get any pay, the goal of going to this particular office ceases to be active, etc. In summary, Brunswik argued that behavior can be usefully described only by reference to the focal units to which it belongs. One can be more or less detailed or molecular in one's description by referring to more inclusive or less inclusive foci, but without such reference predictions and explanations cannot work.

From the lens model one can see that the habit-motive confusion may stem from the *relativity* of these terms. The lowest hierarchical unit involved is apt to be treated as a habit, and the higher orders involved are apt to be seen as motives (controlling the habit). When we observe tooth-brushing relative to washing hands, using deodorants, etc. we treat it as a habit we have acquired in the course of trying to keep clean and good smelling (superordinate motive). On the other hand, when we consider behaviors such as brushing the teeth with one's left hand, looking for the tooth brush on the floor, rushing to the drug store to buy a new one, etc. these are seen as involving learned habitual components controlled by a motive for tooth brushing. Thus the hierarchical lens model helps dissolve the confusion generated by the attempts to distinguish between habits and motives as simple observables.

Brunswik maintained a consistent methodological behaviorism, dealing only with objectively defined environmental and behavioral variables. He also refused to enter into speculations about what goes on inside the organism, and maintained that one could formulate a complete psychology in terms of the distal objects achieved. Sample: Cats may, among other things, be characterized by the fact that certain distal objects (mice) disappear in their presence. Brunswik's many important contributions to psychology cannot be surveyed here. We shall only in passing mention that he emphasized the *probabilistic* nature of important environmental relationships and that the organism must adjust to these in order to survive.

Brunswik's importance for the study of motivation is that he explicitly and generally described the structure of behavior, and thereby the *logic* involved in determining whether or not something is a goal (focus). In his terms, McDougall's and Klineberg's taxonomical problem may be rephrased as follows: what are the most general and universally occurring classes of goals, i.e. classes of variables and situations towards which human behavior tends to converge?

Miller, Galanter and Pribram's 'subjective behaviorism'

In 1960 Miller, Galanter and Pribram published their important book *Plans and the Structure of Behavior*. Although they make no reference to Brunswik, they were very clearly aware of the general structure of behavior that he had depicted in his generalized lens model. They were very strongly influenced by theories of information processing and of *cybernetics* (the study of self-regulating mechanisms), and were concerned with the problem of *simulating* human behavior. By simulation is meant to attempt to write programs which make computers behave as human beings. If successful, such programs may be regarded as models of what may be going on inside the person. Hence, the computer models are a modern version of what are generally called theories. The difference is that the programs are much more explicit and detailed than most psychological theories, that they are fed into a computer, and that predictions are therefore generated mechanically, faster, and at higher levels of complexity than was previously possible. Another difference between computer models and theories is that the former are detailed replicas of all that is supposed to go on inside the person, whereas theories usually consist of abstract principles from which one can only predict a few highly specific quantitative outcomes.

Miller, Galanter and Pribram's main question may be formulated as follows:

What general type of program will generate the well-known typical characteristics of behavior (vicariously mediated, hierarchically organized equifinality)? Their answer is shown in Figure 15.

The unit depicted in Figure 15 is very small and highly simplified,

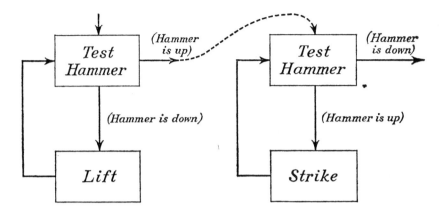

Figure 15. The hierarchical plan for hammering nails. Reproduced from Miller, Galanter and Pribram 1960 p. 36.

but if the plan is the initial (left) focus in the lens model, it should be apparent that it will eventually tend to lead to the right focus (nail flush) via a somewhat variable combination of means, with an elementary hierarchical organization. The hierarchical structure can be further developed by considering that the plan for hammering nails is most likely subordinate to a higher order plan, e.g. for getting a roof ready, which again may be subordinate to a still higher order plan for building a house, etc. Briefly, it appears as if we now have at least the skeleton of a model for the processes that generate the observable behavior of people.

There are two notable features of the concept of plans that deserve some further comment. The first one is that Miller, Galanter and Pribram are perfectly willing to let people *tell them about* their plans. This rules out the interpretation of plans as mere formal theoretical constructs of the psychologist and also the interpretation of plans as neural processes. Presumably subjects cannot be expected to have access to formal constructs of the experimenter or to their own neural processes. Therefore, plans must have *subjective existence for the bearer,* and this brings Miller, Galanter and Pribram to the very threshold of abandoning the behavioristic framework altogether. Their remaining obstacle is a lack of a clear understanding of the role of communication in achieving knowledge of other minds, and of the fact that it is not physical behavior patterns, but the *meaning* of behavior that is the raw datum for the psychologist. This has been discussed in chapter V and will be taken up again in the last chapter of this book.

The other important feature of the concept of plans is that the theoretical problem of distinguishing between motives and habits is eliminated. Plans are both activating and directing, both evaluative and cognitive. The problem of what are the highest order superordinate plans of persons is left open. To be sure, in the example of hammering nails, we may continue to ask why, after we have unraveled a plan to build a house. However, when going beyond a certain limit of generality, one is likely to get such answers as 'I do it because I am trained for it', 'I like it', 'it makes my life meaningful', 'it makes me happy to be a house builder', etc. The diminishing return in these questions indicates that the concept of plan does not encourage asking questions about ultimate driving forces in the tradition of McDougall, Klineberg, and others. Rather, the plans that people have seem to be entirely a matter of historically determined developments and can often be traced far back into their childhood. This would seem to exclude systematic classification. On the other hand, the concept of plan definitely admits and encourages the type of psychological research that takes as its subject matter the entire life cycle of persons and attempts to develop methods of tracing the influence of what might be labeled guiding master plans, including basic philosophic assumptions (see Bühler and Massarik, 1968, and Ellis, 1962).

In conclusion: The advance of Miller, Galanter and Pribram beyond Brunswik lies not only in their outline of processes that may generate the structure of overt behavior described by Brunswik, but, above all, in their emphasis on the subjective existence of these processes. Plans involve future oriented activities carried out *by* persons, whereas Brunswik admitted only autonomous causal chains occurring *in* organisms.

Absence of invariant psychophysiological relationships

The preceding has left one important problem unanswered. We have earlier shown that the belief in invariant relationships between external physical stimuli and subjective experiences is unwarranted (chapter VIII), and that the same is true with respect to physically defined external situations and learning and transfer (chapter IX). However, it may still be argued that the internal bodily stimuli of emotions and motives directly influence experience and behavior, and that, consequently, we must retain a place for biological determinants in a psychology of plans.

An increasing number of recent studies seem to indicate that there are no strictly invariant relationships between bodily stimuli and emotional and motivational states. A small sample of these studies will be briefly described here. For further references see e.g. Heckhausen and Weiner (1972).

Hunger and thirst. We have already mentioned that dissonance theory yields some paradoxical predictions using a forced compliance paradigm (see pp. 205-206). In this paradigm an unpleasant request is made of the subject and the offered reward is insufficient compared to the required behavior. Because the action and the small reward are experienced as dissonant, one has predicted (and frequently found) that the subject may change his evaluation of the originally unpleasant task in such a way that its aversiveness decreases. This paradigm was applied by Brehm (1962) to the experience of hunger and thirst. He asked a group of subjects to undergo prolonged food or water deprivation, without providing an appropriate reward. The lack of incentive for this voluntary deprivation was expected to create a state of dissonance. As predicted, individuals who agreed to this deprivation rated themselves as less hungry or thirsty and drank less water when given the opportunity than subjects given adequate compensation for their compliance.

The need for food and water is a constant feature of our internal environment, but its impact is to some extent regulated by cognitive processes.

Pain. In a study utilizing the forced compliance paradigm, Grinker (1967) showed that subjects given no 'reason' to undergo continued avoidance conditioning are less likely to display an avoidance response (eyelid closure prior to a puff of air to the eye) than subjects who had been given an adequate incentive. Apparently the experimental subjects tended to experience the aversive stimulus as less painful than the control subjects and hence were less motivated to avoid the air puff.

Fear. One might assume that the bodily stimuli in a state of fear are unambiguous and therefore have an invariant effect on a person's experiences. A study by Nisbett and Schachter (1966) is relevant here. They informed some of their subjects that their naturally occurring fear symptoms toward an impending shock were due to a pill which they had been given. These subjects then manifested fewer symptoms of fear than subjects who ascribed their symptoms to the fear of shock.

Anger. In a classical study by Schachter and Singer (1962), subjects were injected with epinephrine, an activating agent. While under this induced arousal they were, among other things, placed in a situation in which another person acted angrily. The subjects who had been injected with epinephrine became more angry in the anger-producing situation than subjects who had merely been given a placebo pill. It should be added that the injected subjects also became more euphoric than the control subjects when placed in an euphoria-producing situation. Hence, again, it is clear that emotional experience is dependent on how the person happens to conceive the nature of his internal states.

In another experiment, Berkowitz, Lepinsky and Angulo (1969) had stooge anger subjects. Some subjects then were given some false measures of their physiological reactions, supposedly revealing their anger toward the stooge. The result was that subjects thus given evidence of their anger displayed more aggressiveness toward the stooge than subjects believing they were not overly upset.

Sex. In a study by Valins (1966), subjects were given false information concerning their internal arousal. While viewing slides of nude females, males overhead false heartrate feedback which indicated that they were excited by some of the pictures, but not by others. The subjects subsequently rated the slides paired with the false arousal information as more attractive, and were more likely to select them for further viewing than slides associated with a normal heart rate.

The preceding sample of studies should be sufficient to indicate rather conclusively that the experience of bodily states, rather than the bodily states themselves, determines emotionality and actual motivation. This experience, just as the experience of external stimuli, is partly dependent on various kinds of contingent information, such as context, learning, and probably also motivation. The latter means that one could probably influence the experience of given bodily symptoms of emotion by introducing proper payoff matrices (cf. the discussion on pp. 169-170). A general consequence of the preceding is that psychophysiology, no less than psychophysics and learning, resists any attempt to find invariant principles linking the physical and the mental. The conclusion seems to be that the study of why men act as they do must be largely focussed on that which is not in observable behavior, nor in the external physical world, nor inside the body, but rather in the mind. What this means will be summarized and expanded in the next and final chapter.

Questions after Chapter X

1. Are you really convinced that all attempts to classify human motives are fruitless, or do you have doubts and objections?

2. Compare the lens model (p. 217) and the plan model (p. 220) with the common-sense model of action (p. 101). What important differences, if any, are discernible?

3. How can psychophysiology still be regarded as important, even though there may exist no strictly invariant links between experience and bodily states?

XI. Humanistic psychology as a framework for practice and research

A common, rather bitter, joke among psychologists is that 'psychology first lost its soul, and then its mind'. The gap between our daily common-sense understanding and much psychological theorizing and methodology has become very wide indeed, and we must attempt to reduce the gap and diminish the dissonance. Here, we will summarize the point of view developed in this book and elaborate it further in some respects. Our goal is a formulation with which psychologists and other people can truly *live*, not only in the consulting room and the laboratory, but also in the outside world. The position will be presented in the form of a connected series of statements accompanied by comments and elaborations.

Psychology must primarily be a study of the other person

The reason for this is that introspection by the researcher is a process in which what is observed is directly influenced by the initial theoretical position and the connected expectancies. It is not denied that the researcher's opinions and expectancies may influence the subject too. This occurs via the instructions given, the problems posed and the questions asked, the arrangement of the study, etc. However, this influence can, in principle, be analyzed and controlled. The influence of the researcher's theoretical position and expectancies on his own experiences and performance cannot be in the same way analyzed into separate components and controlled.

It should be noted that the above only concerns the researcher's own introspection. There is by no means a rejection of introspection in the other person. The other person's direct reports of his interpretations and experiences are valuable data, as long as they are not influenced by knowledge of the researcher's theoretical position.

It follows from the preceding that an open dialogue between the psychologist and his subject is a rather doubtful method of obtaining data, since the psychologist will then directly influence what he observes. In order to give a complete account of the interaction of psychologists with the public, it should be pointed out that research is only one phase in the process. Another necessary phase is the communication of results to the public (via textbooks, popularizations, etc.). In this phase psychologists may potentially influence people profoundly, and they must, in principle, take this into account when moving into the next research phase. The interaction of the two phases has not so far created any noticeable difficulties. The number of research psychologists is so small and their findings so unimportant from a practical point of view, that the popularization of psychology has not yet led to 'contamination' of 'naive' subjects to any appreciable extent. However, note that, e.g., widespread publication of such sales techniques as are described on pp. 206-208 may rapidly lead to an awareness of retailers and others which renders the techniques less useful. In general, to the extent that psychological techniques become really useful, the second phase of the interaction with the public becomes more important, and the dictum that psychological techniques should be kept secret (p. 53) becomes more controversial.

Psychology must take for granted that other persons are conscious, i.e. that a world exists for them

This is an assumption without which we cannot live. It is directly or indirectly presupposed in almost all our daily activities. Attempts to question it must remain philosophical exercises, theoretically interesting perhaps, but never of direct practical consequence.

To be sure, one may conduct studies of under what conditions people ascribe various degrees of consciousness to a person. Probably such indicators as responsiveness, signs of discrimination and recognition, and ability to participate in a normal process of communication are crucial in this respect. However, even for such studies the assumption that others *can* be conscious is *a priori*. The analysis of the conditions of judgment is secondary and only makes sense given the *a priori* assumption.

Psychology is the study of subjective worlds

It is well known that discussions about how the domain of a science shall be delimited can be rather unfruitful, and that they can often be best understood as serving the purposes of competition between different professions and schools of thought. Nevertheless, it may in this case have some heuristic value to clarify what becomes the domain of psychology, given the present position. At the very least, it serves as a background against which methodological requirements may be evaluated.

Subjective worlds are worlds that exist for individuals. The psychologist always asks about the subjective, about how the person experiences the world, including himself, what he likes and dislikes, what he thinks is right and wrong, what he wants to do, what he attempts to do, etc. This means that the subject matter of psychology has another mode of existence than the subject matters of natural science and of sociology. Natural science studies phenomena which exist in themselves, independently of human beings. Sociology studies phenomena which exist *for* people, but independently of any given individuals.

It is important to consider the relationships between these different kinds of realities and to note that they presuppose each other. A more stringent analysis of these complex matters lies outside the scope of this book (see e.g. Berger and Luckman, 1967). However, a few salient points should be brought forward here. If there were no physical reality, i.e., no aspects of the world *independent* of people, there could hardly be any basis for communication. There would be no synchronization of when different individuals would experience, e.g. changes in the external situation, no synchronization of when they recognize repetition or regularity, etc.

A special case of the fundamental importance of physical reality for communication involves experimental psychology and was formulated by the author in a previous paper as follows (Smedslund, 1966, pp. 393-394):

If two proximal stimulus situations are physically identical, no subject will be able to discriminate between them. This inference is the basis for the operational definition of *psychological change.* If the subject's behavior changes from one presentation of a proximal stimulus situation to the next, then the change must derive from a change within him which is not dependent on any change in outside stimulation. In intersubjective comparisons the same procedure defines *individual differences.*

This inference reflects the necessary working assumption that the 'grain' of the objective physical world as we conceive it today, always is finer than the 'grain' of any subject's world. Briefly, *the intersubjective physical descriptions are employed in psychology in order to control the input from outside the subject, enabling one to eliminate irrelevant external influence and to single out psychological change and difference for study.*

This quotation clearly implies that if we did not rely on physical reality, experimental psychology would be impossible.

Conversely, physical descriptions presuppose a) individual observers (i.e. subjective worlds) and b) communication between these, which again presupposes the existence of a supraindividual social reality (in the form of a common language, etc.)

Social and subjective realities also mutually presuppose each other, Social reality presupposes the participation of many individuals, i.e. many subjective realities. The converse is also true. The very act of getting to know a person's subjective world, through communication, presupposes the existence of a common social reality. It is difficult to even conceive of a human mind developing outside of communion with others. If there were such a mind (a monad) we could by definition not know anything about it, since knowing another mind can only occur through communication (see below).

The tight interrelatedness of the different kinds of realities from an epistemological point of view is paralleled in practice. We can never understand the subjective world of a person in isolation, but only as it relates to the concurrent social and physical realities. It is clear from the presentations of Levi Strauss (1966) and others that, e.g., the task of describing a native's botanical classifications would be impossible, if the anthropologist did not know enough botany to identify the species involved. Similarly, we are hard pressed to do anything about a person's feelings of anxiety if we do not know anything about the concurrent social and physical events involved.

As we have shown in the preceding three chapters, there are no strictly invariant relationships between the physical and the mental, nor are there any immutable rules that cannot be broken by the individual. However, this relative independence of the mental can only be described and investigated against an objective background. There may be no psychophysical invariants, but people's experiences are generally related to the physical reality, there may be no totally compelling moral absolutes, but people are generally orienting themselves relative to the rules in society, etc. In summary, even though psychology is the study of subjective worlds, it always must treat its subject matter *within* the larger framework of the surrounding social and physical worlds. Concretely, the psychologist does not deal with persons in a vacuum, but with persons *in* the social and physical world. Persons act, and their actions have physical as well as social antecedents, contexts, and consequences. Even though the psychologist's main concern is with the subjective aspects of action (reasons, intentions, interpretations, etc.), it is obvious that he can only achieve a practically useful understanding if he takes into account the relevant objective (physical and social) context of the actions. The reader should note that the tripartition subjective-social-physical is in some ways similar to the phenomenological tripartition into *Eigenwelt* — *Mitwelt* — *Umwelt* (see, e.g., May et al. 1958, pp. 61-65).

There is, in principle, only one way in which one can get to know a person's subjective world, namely through communication

This follows directly from consideration of the nature of the task. In natural science one seeks to establish statements of the general form 'x is the case', whereas in psychology the elementary statements have the form 'for P x is the case'. 'x is the case', can, in principle, be directly verified by the researcher. On the other hand, 'for P x is the case' can only be verified if P utters 'x is the case' or in other ways expresses himself or behaves in a way equivalent in meaning to this utterance. There are two important preconditions for this verificational procedure to be valid. The first one is that P is telling (expressing) the truth, i.e. that P is not intentionally trying to mislead the observer. This problem has been discussed earlier (p. 46) and, in order to simplify, it will here be taken for granted that deceit is not involved. The second precondition is that *what P means by 'x is the case' is identical with what the observer believes P means by 'x is the case'.* The achievement of psychological knowledge is dependent on such commonality in meaning, and this is what we refer to when we assert that psychologists are dependent on communication. Communication is the exchange of messages that *mean* the same to the participants.

The raw data of psychology are the public (social) meanings of the subject's expressions and actions

The only bridge crossing the gap between the psychologist and the subjective world of his subject or client is that of communication. In this process the utterances or messages function as a kind of 'half-way house' since their meaning is both public and private. For a more general discussion of 'half-way houses' with a somewhat different perspective, see Weisskopf-Joelson (1968, p. 369).

It should now be clear, as has been known to practitioners all along, that the attempt to treat messages as physical events and the effort to reconstruct their significance by means of learning theory, etc., are doomed to fail.

The subject's utterances and expressions have immediately accessible public meaning, and these are the data of psychology. Given the full context, there is usually a strong tendency to consensus among independent observers belonging to the given society, as to what this meaning is. No sharp dividing line between data and interpretation is implied. All data are interpretations in the sense that they are selective and reflect implicit assumptions. The term 'raw data' is simply used to indicate the level at which observations are reported and at which intersubjectivity (within the given society) is required.

It should be noted that we describe observations down to a detail beyond which variations are not expected to make any difference in meaning relevant for the given purpose. Depending on this purpose we may, for example, report:

a) he said he was probably going home,
b) he said 'I think I will go home',
c) he said '(phonemic transcription)',
d) he said '(phonetic transcription)',
e) videotape of the performance, etc.

In all these examples we normally assume that the person meant by what he said the same as he would be expected to mean by any normal adult member of the same community (society) who observed him in the full context.

Commonality in meaning is tested by means of logic

Sometimes we may doubt whether the preconditions of communication are met and then we must ask the following question: How do we know that when P utters 'x is the case' he means what we think he means by 'x is the case'? In other words, how can we control that there is a real commonality in meaning? As has already been mentioned on pp. 82-83, the only way to check this is to observe the extent to which there is agreement on what is *equivalent to, implied by, contradicted by,* and *irrelevant to,* the given expression. Naturally, this presupposes that we have at least some means of communicating agreement. If x and y are synonymous formulations in the given language and context, we would expect P to affirm that 'y is the case' (equivalence). Also, if it follows from 'x is the case' that 'z is the case', then we would expect P to affirm that 'z is the case' (implication). Furthermore, if x and v are logically incompatible, we expect P to reject as false the statement 'v is the case'. Finally, if w has no logical relationship to x, we expect P to affirm that whether 'w is the case' or not does not affect the truth-value of 'x is the case' (irrelevance). The preceding should not be construed to mean that the procedures are restricted to verbal behavior. If, for example, someone looks at you in a loving and tender way and stretches her (his) hand toward your face, you expect to be caressed rather than hit on the nose (implication), etc.

If the preceding four procedures generate disagreement, the proper conclusion is that there is no complete commonality in meaning, rather than that the subject is not logical. We have already (pp. 82-83) pointed out that understanding (achieving commonality in meaning) and logic presuppose each other, and that we always have to take logic for granted in trying to judge the degree of understanding. We can only understand that which is logical.

We have criticized those traditions in experimental psychology that, ostensibly, study degrees of logicality in subjects, by pointing out that this approach leads to counterintuitive and in the last resort absurd conclusions. More precisely, the circular relationship between understanding and logic leaves us with three possible strategies.

The first strategy is always to assume that lack of agreement means faulty logic, but this leads directly into absurdity. It would imply that, e.g., apparent lack of understanding of a language is not really lack of understanding, but simply reveals a total (and entirely mystical) loss of logic as soon as the language is introduced.

A second strategy is to assume that sometimes lack of agreement stems from faulty understanding, sometimes from faulty logic, and sometimes from both. However, this strategy, which seems to be used in experimental psychology and sometimes elsewhere, appears to be quite arbitrary, since no unequivocal criteria can be found for *when* it is appropriate to select one of the three alternative interpretations. Typically, people appear to ascribe breakdown of communication to lack of understanding, for instance, when the other person is a foreigner to the given culture, an outsider to the given profession, etc., whereas the breakdown is ascribed to madness when he is a member of the culture or profession, etc. In the case of children, some experimental psychologists (notably of the Piaget tradition) tend to ascribe the difference between adult and child to illogicality on the part of the latter, whereas ordinary people would tend to ascribe it to lack of understanding of the situation and the terms involved. In general, our attributions may reflect whether or not we hope to achieve agreement reasonably easily. The foreigner only has to learn our language and our customs in order to become 'normal', but with the massively 'insane' the prospects may appear dim. However, there seem to exist no compelling criteria for deciding when a lack of communication should be attributed to lack of understanding and when it should be attributed to a lack of logic. Hence, this strategy is inherently unsatisfactory.

There remains only the third strategy, namely always to interpret breakdown in communication as a symptom of lack of understanding in the sense of lack of commonality in meaning, and always to take logic for granted. This is what we typically do in everyday life, and it becomes problematic only when the subject is confronted with complex formal logical derivations. Here we sometimes feel that it is the ability to judge logical relationships that breaks down. However, this may usually be attributed to limits in our capacity to keep complicated premises in mind. The studies of Henle (1962) illustrate this point very well. She found that many subjects who failed in syllogistic reasoning had other premises in mind than the correct ones, and that, given these subjective premises, their reasoning was logical. This matter cannot be conclusively decided on empirical grounds, but the example indicates how one can always save the assumption that the subject's elementary logical ability is intact.

In order to prevent misunderstandings, a few additional comments on the matter of logic are necessary.

First, the preceding may seem to imply that, by reducing all apparent illogicality to lack of commonality of meaning, one denies the existence of the illogical, irrational. However, this is not a correct description of the present position. What we have said is that understanding and logic presuppose each other, and that one can always attempt to interpret breakdown in communication as reflecting lack of understanding rather than lack of logic. In other words, we can only understand that which is correctly logical, and in attempting to understand we attempt to discover the logical structure involved. When we do not succeed in this, we have failed to understand, and we can only give negative descriptions, such as 'not-transitive', 'contradictory', 'unclear', 'confused', etc. In summary, we neither deny nor affirm the existence of the illogical (irrational), we merely assert that only the logical can be understood.

Second, it is necessary to clarify an ambiguity in our usage of the term 'logical'. When we state that relations between subjective or intentional phenomena are logical, we mean that they are of a *kind* that differs, e.g., from causal relations. When, on the other hand, we state that understanding presupposes logic, we mean that understanding presupposes *correct* logic, and thus commonality in logical judgment.

Third, one must ask how we can ever understand *change* and the *new* within a logical framework. Events in a static subjective world, or in a world where all changes are elicited from outside and merely release readymade unchanging dispositions can be described in a logical framework.

We have already several times pointed out that there is a logic of change (pp. 191, 194, 197) and that we understand change when we know the person's reasons for change. Obviously, if we are unable to find any plausible reason for a person's change, then we do not understand it. Again, we do not deny or affirm the existence of changes without reasons, but merely assert that our understanding depends on the finding of reasons, from which the change follows logically.

We do not automatically leave it to the person to determine his reasons, although we usually acknowledge that he is the best judge. Sometimes the person is unable to state his reasons very clearly, sometimes he is unwilling to reveal them and tries to cover up by deceit. Finally, we can readily admit that people may fool themselves and believe that they have changed for reasons that are not the real ones. It is important to recognize exactly what is involved in determining what are the *real* reasons for a given change. The real reasons are a set of reasons that fit what the person has experienced and how he changes, and that he himself frequently comes to recognize once they are communicated to him. Sometimes the person does not accept or recognize the assumed real reasons, but, even then, the psychologist may feel that they cover the observations better than those that the person believes in. Such disagreements are frequent, one must live with them. The only way they are ultimately resolved is through the achievement of consensus (agreement). The extraordinary popularity of psychoanalytic theory seems to stem, at least partly, from the power to define what is real, given to the user of the theory. The mere usage of concepts such as 'repression', 'denial', 'displacement', 'projection', 'sublimation', etc., presupposes that the user has access to the *truth*, whereas the person described does not know himself. The concepts appear to mediate factual and neutral descriptions, whereas, actually, they give the user exclusive rights to define reality.

The psychologist is acting under ethical constraint

The humanistic position emphasizes that the psychologist and his subject/client/student are *fellow human beings* living together in society. We have already discussed some of the implications of this from several points of view (chapters I, II, and III). The main ones are that there must be mutual respect and compassion. It remains to comment on the obvious fact that a common frame of reference for judgment of what is *good* and what is *bad* cannot always be found. Actually, there are frequent disagreements and conflicts about this; in other words, ethical constraints are *ambiguous*. Ideological conflicts reach far into the subculture of psychology itself, and are reflected in such various slogans as 'psychology should serve the interests of the People against the Establishment', 'psychology should serve the interests of freedom (variously defined)', 'only a Marxist psychology is valid', 'the psychologist should first of all be committed to the ideals of Science, he should above all search for the Truth', 'psychology should be detached from all ideologies and religions', etc.

The position taken here is that the psychologist should recognize his roles in society, his membership in the subculture, and his personal characteristics. With this recognition as a background, he should fight to maintain a) the critical attitude which is the essence of our scientific commitment, and b) the basic respect and compassion for his fellow human beings which is incompatible with dealing with them as mere objects. Beyond this, psychologists cannot be expected to agree. Although it may appear intolerable, there do exist Fascist psychologists, Capitalist psychologists, Communist psychologists, Moslem psychologists, Buddhist psychologists, Anarchist psychologists, Ivory Tower psychologists, etc. Subjectively, they all think they carry the banners of Love and Reason, but knowing this cannot prevent us from seeking our allies and joining the battle.

General conclusion

Although it may not have been apparent, we have tried to avoid restricting the field of permissible activities in psychology unduly. Only those endeavors that lead nowhere or to absurd outcomes have been warned against. Most of the considerable piecemeal wisdom that psychologists have accumulated has been left out of this book, both because it has been described well elsewhere, and because we have wanted to concentrate on a few salient characteristics of what it means to become a psychologist. It remains to see whether what is said has any real impact. Critical readers may well ask whether or not what has been written in this book makes any real difference in what we actually *do* as psychologists. If it makes no difference it can perhaps be safely ignored as another instance of academic hairsplitting. This question can only be answered by subsequent history. The effects of reading something need not become immediately visible in clear and concrete changes in professional practice. The effects may just as well be in the form of deeper changes over time that gradually penetrate what we do. We cannot stop believing that theoretical reflection has practical value.

How, then, can psychologists be of help? Surely not by lingering in the aftermaths of the hopeless struggle to become a respectable natural science. Not by everyone retreating into those remaining sanctuaries of hybrid natural and social science (however valuable they may be): sensory psychology, neuropsychology, psychopharmacology, psychosomatic medicine, ethology, psychometrics, etc. Not by escaping into mere and sheer concrete practice with the dream of becoming a well-known (and well-off) psychotherapeutic guru. Hopefully not by dropping psychology altogether for marching and actioning under the banners of some absolutizing creed.

Those colleagues who prefer it should be left undisturbed in their armchairs or among their cherished instruments. In the affluent part of the world we can afford this, and we need the free, strange, and sometimes seemingly useless intellectual adventures. Perhaps we also profit from having some old and wise therapists and some clever computer-minded laboratory geniuses around. Yet, it cannot be denied that the considerations in this book are strongly biased in one particular direction. They reflect a growing suspicion that we have been too afraid to explore systematically the gold mines of our unreflected common sense for subtle and efficient ideas about how to *help,* how to *educate,* and how to *liberate* people. We know much about how to design studies wisely and how to evaluate outcomes realistically. What we still do not know very much about is how to formulate and realize efficient concrete procedures that work *better* than those that have evolved in society. The psychological practitioner still works very much like what Levi-Strauss (1966, Chapter 1) calls a 'bricoleur', i.e. by assembling concrete culturally given fragments in order to produce a practical solution for a given situation. This can be reasonably efficient, but we cannot expect anything but very slow advances. The scientific attitude, on the other hand, is consistently critical and oriented toward systematic and general analyses of abstract concepts. The scientist is also truly a revolutionary in the sense that his critical attitude leads him to transcend every given cultural boundary in search of new and better concepts and procedures.

The paradox of psychology is that one is forced to work as a bricoleur since one must depend on the given cultural framework, depend on one's common sense; yet at the same time one should try to do this in a systematic and scientific way. Perhaps what we are saying is that, in psychology, one must become a good bricoleur before one can become a good scientist.

Becoming a psychologist is more than ever becoming an adventurer in intellectual landscapes which are at the same time strangely well known and utterly baffling. But as we, hopefully, become more adept in our profession, we must face the dilemma of how to manipulate without losing compassion, how to influence without losing respect, how to help without governing.

Questions after Chapter XI

1. How did the notion that other persons are conscious come about?

2. Discuss and try to clarify further the mutual dependence of the subjective, the social, and the physical worlds.

3. Does the notion of a 'logic of change' make sense to you? Discuss the implications of this notion in terms of concrete examples from your own experience.

4. What, if anything, do you feel you have learned from this book? How will what you have learned affect your future activities?

References

Anastasi, A. *Differential psychology. Individual and group differences in behavior.* New York: Macmillan, 1958.

Atkinson, J. W. *An introduction to motivation.* New York: Van Nostrand, 1964.

Attneave, F. *Applications of information theory to psychology.* New York: Holt, 1959

Bakan, D. *On method. Toward a reconstruction of psychological investigation.* San Fransisco: Jossey-Bass, 1968.

Bandura, A. *Principles of behavior modification.* London: Holt, Rinehart and Winston, 1969.

Bennett, G. K., Seashore, H. G., and Wesman, A. G. *Differential aptitude tests, manual,* 4th ed.) New York: Psychological Corporation, 1966.

Berger, P. L., and Luckmann, T. *The social construction of reality. A treatise in the sociology of knowledge.* Garden City, N.Y.: Doubleday, Anchor Books, 1967.

Bergmann, G.. and Spence, K. W. The logic of psychophysical measurement. *Psychological Review,* 1944, *51,* 1-24.

Berkowitz, L., Lepinski, J. P., and Angulo, E. J. Awareness of own anger level and subsequent aggression. *Journal of Personality and Social Psychology,* 1969, *11,* 293-300.

Berlyne, D. E. *Structure and direction of thinking.* New York: Wiley, 1965.

Berne, E. *Games people play. The psychology of human relationships.* London: Andre Deutsch, 1966.

Bower, G. M. Mental imagery and associative learning. In L. Gregg (Ed.) *Cognition in learning and memory.* New York: Wiley, 1969.

Brehm, J. W. Motivational effects of cognitive dissonance. In M. R. Jones (Ed.), *Nebraska symposium on motivation.* Lincoln: University of Nebraska Press, 1962, pp. 51-77.

Brown, J. S. Problems presented by the concept of acquired drives. In *Current theory and research in motivation. A symposium.* Lincoln, University of Nebraska Press, 1953.

Brown, R. *Words and things.* New York: Free Press, 1958.

Brown, R. *Social psychology.* New York: Free Press, 1965.

Brunswik, E. *The conceptual framework of psychology.* Chicago: University of Chicago Press, 1952.

Brunswik, E. *Perception and the representative design of psychological experiments.* Berkeley: University of California Press, 1956.

Bühler, C., and Massarik, F. (Eds.). *The course of human life. A study of goals in the humanistic perspective.* New York: Springer, 1968.

237

Conklin, H. C. Hanunóo color categories. *Southwestern Journal of Anthropology,* 1955, *11,* No. 4.

Cronbach, L. J. *Essentials of psychological testing.* New York: Harper, 1960.

Eisler, H. and Ekman, G. A mechanism of subjective similarity. *Acta Psychologica,* 1959, *16,* 1-10.

Ellis, A. *Reason and emotion in psychotherapy.* New York: Lyle Stuart, 1962.

Estes, W. K., Koch, S., MacCorquodale, K., Meehl, P. E., Mueller C. G., Jr., Schoenfeld, W. N., and Verplanck, W. S. *Modern learning theory.* New York: Appleton-Century-Crofts, 1954.

Festinger, L. *A theory of cognitive dissonance.* Evanston, Ill.: Row, Peterson (reprinted by Stanford University Press, Stanford, Cal., 1962).

Fiske, D. W. and Maddi, S. R. (Eds.) *Functions of varied experience.* Homewood, Ill.: Dorsey, 1961.

Flavell, J. H. *The development of role-taking and communication skills in children.* New York: Wiley, 1968.

Frazer, J. G. *The golden bough.* (Abridged Edition) London: 1922.

Frenkel-Brunswik, E. *Psychoanalysis and the unity of science. Proceedings of the American Academy of Arts and Sciences,* 1954, *80,* No. 4, 271-350.

Friedman, N. *The social nature of psychological research. The psychological experiment as a social interaction.* New York: Basic Books, 1967.

Galanter, E. Contemporary psychophysics. In *New directions in psychology. I.* New York: Holt, Rinehart and Winston, 1966.

Garner, W. R. *Uncertainty and structure as psychological concepts.* New York: Wiley, 1962.

Goffman, E. *Interaction ritual. Essays on face-to-face behavior.* Garden City, N.Y.: Doubleday, Anchor Books, 1967.

Golding, W. *Lord of the flies.* London: Faber & Faber, 1969.

Grave, S. A. Common sense. In Edwards, P. (Editor-in-chief). *The encyclopedia of philosophy.* New York: Macmillan, 1967.

Griffin, J. H. *Black like me.* Boston: Houghton Mifflin, 1960.

Grinker, J. *The control of classical conditioning by cognitive manipulation.* Unpublished doctoral dissertation, New York University, 1967.

Hamsun, K. *Victoria.* New York: Knopf, 1929.

Havighurst, R. J., Bowman, P. H., and Liddle, G. P. *Growing up in River City.* New York: Wiley, 1962.

Heckhausen, H. and Weiner, B. The emergence of a cognitive psychology of motivation. In P. C. Dodwell (Ed.), *Psychology, 1972.* London: Penguin, 1972.

Heider, F. *The psychology of interpersonal relations.* New York: Wiley, 1958.

Henle, M. On the relation between logic and thinking. *Psychological Review,* 1962, *69,* 366-378.

Hilgard, E. R. *Theories of learning.* New York: Appleton-Century-Crofts, 1956.

Insko, C. I. *Theories of attitude change.* New York: Appleton-Century-Crofts, 1967.

Kelly, G. *The psychology of personal constructs.* (2 vols.) New York: Norton, 1955.

Kiesler, C. A., Collins, B. E., and Miller, N. *Attitude change: a critical analysis of theoretical approaches.* New York: Wiley, 1969.

Klineberg, O. *Social psychology.* New York: Holt, 1940.

Krech, D. Notes toward a psychological theory. *Journal of Personality,* 1949, *18,* 66-87.

Laing, R. D. *The politics of experience.* London: Penguin, 1967.

Levi-Strauss, C. *The savage mind*. Chicago: The University of Chicago Press, 1966.

Madsen, K. B. *Theories of motivation. A comparative study of modern theories of motivation*. Kent, Ohio: Kent State University Press, 1968.

Martin, E. Transfer of verbal paired associates. *Psychological Review*, 1965, *72*, 327-343.

May, R., Angel, E., and Ellenberger, H. F. (Eds.) *Existence*. New York: Basic Books, 1958.

Meehl, P. E. On the circularity of the law of effect. *Psychological Bulletin*, 1950, *47*, 52-75.

Meehl, P. E. and Rosen, A. Antecedent probability and the efficiency of psychometric signs, patterns, or cutting scores. *Psychological Bulletin*, 1955, *52*, 194-216.

Milgram, S. Some conditions of obedience and disobedience to authority. *Human Relations*, 1965, *18*, 57-75.

Miller, G. A. The magical number seven, plus or minus two: some limits on our capacity for processing information. *Psychological Review*, 1956, *63*, 81-97.

Miller, G. A., Galanter, E., and Pribram, K. H. *Plans and the structure of behavior*. New York: Holt, 1960.

Mills, T. M. *The sociology of small groups*. Englewood Cliffs, N.J.: Prentice-Hall, 1967.

Neisser, U. *Cognitive psychology*. New York: Appleton-Century-Crofts, 1967.

Nisbett, R. E. and Schachter, S. Cognitive manipulation of pain. *Journal of Experimental Social Psychology*, 1966, *2*, 227-236.

Osgood, C. E. The similarity paradox in human learning: a resolution. *Psychological Review*, 1949, *56*, 132-143.

Osgood, C. E. and Tannenbaum, P. E. The principle of congruity in the prediction of attitude change. *Psychological Review*, 1955, *62*, 42-55.

Paivio, A. On the functional significance of imagery. *Psychological Bulletin*, 1970, *73*, 385-392.

Piaget, J. and Inhelder, B. *La genèse de l'idée de hasard chez l'infant*. Paris: Presses Universitaires de France, 1951.

Piaget, J. and Inhelder, B. *The psychology of the child*. London: Routledge & Kegan Paul, 1969.

Postman, L. The history and present status of the Law of Effect. *Psychological Bulletin*, 1947, *44*, 489-563.

Postman, L. Is the concept of motivation necessary? *Contemporary Psychology*, 1956, *1*, 229-230.

Poulton, E. C. The new psychophysics: six models for magnitude estimation. *Psychological Bulletin*, 1968, *69*, 1-19.

Professional-ethical directives for members of the Norwegian Psychological Association (passed on February 21, 1959).

Raven, J. C. *Guide to using the coloured progressive matrices sets A, Ab, B*. (Revised order, 1956). London: H. K. Lewis, 1965.

Rommetveit, R. *Selectivity, intuition and halo effects in social perception*. Oslo: Oslo University Press, 1960.

Rosenthal, R. *Experimenter effects in behavioral research*. New York: Appleton-Century-Crofts, 1966.

Rubenowitz, S. *Emotional flexibility-rigidity as a comprehensive dimension of mind* Stockholm: Almqvist & Wiksell, 1963.

Schachter, S. and Singer, J. E. Cognitive, social, and physiological determinants of emotional state. *Psychological Review,* 1962, *69,* 379-399.

Schütz, A. *Collected papers. I. The problem of social reality.* The Hague: Martinus Nijhoff, 1967.

Scott, W. A. and Wertheimer, M. *Introduction to psychological research.* New York: Wiley, 1962.

Skinner, B. F. Are theories of learning necessary? *Psychological Review,* 1950, *57,* 193-216.

Smedslund, J. The utilization of probabilistic cues after 1100 and 4800 stimulus-presentations. *Acta Psychologica,* 1961, XVIII, 383-386.

Smedslund, J. The concept of correlation in adults. *Scandinavian Journal of Psychology,* 1963, *4,* 165-173.

Smedslund, J. *Concrete reasoning. A study of intellectual development. Monographs of the Society for Research in Child Development,* 1964, *29,* No. 2, 39 pp.

Smedslund, J. Constancy and conservation: A comparison of the systems of Brunswik and Piaget. In Hammond, K. R. (Ed.), *The psychology of Egon Brunswik.* New York: Holt, Rinehart and Winston, 1966.

Smedslund, J. Mental processes involved in rapid logical reasoning. *Scandinavian Journal of Psychology,* 1968, *9,* 187-205.

Smedslund, J. Psychological diagnostics. *Psychological Bulletin,* 1969, *71,* 237-248.

Smedslund, J. Circular relation between understanding and logic. *Scandinavian Journal of Psychology,* 1970, *11,* 217-219.

Stern, A. *Sartre. His philosophy and existential psychoanalysis.* New York: Dell Publishing Co., 1967.

Thorndike, E. L. *Human learning.* New York: Appleton-Century-Crofts, 1931.

Thorndike, R. L. and Hagen, E. *10,000 careers.* New York: Wiley, 1959.

Valins, S. Cognitive effects of false heart-rate feedback. *Journal of Personality and Social Psychology,* 1966, *4,* 400-408.

Vernon, P. E. *Personality assessment. A critical survey.* London: Methuen, 1969.

Vygotsky, L. S. *Thought and language.* Cambridge, Mass.: The M.I.T. Press, 1962.

Wason, P. C. and Johnson-Laird, P. N. (Eds.) *Thinking and reasoning.* Selected readings. Harmondsworth: Penguin, 1968.

Watzlawick, P., Beavin, J. H., and Jackson, D. D. *Pragmatics of human communication. A study of interactional patterns, pathologies, and paradoxes.* New York: Norton, 1967.

Webster's Third New International Dictionary. Unabridged. Springfield, Mass.: Merriam, 1967.

Weisskopf-Joelson, E. *Meaning as an integrating factor.* In Bühler, C. and Massarik, F. (Eds.) *The course of human life. A study of goals in the humanistic perspective.* New York: Springer, 1968.

West, M. *Children of the sun.* London: Pan Books, 1966.

Wisdom, J. *Other minds.* Oxford: Blackwell, 1952.

Zimbardo, P. G., Weisenberg, M., Firestone, I., and Levy, B. Communicator effectiveness in producing public conformity and private attitude change. *Journal of Personality,* 1965, *33,* 233-256.

Zimbardo, P. G. and Ebbesen, E. B. *Influencing attitudes and changing behavior. A basic introduction to relevant methodology, theory, and applications.* Reading, Mass.: Addison-Wesley, 1969.

Index

negative reinforcement 191
Neisser, V. 173
neutral science 26-27
Nisbett, R. E. 222
nonreinforcement 191
norms and values 113-115
Norwegian Psychological Association
49, 73

O

objective order of people 129
observations 32-33
open admission 70-73
opinions 203-204
order, subjective and objective 137-140
ordering 123-125
Osgood, C. E. 196, 197
ought and may 98
overcommunicating attention 58
overlearning 181

P

pain 222
Paivio, A. 201
parallel-forms method 154
Parmenides 29
Pavlov, Ivan Petrovitch 184-186
payoff matrix 169-170
perceiver, other persons as 99-100
perception 98
personality trait 132-137
personality structures 125
phobias 202-203
physical characteristics 141
Piaget, Jean 34, 91, 92, 84, 94, 197
Piaget tradition 231
pleasure 102-106
positive reinforcement 191
Postman, L. 193, 214
potential subject/client 22
Poulton, E. C. 177
power-function 176
practical understanding 16-17, 21
prescriptions 25
presence vs. absence 34-35
Pribram, K. H. 200, 201, 219-221
primary reinforcement 186

principle of association 187
principle of postremity 187
professional ethics 49-54
psychological investigation, psychologist
    subjected to 20
psychological similarity 194
psychological sub-culture 65-76
psychologist as practitioner 49-64
psychologist as researcher 25-48
psychophysics 163-178
psychophysics, internal and external 164
punishment 191

R

Raven, J. C. 153
recovery 185
reflection 29-31
reflexive undertaking 18
reflexivity 18-19
relevance 27-28
remembering 199-201
representative sample 153
representativeness 37-38
researcher 26-27
researcher as a high-status person 41-43
reward 191
Rommetveit, R. 127
Rosenthal, E. 27
Rubenowitz, S. 135-137

S

samples 37-38
Sartre, Jean-Paul 29, 31
satisfaction 105
scaling 176-178
Schachter, S. 222, 223
Schioldborg, Per 13
Schütz, Alfred 21, 68
scientific knowledge 26
Scott, W. A. 39
Seashore, H. G. 159
second signal system 186
self-consciousness 57
self-expression 58
semitechnical language 67-69
sex 223
significance 40-41